BODIES FOR SALE

Do people have a moral right to sell their kidneys, or other body parts? Is it wrong to receive money for being a surrogate mother? Can we – and should we – patent DNA? How ethical is the 'commodification' of the human body?

Bodies for Sale: Ethics and Exploitation in the Human Body Trade explores the philosophical and practical issues raised by activities such as surrogacy and organ trafficking. Stephen Wilkinson asks what it is that makes some commercial uses of the body controversial, whether the arguments against commercial exploitation stand up, and whether legislation outlawing such practices is really justified.

In Part One Wilkinson explains and analyses some of the notoriously slippery concepts used in the body commodification debate, including exploitation, harm, and consent. In Part Two he focusses on three controversial issues (the buying and selling of human kidneys, commercial surrogacy, and DNA patenting) outlining contemporary regulation and investigating both the moral issues and the arguments for legal prohibition.

Combining philosophical analysis with a detailed examination of current practice, *Bodies for Sale* is a comprehensive introduction to the ethics of body commodification and will be of interest to students of philosophy, politics, and law as well as anyone with a serious interest in healthcare ethics and policy.

Stephen Wilkinson is Senior Lecturer in ethics and philosophy at Keele University. He has published a number of papers on applied ethics and philosophy, one of which won the 1999 *Philosophical Quarterly* International Essay Prize.

BODIES FOR SALE

Ethics and exploitation in the human body trade

Stephen Wilkinson

First published 2003
by Routledge
11 New Fetter Lane, London EC4P 4EE

Simultaneously published in the USA and Canada
by Routledge
29 West 35th Street, New York, NY 10001

Routledge is an imprint of the Taylor & Francis Group

© 2003 Stephen Wilkinson

Typeset in Palatino by RefineCatch Limited, Bungay, Suffolk
Printed and bound in Great Britain by
MPG Books Ltd, Bodmin

British Library Cataloguing in Publication Data
A catalogue record for this book is available from the British Library

Library of Congress Cataloging in Publication Data
Bodies for sale: ethics and exploitation in the human body trade/
Stephen Wilkinson, editor.
p. cm.
Includes bibliographical references and index.
1. Sale of organs, tissues, etc. I. Wilkinson, Stephen, 1965–
RD120.7 .B636 2003
174′.29795 – dc21
2002036785

ISBN 0–415–26624–6 Hbk
ISBN 0–415–26625–4 Pbk

FOR MY PARENTS

CONTENTS

PREFACE

The completion of this work was made possible by grants from the Arts and Humanities Research Board and from Keele University. I'd like to record my gratitude for both awards.

Several Keele University colleagues deserve thanks for their help. Eve Garrard and David McNaughton have been superb readers of my work for the last eight years, providing just the right combination of encouragement and incisive criticism. Sally Sheldon has provided many hours of stimulating and informative discussion about healthcare law and ethics. Angus Dawson and Jo Rogers deserve special credit for (amongst many other things) managing our professional ethics programme so efficiently during my unexpected absence. Other Keele colleagues who have helped in one way or another include Chris Daly, André Gallois, and John Rogers.

To turn to people outside Keele, Bob Brecher, David Resnik, and Adrian Walsh have each read and provided very helpful comments on large parts of the typescript, for which I am extremely grateful, while the list of others to whom I am indebted in one way or another includes: Ruth Chadwick, Heather Draper, Bobbie Farsides, John Harris, Catriona McKinnon, Sue Millns, Richard Norman, and Philip Stratton-Lake. I would also like to thank the anonymous readers appointed by Routledge for their very useful comments on the typescript, Pauline Marsh for her meticulous copy-editing, and Richard Wilson for his very thorough work on the proofs.

An early (and much shorter) version of Chapter 9 ('Patenting life') appeared in *Imprints* ('Intellectual property rights and the human body: is "gene patenting" a special case?', *Imprints*, 2001, vol. 5, pp. 132–160 (http://go.to/imprints)). I would like to thank the editors for permitting me to retain full ownership of the material and Alan Carling for his useful referee's comments.

Last but not least, I'd like to thank my parents. Without their unwavering support over many years, this book wouldn't exist.

1

INTRODUCTION

The commercial exploitation of the human body is nothing new. Indeed, prostitution is commonly described as 'the oldest profession'. Since the 1980s, however, concerns have been voiced about the new ways in which biomedical technologies allow us to use the human body for profit. Some people argue that this 'commercialisation' or 'commodification' of the human body is wrong and should be banned. Others take a more permissive view, arguing (for example) that people have a moral right to sell parts of their bodies. *Bodies for Sale* is both an introduction to this debate, the 'body commodification' debate, and a critical assessment of the main arguments and concepts deployed within it.

The book is divided into two parts. Part I ('Concepts') explains and analyses some of the notoriously slippery concepts used in the body commodification debate. These include coercion, commodification, exploitation, harm, and objectification. Drawing on some of the conceptual work in Part I, Part II ('Practices') consists of a detailed discussion of three examples: the buying and selling of human kidneys, commercial surrogacy, and DNA patenting. Each chapter starts by explaining contemporary regulation and/or practice and then scrutinises both the ethical objections to the practice in question and the arguments for prohibiting it.

1.1 Concepts

Part I starts with the idea of exploitation. Many commercial practices – including organ sale, prostitution, and paid surrogacy – have been the subject of attacks couched in terms of exploitation. Hence, in order to understand the case against such practices, we need to know what exploitation claims mean. Indeed, I'd go further and suggest that exploitation is the single most important and widely deployed moral concept in the body commodification debate. If this is so, then vying for second place in the important moral concepts league table are 'commodification' and 'objectification'. These, and their relationship with exploitation, are the subjects of Chapter 3.

1

Chapter 4 looks at a concept which is less straightforward than it might at first appear – harm. Accusing commercial practices of being exploitative and accusing them of being harmful are common moves in the body commodification debate. Chapter 4 therefore aims to improve our understanding of such charges by exploring the connection between exploitation and harm and by looking at the nature of harm. The question of whether the commercial utilisation of the body is harmful is vitally important, especially given the widespread acceptance of Mill's *harm principle*, according to which 'the only purpose for which power can rightfully be exercised over any member of a civilised community against his will is to prevent harm to others'.[1]

Chapter 5 gives an overview of the idea of valid consent. This has both a primary and a secondary role within the body commodification debate. The primary role is that it's thought by many to explain directly the wrongness of certain commercial practices. For example, it has been argued both that surrogate mothers and people who sell parts of their bodies (for example, kidneys) don't, or can't, validly consent. For this reason, so the argument goes, such practices are wrong, since interactions that are as intimate, or as dangerous, as these must be properly consensual. Consent's secondary role is the contribution that it makes to the justification of exploitation claims. For, as we'll see, most (maybe even all) instances of exploitation appear to involve a consent that is somehow defective or inadequate.

Finally in Part I, Chapter 6 analyses the concept of coercion. The relevance of this is that accusations of coercion frequently underpin attempts to show that particular commercial practices involve the wrongful use of people or the violation of their autonomy, or that any consent given is invalid. For example, it's sometimes said that only people who were coerced would 'volunteer' to sell a body part or to provide 'sexual services'.

1.2 Practices

To turn now to Part II, organ sale, commercial surrogacy, and the patenting of human DNA are really only examples (though, I believe, representative ones) and form part of a much larger debate about the desirability (or otherwise) of permitting the commercialisation of the human body. This debate, which has in recent years attracted considerable attention from scholars in a variety of disciplines, has both theoretical and practical aspects. On the theoretical side (the concern of Part I) concepts such as exploitation, personhood, property, and self-ownership are re-examined. On the applications side (the concern of Part II) a number of body-commercialising practices have been subjected to scrutiny by moral philosophers, legal academics, and others. Table 1.1 provides a framework within which to place these various practical issues.

Table 1.1 Ways of commercialising the body

	Types of entity	Specific examples
Commercialisation of physical objects	Body products	Paying blood and gamete 'donors'
	Body parts	Paying 'donors' of kidneys and other solid organs
Commercialisation of abstract objects	Representations of the body	Commercial modelling and pornography
	Genetic information	DNA patenting, control/ownership of personal genetic data
Commercialisation of bodily services	Sexual services	Prostitution
	Reproductive services	Paid surrogacy
	Other services	Paying research subjects

We can usefully divide the issues into three categories. First, there is the commercialisation of *physical objects*. This includes, most obviously, the sale by individuals of particular body parts (such as kidneys) and of bodily products (such as blood and semen). Second, there is the commercialisation of *abstract objects*. This category includes informational and intellectual property, as well as such things as images of individuals' bodies. Hence, interestingly, such apparently disparate practices as DNA patenting, pornography, and voyeurism might fall into the same general category. Finally, there are so-called *bodily services*. Two of the most hotly contested practices in this category are reproductive services (especially paid surrogacy) and paid sex work. Payment for being a subject in biomedical research should also be placed in this final grouping.

The practices selected for sustained discussion in Part II serve as representatives of each of these three categories: solid organs (for example, kidneys) are *physical objects* and surrogacy is (arguably) a bodily *service*, while DNA patenting involves the acquisition of *abstract property*. Hence, while we won't examine in detail every individual aspect of the human body which is, or could be, a contested commodity, we will – to some extent – cover the whole range by looking at representative examples. I don't, of course, wish to deny that there are important differences between the individual practices within each category. Later on, for example, I'll point to some differences between selling blood or semen and selling solid organs like kidneys, and will suggest that paid

3

surrogacy is different in morally relevant respects from prostitution. However, argumentative moves which are made against organ sale do tend also to be used against the sale of blood and gametes, while argumentative moves which are made against prostitution tend also to be used against paid surrogacy. In learning how to deal with the case against one commercial practice, then, we learn a lot about how to deal with similarly structured arguments against other commercial practices. A key part of the philosopher's job is to explain and draw people's attention to structural similarities of this kind.

Finally, I should mention in passing an important issue that could usefully have been addressed in a book like this, but which hasn't been discussed in any detail owing to space limitations: the 'retention' of human organs. This, particularly the retention of dead children's organs without explicit parental consent, is very newsworthy in the UK at the time of writing and was the principal concern of the Redfern Report.[2] Redfern was an investigation into organ retention at Alder Hey (the Royal Liverpool Children's NHS trust) and focussed particularly, though by no means exclusively, on the behaviour of pathologist Professor van Velzen. According to Redfern, van Velzen was guilty (amongst other things) of:

> order[ing] the unethical and illegal retention of every organ in every case for the overriding purpose of research ... ignoring written consents to limited post mortem examination ... lying to parents about his post mortem methods and findings ... [and] causing an unnecessary excessive, illegal and unethical build up of organs following post mortem examination, ostensibly for research but with no likelihood that the bulk of the organs stored in containers would ever be used for research.[3]

Professor van Velzen's behaviour certainly failed, in many respects, to conform to the profession's accepted standards. However, it emerged during the course of investigations that the practice of retaining dead children's tissues and organs without explicit parental consent was not confined to Alder Hey:

> In Bristol, Liverpool and some other parts of the country, many parents were not aware that their children's organs had been retained beyond the time of burial or cremation. Nor did they consider that they had given consent for this to happen. When the existence of relatively large collections of children's hearts, brains and other organs was revealed publicly, there was an outcry.[4]

This 'outcry' prompted the setting up of the Retained Organs Commission (ROC) in 2001. The ROC, chaired by Professor Margaret Brazier (whose investigations are still in progress at the time of writing), was charged with responding to the 'deep concerns' described in Redfern and with providing advice to the government on the taking and retention of organs and tissue at post-mortem examinations.[5]

While it has not been possible to address directly these issues here, I do believe that some of the arguments and concepts explored in later chapters – for example, what I have to say about exploiting and objectifying bodies – could in principle be fruitfully applied to the 'organ retention' debate.

Part I

CONCEPTS

2

EXPLOITATION

> Although we frequently claim that some act, practice, or transaction is exploitative, the concept of exploitation is typically invoked without much analysis or argument ... exploitation is often utilized as if its meaning and moral force were self-evident. They are not.[1]

Why do we need an analysis of the concept of exploitation? One reason, a general one, is that although exploitation is a heavily used and widely accepted moral concept, moral philosophers have paid relatively little attention to it. As Wertheimer notes,

> despite the frequency and ease with which we make exploitation claims in ordinary moral and political discourse, I think it fair to say that with the major (and I do mean major) exception of the Marxist tradition, exploitation has not been a central concern for contemporary political and moral philosophy.[2]

A second reason for looking at exploitation, one with special relevance to this project, is that asserting that 'markets' are somehow exploitative is perhaps the commonest way of arguing against them. Many commercial practices – including organ sale, prostitution, and paid surrogacy – have been the object of attacks couched in terms of exploitation. So in order to understand the case against such practices, we need to know what exploitation claims mean. As we'll see shortly, though, saying exactly what exploitation is isn't easy. For it's a complex and contested concept and the subject of several competing theories.

2.1 Introducing exploitation

To exploit something, in the most general sense, is simply to put it to use, not waste it, take advantage of it.[3]

In the broadest sense, to exploit something, e.g. a natural

resource, means to use it for a purpose. Such exploitation is morally neutral.[4]

The word 'exploitation', like the related expressions 'use' and 'take advantage of', is sometimes used *evaluatively* or *normatively* and sometimes not; it has both *moral* and *non-moral* senses.[5] Hence, as Schwartz reminds us (above), we can talk entirely neutrally of exploiting (or of using) a resource, or an opportunity, or a talent, and when we speak of exploitation in this way we do not thereby express moral disapproval.[6] But, at the same time, as Onora O'Neill suggests:[7]

> Few moral criticisms strike deeper than the allegation that somebody has used another.[8]

On the other hand, Wertheimer (drawing on Williams) plausibly suggests that exploitation is a *thick moral concept* – one 'such as *treachery* and *promise* and *brutality* and *courage*, which seem to express a union of fact and value'.[9]

Sometimes, it's hard to tell whether 'exploitation' is being used normatively or not, and at times people deliberately take advantage of this ambiguity. When people do this they rarely lay out their arguments in formal terms. However, we can see how they might trade on this ambiguity by thinking about the following schematic example:

1 'Factory farming' involves the commercial exploitation of animals.
2 Exploitation is a bad thing.
3 Therefore 'factory farming' is a bad thing.

In (1), 'exploitation' is used in its non-moral sense. Hence, (1) appears (and is) obviously true. (If 'exploitation' were used in its moral sense in (1), then (1) might still be true, but it wouldn't be *obvious*, and we'd have to argue for it independently.) In (2), 'exploitation' is used in its moral sense and so (2) is supposed to be an obvious *a priori* truth. (3) The conclusion then *appears* to follow – but doesn't really – from (1) and (2). In order for (3) to follow from (1) and (2) we'd need 'exploitation' to be used in the same sense throughout. But if we use it in its moral sense throughout then (1) loses its obviousness – and, if we use it in its non-moral sense throughout, (2) becomes false, since exploitation in the non-moral sense clearly isn't always bad. So, either way, the argument is flawed. As I've said, people who take advantage of this ambiguity hardly ever present their arguments in such a formal way as this. However, what I've just said does capture the underlying structure of what they're doing (sometimes intentionally, sometimes not).

Except for these equivocal cases, the non-moral use of 'exploitation' is irrelevant to our present concerns and from now on I'll concentrate just on its moral sense (or senses).[10] We can usually get a good (though not infallible) idea of whether 'exploitation' is being used normatively or not by seeing what it's being applied to. For example, when it's applied to inanimate objects, it's normally being used non-morally, but when it's applied to persons, it implies moral criticism.[11] Thinking along these lines, Robert Goodin even goes as far as to say that 'an act of exploiting a person always constitutes a wrong'.[12] And, as Jonathan Wolff points out, similar things can be said about the word 'use':

> There can be no doubt that the idea of exploitation is closely related to some notion of use ... exploiting someone is using someone. Generally, when we say 'x used y', where y is a person, we intend this to be a form of criticism of x's behaviour.[13]

One way of dealing with this is to say not that 'exploitation' has a moral and a non-moral sense, but that it has just one sense (it means *use*) accompanied by different 'connotations' in direct contexts, this difference being explained by the fact that while using persons is wrong, using inanimate objects is not.[14] However, things are not that simple, since:

> using other *people* may be OK, as students use teachers to learn. But it is odd to describe such cases as exploitation. Among people, the word implies *merely* using others, taking wrongful advantage for one's own purposes.[15]

So the point is not just that using people is wrong, while using other things is OK. For there is (normally) nothing wrong with using people 'as students use teachers', or as patients use their doctors, or as children use their parents. Rather, the concept of exploitation, when applied to persons, is part of an attempt to pick out those uses of persons which are morally wrong, distinguishing them from those which are innocent. Hence, while it's true that 'exploit' means *use* when applied to persons, there is much more to be said. 'Exploitation' means something more specific, *wrongful use*. In fact, it means something even more specific than that since, as Wolff points out, not all 'improper uses' of persons are exploitative:

> 'exploits' as a moral criticism seems very close to 'improperly uses', although there are some improper uses of people – for example as a punch bag – which would not normally be thought of as forms of exploitation.[16]

We can start our analysis of exploitation, then, by schematically defining 'exploiting a person' as *wrongfully using her in one or more of a limited set of ways*. The main aim of sections 2.2–4 is to say what these ways are and why they constitute wrongdoing, but, before proceeding with this task, we must make three further clarificatory points.

The first is a concern that what I have said so far might be taken to imply that only persons – and not, for example, animals, or nature – can be exploited (in the moral sense).[17] Given certain very widely held and plausible assumptions about persons, it's particularly easy to see how the idea of exploitation applies to them; the concepts 'exploitation' and 'personhood' are, we might go as far as to say, made for each other. That said, there is no reason in principle why exploitation shouldn't be extended (and in its normative sense) to animals, or perhaps even to nature or to works of art. In each case, whether one thinks that the thing in question can be exploited will depend on what one thinks of its moral (or other evaluative) status. For example, someone who regards horses as quasi-persons will think that horses can be exploited just as humans can be. Or someone who thinks that nature is 'sacred' may think that it can be wrongfully used in exploitative ways. Nothing that I have said so far rules these possibilities in or out, since everything depends on what one thinks about the moral status of horses, nature, etc. My own focus, however, will be almost entirely on the exploitation of persons.

The second clarificatory point concerns my suggestion (above) that wrongfulness should be built into the definition of 'exploitation'. This might, understandably, be taken as an endorsement of *absolutism* about exploitation: the view that to exploit is always (and necessarily) wrong. The definition I propose is not, however, meant to be absolutist. Rather, my 'weaker' view is that exploiting persons (in the moral sense) is wrong *other things being equal* or, more specifically, *in the absence of other (sufficiently strong) countervailing moral considerations*. Take, for example, a case in which we have to choose between:

1 exploiting an individual (without seriously harming her) and in so doing saving the world from a nuclear catastrophe which would kill billions; and
2 not exploiting the same individual, thereby not averting a nuclear catastrophe in which billions die.

What ought we to do? Obviously, we would like to know more about the case before making a final decision. But it nonetheless seems clear that most of us have a strong preliminary intuition in favour of (1). In other words, we are not absolutists about exploitation, even if we think that the exploitation involved in (1) is regrettable and *prima facie* wrong. This intuition is compatible with what I want to say about exploitation, that it is wrong *in the absence of other (sufficiently strong) countervailing moral considerations*. For here we obviously have countervailing moral considerations: the fact that if we don't exploit, billions will die. If those considerations were absent, if there were no nuclear threat, then we probably *would* want to say that we shouldn't exploit. We should bear in mind throughout, then, that the fact that there is a genuine or valid exploitation objection to a practice doesn't necessarily mean that that practice is wrong 'all things considered'. For there may be countervailing moral considerations which are more important or 'weighty' than the fact that there's exploitation. *A fortiori*, that a practice is exploitative isn't always a sufficient reason for banning it, since there can be sound policy reasons for permitting the continuation of exploitation.

The third and final clarificatory point is that exploitation need not be intentional, although whether it's intentional or not may impact on our views about the exploiter's blameworthiness and character. Wertheimer makes the point well:

> A may exploit B even though A believes the terms of the transaction are eminently fair – if they are not. And A may exploit B while (and perhaps even because) A is unaware of the effects of the transaction on B. Free riders frequently do not understand that they are riding free. Of course, as with other forms of wrongdoing, we can distinguish between the wrongness of the act and the agent's culpability for that act. We may regard intentional exploitation as worse than negligent exploitation, and there may even be completely non-culpable exploitation.[18]

Thus, even if it were true that *all* capitalists and husbands (for structural reasons) exploit their workers and wives (respectively), it needn't be true that they all *intend* to do so. For some of them (naively perhaps) sincerely believe that they are benefiting and/or treating their workers and wives fairly.

2.2 Wrongful use and disparity of value

Within the moral sense of 'exploitation', John Harris usefully distinguishes between 'two differing conceptions'. The first of these is:

> the idea of *wrongful* use and may occur when there are no financial or commercial dimensions to the transaction. A classic case here would be where it is claimed that lovers may exploit one another, that is, use one another in some wrongful way. The most familiar of such wrongful ways in this context might be where it is claimed that one partner uses the other or treats the other merely as a 'sex object'.[19]

While the second conception

> involves the idea of some disparity in the value of an exchange of goods and services.[20]

Being underpaid for one's work by an unscrupulous boss is a classic example of exploitation in this second sense, as is being made to pay exorbitant prices for scarce goods by profiteers during emergencies, such as in wartime. In each case, there is a disparity of value; you are *underpaid* in one case and have to *overpay* in the other.

Sometimes both kinds of exploitation are present in the same situation. Prostitution is a good example of this. Most street prostitution is believed to be exploitative in the 'disparity of value' sense for reasons which include the fact that the women involved don't receive, or don't keep, enough money. But many people also argue that, even if there were no problems with underpayment, etc., prostitution would still be exploitative in that it involves the wrongful use of women (or others) as 'sex objects'.[21] Goodin, for example, says that:

> we would certainly want to say that prostitutes are exploited by their clients and pimps, *however well the prostitutes might be paid.*[22]

The two kinds of exploitation can, however, also function independently of one another. Consider, for example, Harris's example of the lover who says that she is treated as a sex object. Her complaint clearly appeals to wrongful use exploitation and, equally clearly, does *not* appeal to 'disparity of value' exploitation. For she is hardly likely to be impressed if her lover attempts to deal with the sex object complaint by offering to pay her for sex. Conversely, if a philosophy professor complains that she is underpaid for her philosophical labours by an *exploitative* university administration, she is (rightly or wrongly) complaining *only* about 'disparity of value' exploitation. For the chances of her thinking that employing people to teach philosophy and to do philosophical research is a *wrongful use* of them (no matter what the pay) are pretty remote.

The word 'exploitation', then, appears to be used in three different ways. We have first to distinguish between its moral and non-moral occurrences and then, within the moral ones, between 'wrongful use' and 'disparity of value' claims. How should we respond to the fact that ordinary moral thought contains these different conceptions of exploitation?

One response, a highly revisionary one, is to insist that we choose between the conceptions, providing philosophical arguments to show why one is better and adequate on its own and why the other should be abandoned. Sensat, for example, distinguishes between two frameworks for theories of exploitation. One of these, corresponding to the 'disparity of value' conception, views exploitation as 'basically a misdistribution of the benefits of social cooperation', while the other, corresponding to the wrongful use conception, views it as 'a certain kind of use of what is exploited, namely a use which is contrary to its nature'.[23] He then proceeds to argue against the former, which, he says, is 'fundamentally flawed'; for exploitation is *really* all about wrongful use, and those who think otherwise are mistaken.[24]

A second approach is to produce a 'higher-order' and/or more general theory of exploitation which somehow incorporates both conceptions. An example of this can be found in Jonathan Wolff's paper 'Marx and exploitation', where he offers us the following 'general analysis of exploitation':[25]

> to be an exploiter is to use another's circumstances to obtain their actual compliance with a situation without having sufficient regard to whether that situation violates fairness, flourishing, or suffering norms. To be exploited is to be treated in this way.[26]

Wolff's analysis (and this is not meant as a criticism) is what we might call *enablingly vague*. The precise content of 'fairness, flourishing, or suffering norms' is unspecified, and a variety of different philosophical theories about such norms can be plugged into Wolff's general definition, yielding a more substantive account. As regards wrongful use and disparity of value, it's easy to see how Wolff's definition could incorporate both. For wrongful use is (on most views) likely to violate at least one of our 'fairness, flourishing, or suffering norms', while 'disparity of value' will, at least in the standard case, be unfair and may violate the other norms too.

The third and final response is to regard the two 'exploitations' as entirely distinct moral phenomena, which just happen, by an accident of history, to be attached to the same English word. On this view, the word 'exploitation' is rather like the word 'bank', which can refer to two unrelated things: a financial institution, or the side of a small hill or mound. Another example, closer to home, is the word 'right', which (as well as its non-moral sense, *the opposite of left*) means two different things within ethics. There is an *action being right*, the right or correct thing to do, as in 'it was right for her to save that drowning child'. And then there is *someone having* a right, which here means an entitlement to something, as in 'I have a right to life.'

My aim here is not to provide a complete philosophical theory of exploitation but rather (following Wood)

> to clarify the concept ... by exploring what I think people mean when they object to behavior or social arrangements as

exploitative, and identifying the moral convictions which give such objections their force.[27]

In so doing, I hope to improve our understanding of how, and whether, exploitation objections to the commercialisation of the body work. Given this, my general strategy in what follows will be to remain as neutral as possible with respect to the theoretical options outlined above. I'll proceed *as if* there are two distinct types of exploitation, corresponding to Harris's 'two conceptions'. This may or may not, ultimately, be the correct theory of exploitation. It does seems to me, though, that each 'conception' (rightly or wrongly) has an independent role in our moral thought and that each contains, or can be used to articulate, an important (and independent) ethical insight. Since the aims here are more applied than theoretical, these facts are enough to justify the structure of what follows – my offering two semi-independent accounts of the two 'exploitations'. I should add, though, that it seems unlikely that the two 'exploitations' are completely unrelated things which just happen to be referred to by the same word, since, as we shall see, they do share a number of important features.

2.3 Benefit

Many people seem to think that exploitation (at least in the 'pejorative' sense) has to be unfair or unjust, and that the injustice consists in a redistribution of harms and benefits, with the benefits flowing from the exploited to the exploiter.[28]

This section aims to explain the connection between benefit and exploitation. In particular, we're going to take a look at the idea that exploiters necessarily derive benefit from their exploitative behaviour. Versions of this position are endorsed by, amongst others, Feinberg and Wertheimer:[29]

Common to *all* exploitation of one person (B) by another (A) . . . is that A *makes a profit or gain* by turning some characteristic of B to his own advantage.[30]

A cannot exploit or take advantage of B unless A obtains some advantage through the transaction with B.[31]

This view, which states a (putative) necessary condition for the occurrence of exploitation, I term the *benefit condition*.

To some people, it seems just obvious that exploiters are getting something, or gaining some kind of advantage, when they exploit. Why else would they do it? If, however, an argument is needed, perhaps the best is that the benefit condition is an effective way of distinguishing exploitation from abuse (as well as from certain other forms of wrongdoing, including discrimination and oppression). This appears to be one thing that moves Wertheimer to endorse a version of the benefit condition:[32]

> It has been alleged, for example, that medical students are frequently abused by oral insults and denigration and that this abuse may leave 'long-lasting emotional scars'. By contrast, it is also sometimes claimed that medical interns are exploited, that they work long hours for low pay. The contrast is just right. There is no reason to think that anyone gains – at least in any normal sense – from abuse, but it is at least plausible to think that the hospitals or patients gain from the exploitation of interns.[33]

Wertheimer's version of the benefit condition is what we might call robustly objective. For him, in order for A to exploit B, A must derive actual benefit:

> A does not actually exploit B unless A gains from the interaction, even if A *seeks* to gain from the transaction. We can distinguish between the claim that A *exploits* B and the claim that A *acts exploitatively* towards B.[34]

So, for Wertheimer, people who attempt exploitatively to derive benefit from others, but fail to derive the benefit envisaged, don't count as having exploited at all, although they have 'acted exploitatively'. Someone who rejects this 'objective' benefit condition is Sensat:

> Exploitation . . . need not further exploiters' real interests at all. Indeed, if exploitation involves something like Kant's treating persons merely as means, then exploitation may be a type of heteronomy and thus *never* in exploiters' highest-order interests.[35]

In support of this, he offers us the example of

> the man who, relying on certain power advantages, gets a woman to engage in public displays of deference and submissiveness toward him in order to boost his status as defined by the standards of a misogynous culture. While the woman's behavior is degrading to her and violates rather than realizes her nature, the man's use of the woman does nothing to further his real interests. Though it does foster the achievement of a goal which he has set for himself.[36]

Sensat's remarks show that we should reject the benefit condition, or rather the 'objective' version of it. The objective version says (implausibly) that exploiters always actually derive benefit. But a more plausible version would be subjective, appealing not to the exchange of benefits, but to the exploiter's aims and intentions: the idea being that exploiters always *aim* to derive benefit from their exploitative behaviour.

Although exploitation need not be intentional (i.e. not all exploiters mean to exploit), there may nonetheless be necessary conditions for the occurrence of exploitation which cite the exploiter's intentions. The subjective benefit condition is one such (putative) necessary condition, saying as it does that in order to exploit, one must intend to derive benefit. Exploiters (or attempted exploiters) can fail to be successful in at least two different ways. First, they can simply not get the exploitee to do, or give them, what they want. At least some of these cases will be cases of merely attempting to exploit, or what Wertheimer calls 'acting exploitatively' (without actually exploiting). Second, they can be mistaken about the value of what they demand and so fail to derive any real benefit from it, even if they get what it was that they originally wanted (under a non-evaluative description). Sensat's case is a failure of the second kind and shows very well why the subjective benefit condition is to be preferred to an objective version. The reason is that it would be more than a little odd if we said of someone, such as Sensat's misogynist, that he wasn't *really* an exploiter because the thing that he was trying to extract from the exploitee wasn't *really* of any value. Sensat, then, has provided us with a good counter-example to the objective benefit condition, and shown that it is rather a subjective benefit condition that we should be considering.[37]

However, even the subjective benefit condition faces problems of its own. The most obvious is that there could, it seems, be cases in which A exploits B not in order to benefit herself, but solely in order to affect (either positively or negatively) a third party, C. A good example of this is biomedical research on human subjects. This can, of course, be exploitative under certain conditions, but it may sometimes be motivated not by self-interest, but by the researcher's desire to do good – for example, finding a cure for AIDS, cancer, or heart disease. Alternatively, consider the following hypothetical:

Anne, Bob, and Carole

Anne employs Bob (for whom she has little regard) under highly exploitative conditions. She does this for one reason only: in order to pay for a lifesaving transplant operation for her sister Carole. Anne derives no material benefits from the arrangement. On the contrary, she (like Bob) works very hard for a minimal wage, saving all the profits for Carole's operation. Furthermore, she doesn't believe that she will derive any emotional or psychological benefits from prolonging her sister's life, since relations between them are at best 'frosty'. Rather, Anne is doing this entirely 'out of a sense of duty'.

One possible response to Anne's behaviour is to say that she must believe that she will derive some kind of benefit, even if it's just the absence of guilt feelings, otherwise she wouldn't do what she's doing. However, this won't work against hypotheticals (in which the fact that she doesn't believe that she stands to benefit can just be *stipulated*) unless attached to the (implausible) view that people only act in ways which they at some level think will benefit them.

Another response, suggested by Feinberg, is to broaden the notion of benefit ('gain' in his terms) in such a way that Anne's behaviour counts as benefiting her:

> A may exploit B for great 'gain' all of which he then gives to charity. Clearly, to accommodate this example we must dilute the sense of 'gain' so that it includes gain either for oneself or for some person or cause that one chooses to benefit. In order to preserve the gain requirement, in short, we must employ an admittedly extended sense of 'gain' including both gain in the strict sense and fulfilment of one's aims, purposes, or desires, including altruistic and conscientious ones.[38]

Wertheimer makes a similar move, introducing the category of *mediated exploitation*:

> Although the paradigmatic exploitation claims involve cases in which A seeks to promote his or her *self*-interest, we need a more protean conception of what counts as a benefit to A, one that includes A's purposes, goals, and values. In some cases, for example, A exploits B *on behalf* of C. Call this *mediated exploitation*. Consider the Legal Aid lawyer who advises her client to reject a generous settlement because she wants to litigate a new legal doctrine that, if litigation is successful, will serve the interests of a larger group. The lawyer may have exploited her client on behalf of others, but she has exploited her client nonetheless.[39]

Of course, one *could* choose to use the word 'benefit' in the ways suggested by Feinberg and Wertheimer, thereby rendering a version of the benefit condition consistent with the Anne, Bob, and Carole case (which, in Wertheimer's terms, looks like an instance of mediated exploitation). However, there are good reasons not to.

19

The first is that saying that Anne benefits from her actions is highly counter-intuitive and appears inconsistent with our ordinary usage of the word 'benefit'. Indeed, what we would probably want to say of Anne's actions (and of many other cases of charitably exploiting) is that they are acts of *self-sacrifice*, rather than *self-benefit*. Now this is not, of course, decisive. For our 'folk' use of the word 'benefit' might involve a mistake or an inconsistency, or be otherwise conceptually sub-optimal. But there should at least be a presumption in favour of ordinary usage, one which can be overturned only by substantive argument.

The second reason, one internal to our interest in producing an account of exploitation, is that if we take benefit to include fulfilment of any of 'one's aims, purposes, or desires', then the benefit condition doesn't really add anything to the idea that exploitation is use. It's obvious that exploitation necessarily involves use, and obvious too that this, in turn, involves the attempted satisfaction of the exploiter's aims, purposes, or desires. Now the benefit condition may or may not be true. But what it's *supposed* to do is to improve our account of exploitation by *adding an additional constraint*, such that not all A's usings of B, but only the ones where A tries to derive benefit from using B, count as exploitation. Given this, Feinberg's suggested broadening of the idea of benefit totally 'emasculates' the benefit condition, giving it no content over and above the idea of use. So, at least for our purposes, we may as well not bother even to discuss Feinberg's 'weak' benefit condition, for it adds nothing to the central insight that exploitation necessarily involves use.

The third and final reason is that some 'aims, purposes, or desires' are clearly self-destructive, so on Feinberg's extended understanding of 'benefit', I count as having benefited myself even when the desires I've satisfied are wholly (and self-consciously) self-destructive ones. What this shows, it seems, is that the broad understanding of benefit should be rejected on general grounds because it trivialises and renders redundant the idea of benefit, collapsing it into the idea of desire satisfaction.

A better response to Anne, Bob, and Carole is to abandon the benefit condition (in both its objective and subjective forms). For, really, there is in principle no reason why A could not exploit B for reasons which have nothing at all to do with A's welfare. And there could also be cases in which A exploits B in order to *harm*, rather than benefit, herself.[40] Consider, for example, the following:

> The Slave Owner, having killed her father during a heated argument, is filled with self-loathing and guilt. She decides (calmly and rationally) that she wants to be mutilated as a penance. She sends The Slave to purchase the necessary equipment and orders her to carry out the mutilation. Although The Slave is not exactly keen on The Owner, she

nonetheless has moral qualms about mutilating her and also finds the whole idea physically repulsive. However, The Owner insists that The Slave must go through with it, threatening to have her and her family tortured if she doesn't do what she wants.

Presumably we *do* want to say that The Slave is exploited here because, in most respects, the situation is just like any other case of forced labour. The Slave is coerced and made to do what The Owner wants – which, here, just happens to be mutilation. However, it's also clear that The Owner's goals are not (or, at least, need not be) self-beneficial. Hence, we have another counter-example to the benefit condition. (A more realistic case like the above might be where someone – again for reasons of 'self-loathing', rather than pleasure – hires a prostitute, under exploitative conditions, to perform harmful 'sadistic' acts.)

What we should say then is not that exploiters necessarily use others to benefit themselves, but that *they necessarily use others to foster the achievement of their own goals*: goals which may or may not be selfish and may or may not coincide with the furtherance of their real interests.[41] In reality, of course, most of the goals that people have are self-interested ones. Hence, exploiters do normally use others to benefit themselves, which is why the benefit condition strikes us as initially plausible. But attempting to benefit oneself is not a necessary part of being an exploiter. This proposal, which we might term the *use condition*, is in substance more or less the same as Feinberg's 'expanded' benefit condition, but (for reasons given earlier) I prefer to drop talk of benefit, instead of expanding the notion of benefit.

2.4 Use

There are various things about people which we exploit. We might exploit their strong backs or weak minds. We might exploit their fears, ignorance, superstitions, gullibility, or naiveté. We might exploit their generosity, loyalty or trust. We might exploit their bad luck, their joblessness, homelessness or illness. All those things, however, are merely *attributes* of people and their circumstances. Exploiting a person's attributes is not the same as exploiting a person. Each of us can sometimes exploit some of our *own* attributes – a runner her stamina, a boxer his reach, etc. We would not thereby be exploiting ourselves; we would just be exploiting certain *things about* ourselves.[42]

This section aims to address two questions. The first is simply: what exactly is use? More specifically, what exactly is the kind of use involved in exploitation? The second relates to the distinction drawn by Goodin above: how does exploiting or using *a person* relate to exploiting or using *a person's attributes*? It won't be possible to answer completely such questions here. However, it will be possible at least to provide a general framework, and to rule certain possibilities out and others in.

One initial linguistic complication and, I suspect, the source of more than a little confusion, is the fact that (as we have already seen) 'use', like 'exploitation', can be used as a moral term. Hence, if B is *exploited* by A, in the moral sense, then we probably also want to say that B is *used* by A, again in the moral sense. Bearing this in mind, the first thing we need to say about use is that 'use' as it occurs in the use condition is *not* a moral term. Rather, for A to use B (in the sense intended) is simply for A to bring it about that that B or, more likely, some part or aspect or behaviour of B, makes a causal or constitutive contribution to the achievement of A's relevant goals (where 'goals' is meant as a general term covering aims, desires, wants, etc). So the use condition (when it's satisfied) is normally satisfied by there being use of one or more of the exploitee's attributes, rather than use of the exploitee *per se*.

As an answer to our questions, though, this is at best schematic. Can anything more be said? One substantive answer is suggested by Wood, who offers a very plausible model of the kind of use which normally occurs when one person exploits another. First, he distinguishes two aspects of the 'standard' exploitative relationship: *advantage-exploitation* and *benefit-exploitation*. We *advantage-exploit* when we 'exploit someone's weakness or vulnerability, which gives us a hold over the person'.[43] (So we might say that to advantage-exploit is to 'take advantage'.) The vulnerabilities which are the objects of advantage-exploitation are often desires and needs. Hence, we can say, for example, that the starving worker's *need* for food and the young 'wannabe' footballer's passionate *desire* to be a soccer star are advantage-exploited by their employers; or that the economically dependent wife's *need* for money and a home is advantage-exploited by her husband; or that the terminally ill patient's desperate *desire* for a 'miracle cure' is advantage-exploited by the bio-medical researchers who recruit her into their clinical trial. However, the idea of vulnerability is wider than that of desire/need, and, as Wolff points out:

> it is easier to give a list of causes of vulnerability than to explain its nature. Typically you are vulnerable if (other things being equal) you are poorer, more ignorant, less intelligent, less cunning, or less ruthless than another, or have some other bargaining weakness with respect to them.[44]

The relationship between advantage-exploitation and the 'full' exploitation of persons is, it seems to me, as follows. One can be advantage-exploited without being exploited (in the moral sense): i.e. advantage-exploitation is not sufficient for exploitation. But one can't be exploited, or at least one can't be the object of disparity of value exploitation, without being advantage-exploited: i.e. advantage-exploitation is necessary for disparity of value exploitation.

The reason why advantage-exploitation isn't sufficient for exploitation is simply that there are entirely innocent, or even beneficent, cases in which one or more of a person's vulnerabilities are advantage-exploited. For example, a friend might advantage-exploit my gullibility in order to give me a surprise party or an unexpected gift which she knows I will enjoy – and enjoy all the more for having been 'taken in'.[45] It would be bizarre to describe such cases as exploitation, although, interestingly, similar cases could be exploitation (or attempted exploitation) if my friend's aims were different: for example, if she advantage-exploited my gullibility by playing a practical joke on me in order to impress third parties.

The reason why advantage-exploitation is a necessary part of disparity of value exploitation is that this form of exploitation normally involves getting the exploitee *to agree to a 'bad deal'* by advantage-exploiting her personal or situational weaknesses. Indeed, Wood is right when he says that without advantage-exploitation, there wouldn't be the required 'control or manipulation of the object of exploitation'. For people (at least if they are fully informed, rational, etc.) are hardly likely to agree to 'bad deals' unless they are advantage-exploited (or otherwise pushed or tricked) into doing so.

Turning now to benefit-exploitation, we benefit-exploit when we take advantage of 'some attribute of the person from which we derive benefit or use to achieve our end'.[46] So to benefit-exploit is to derive benefit or otherwise make use of. Hence, we can say of the earlier examples that the employers and husbands benefit-exploit the capacity of their workers and wives (respectively) to provide productive labour; or that the bio-medical researchers benefit-exploit some useful aspect of their research subjects' bodies.

Like advantage-exploitation, benefit-exploitation is not *sufficient* for the 'full' exploitation of a person. If it were, then exploitation would occur whenever anyone was useful to anyone else (for example, in employment or friendship) and accusations of exploitation would hardly be serious moral criticisms – if indeed they were criticisms at all – given that exploitation would be endemic. It does, however, seem that benefit-exploitation is *necessary* for the 'full' exploitation of a person, since this is entailed by (what I at the end of the previous section termed) the use condition. For the use condition says that (successful) exploiters necessarily use exploitees as means of achieving their goals. And exploitees can contribute to the achievement of their exploiters' goals in this way only if they have one or more usable attributes which are benefit-exploited. Hence, in order for a person to be exploited, one or more of her attributes must be benefit-exploited. (Note that this is compatible with my earlier rejection of the benefit condition, since Wood's idea of benefit-exploitation appeals not only to benefit, but to 'benefit or use'.)

Wood, then, is right to describe the relationship between the two aspects of exploitation as follows:

> As their names are meant to imply, advantage-exploitation and benefit-exploitation constitute a complementary pair, and advantage-exploitation is the foundation of benefit-exploitation. Without benefit-exploitation there would be no *use* of the object of exploitation, while without advantage-exploitation there would be no control or manipulation of the object of exploitation.[47]

So in order to be exploitable (at least in the disparity of value sense) one must be both useful and vulnerable (which presumably everyone is to differing extents). Someone who is entirely useless can't be exploited because she can't contribute to the achievement of the exploiter's goals, while someone who is totally invulnerable can't be exploited because she can't be made to agree to an exploitative deal by having her weaknesses advantage-exploited. This is a helpful insight, since it provides a structure for thinking about why certain people are more exploitable than others. The most exploitable people are those who are *both* very useful *and* very vulnerable. A young woman who was both sexually attractive and poor would be an obvious example. Her sexual attractiveness makes her 'useful' – both directly, as a means of satisfying men's sexual desires, and indirectly, as a way of making money for third parties – while her poverty makes her vulnerable. So her level of exploitability is high. In contrast, people who are equally useful but *not* vulnerable, such as workers with desired occupational skills that are in short supply, are not very exploitable. On the contrary, they tend to do well in market economies, since they can enter into non-exploitative contracts to sell their useful attributes, or the products of those attributes. Indeed, workers like these may well be in a position to exploit employers who need their services. What about people who are vulnerable but not useful? Such people are not exploitable, but only because they are in the unfortunate position of not having anything to exploit. Even worse, given their vulnerability, if they were to acquire any useful attributes, they could only do so at the cost of becoming the potential victims of exploitation.

At several points, I've qualified claims about exploitation by saying that they apply only to disparity of value exploitation. With this in mind, I'd like to end this section by discussing briefly how the preceding discussion of use (in particular, of advantage-exploitation and benefit-exploitation) relates to wrongful use exploitation.

As I've already suggested, benefit-exploitation is required for both types of exploitation. So the first thing to note is that in order for there to be wrongful use exploitation, there must be benefit-exploitation. Where disparity of value and wrongful use differ is in their relationship to advantage-exploitation. I suggested earlier that in order for there to be disparity of value exploitation, the exploitee must agree (or acquiesce) to a bad deal and that the reason why she agrees to it is that she is advantage-exploited: i.e. a weakness or vulnerability is used to make her agree or acquiesce. However, these considerations don't apply to wrongful use exploitation, because this form of exploitation doesn't require the exploitee to agree to a 'bad deal': *both* because she needn't agree at all *and* because, even where there is agreement, the 'deal' agreed to need not be bad (or, at least, need not be bad considered apart from the intrinsic badness of wrongful use itself). This point will be discussed in more detail in Chapter 5. For the present, it will suffice to think again about wrongful use objections to prostitution and, more generally, to treating other persons as sex objects. In the case of prostitution, the whole point of the wrongful use objection is that it's meant to apply *even if* the prostitute consents and *even if* she gets a 'good deal' (financially, etc.). This shows that, where there is agreement, the 'deal' agreed to need not be bad. And, to think more generally about 'sex object objections', it should be obvious that it's possible for A to treat B as a sex object (and thus arguably subject B to wrongful use exploitation) without B having any say in the matter, without B's agreeing to anything at all. Pornography, rape, sexual abuse, and voyeurism could all be examples of this.

The two different types of exploitation, then, differ not only in their relationship with *advantage-exploitation*, but also in their relationship with *consent*. The question of how exactly exploitation relates to consent is one of the most interesting issues within exploitation theory and will be explored further in subsequent chapters.

2.5 Summary and conclusions

This chapter has introduced and provided the first moves in an analysis of the concept of exploitation. Such an analysis is required because philosophers have paid relatively little attention to defining exploitation, because exploitation is a heavily used and widely accepted idea, and because exploitation arguments have special relevance to the principal concerns of this book. Indeed, I'd go as far as to say that exploitation is perhaps *the* single most important moral concept in the body commodification debate.

The main findings of this chapter's investigations are as follows:

1 The word 'exploitation', like the associated expressions 'use' and 'take advantage of', has both a moral and a non-moral sense. Our interest is almost solely in the first of these.

2 Behind the moral sense of 'exploitation' lie two distinct worries: one about *disparity of value*, the other about *wrongful use*. These can usefully be thought of as two different kinds of exploitation.

3 Although not totally unrelated, these two sorts of exploitation are importantly different in a number of respects: for example, the ways in which they relate to consent and to taking advantage of people's vulnerabilities (what Wood calls *advantage-exploitation*). When assessing exploitation objections, therefore, we must be sure to disambiguate 'exploitation' and to establish which of the two types is being referred to.

4 Exploiters normally derive benefit from exploitation, but don't necessarily do so, or even aim to do so, since there can be charitable or self-destructive exploitation.

5 Exploiters always *use* exploitees: i.e. they bring it about that the exploitee, or some part or aspect or behaviour of the exploitee, makes a contribution to the achievement of the exploiter's goals.

3

OBJECTIFICATION, EXPLOITATION, AND COMMODIFICATION

[I]t is impossible to be a person and a thing, the proprietor and the property.[1]

This chapter aims to give an account of three closely related concepts, each of which plays an important part in debates about the commercialisation of the human body. The three concepts are objectification, (what in the previous chapter I termed) 'wrongful use exploitation', and commodification.

3.1 Objectification

If anything a prostitute treats herself like a chair for someone to sit on. Her mind goes blank. She just lies there. You become an object. A lot of clients say, 'Respond. It doesn't seem normal just lying there.'[2]

Let's start with objectification, since this is the broadest of the three concepts. Indeed, I'll argue later that both commodification and wrongful use exploitation are particular types of objectification. Not surprisingly, to objectify is to treat as a mere object. However, treating *objects* as objects doesn't count as objectification. Rather, to objectify is to treat as a (mere) object something which isn't really (or merely) an object. Nussbaum makes the point as follows:

in all cases of objectification what is at issue is . . . treating one thing as another: One is treating *as an object* what is really not an object, what is, in fact, a human being.[3]

Treating things as objects is not objectification, since . . . objectification is making into a thing, treating *as* a thing, something that is not really a thing.[4]

27

In the first of the above quotations, Nussbaum restricts objectification to human beings and, because this book is mainly about the commercialisation of the *human* body, I'll do the same. There is, however, no reason to rule out *a priori* the objectification of extraterrestrials, animals, nature, or works of art – or, indeed, of anything which isn't a mere thing but can be treated as such.

So what exactly is it to treat something as a mere object? Nussbaum plausibly claims that it is impossible simply to read off a definite answer to this question, or indeed a precise definition of 'objectification', from ordinary language. She argues instead that objectification is a 'loose cluster-concept' and proceeds usefully to identify seven ways of treating something as an object, suggesting that 'we sometimes treat any one of these as sufficient' for objectification, 'though more often a plurality of features is present when the term is applied'.[5] The seven ways are described below (in terms of the objectification of persons).

1 *Instrumentality* – the person is treated as merely a tool for, or a means of, achieving the objectifier's goals.
2 *Denial of autonomy* – the person's autonomy is not recognised or not respected.
3 *Inertness* – the person is treated as lacking in agency ('and perhaps also in activity').
4 *Fungibility* – the person is treated as interchangeable with other similar persons (or even with relevantly similar non-persons).[6]
5 *Violability* – the person's right to bodily integrity is not recognised or not respected.
6 *Ownership* – the person is treated as property.
7 *Denial of subjectivity* – the experiences of the person are not recognised or not regarded as significant.[7]

Nussbaum spends a considerable amount of time constructing a complex account of the interrelations between these seven aspects or kinds of objectification and applies this to a variety of literary examples, most of which contain pornography or depict sexual objectification. There's not space to do the same here and, in any case, my own position is that this part of her analysis is basically correct. What I'll do instead is to proceed directly to the question of why we do (and perhaps should) regard her seven forms of objectification as morally bad ways of treating people.

3.2 Kantian underpinnings

[W]hen we use the term pejoratively, as in 'objectification of persons,' we mean, roughly, 'what Kant would not want us to do.' The person is a subject, a moral agent, autonomous and self-governing. An object is a non-person, not treated as a self-governing moral agent.[8]

Margaret Radin (above) suggests that objectification (in the pejorative sense) is very much a Kantian moral concept, and it seems to me (and to Nussbaum) that she's right about this.[9] Underpinning our ethical worries about the objectification of persons are two principles that are broadly Kantian, though one certainly doesn't need to be a fully-fledged Kantian in order to subscribe to them.

The first of these – which is very obviously connected to the first sort of objectification, *instrumentality* – is Kant's well-known doctrine that people should be treated as ends-in-themselves rather than as (mere) means:

> Act so that you treat humanity, whether in your own person or in that of another, always as an end and never as a means only.[10]

The second principle – which is most clearly connected to the fourth kind of objectification, *fungibility* – relates to Kant's less popularly known distinction between *price* and *dignity*:

> In the kingdom of ends everything has either a *price* or a *dignity*. Whatever has a price can be replaced by something else as its equivalent; on the other hand, whatever is above all price, and therefore admits of no equivalent, has a dignity.[11]

According to this second principle, persons have *dignity*, in the sense explicated by Kant, and should be treated and viewed as such. Treating them as fungible (interchangeable) fails properly to respect their dignity and, in Kantian terms, is to regard them as having mere 'price'. This specifically Kantian way in which the term 'dignity' is used should be carefully distinguished from other 'looser' uses of the term, because rather vague ideas of 'human dignity' are often wheeled out during ethical debates about (for example) biotechnology, without there being any clear sense of what exactly dignity is, or why exactly the technology under consideration is an affront to it. Hence, Burley and Harris are quite right to talk of ethical objections often being couched in terms of '*mysterious appeals* to human rights and human dignity'. (They are referring to objections to cloning, but their point applies much more generally.)[12]

Next, I want to show how the wrongness of each of Nussbaum's seven types of objectification is entailed by one or both of these Kantian principles. In so doing, I'll be explaining why the view that objectification is wrong is commonly held, since adherence to the Kantian principles is itself widespread. Furthermore, on the assumption that these Kantian principles not only are but also ought to be believed, I'll be going a long way towards justifying people's hostility to objectification.

The first type of objectifying (*instrumentality*) is easy to deal with since this is exactly what is proscribed by the first Kantian principle: treat people always as ends and never only as means. We'll be returning to look at instrumentalisation in more detail later on in this chapter.

The status of the second type of objectifying (*denial of autonomy*) is less clear because the meaning of 'autonomy' is unspecified. Also, there is an important distinction between *failing to recognise* that a person has the psychological property of being autonomous and *failing to respect* that autonomy (the latter probably being best understood in terms of unjustifiably restricting the person's freedom). Our difficulty then is that there is more than one way of understanding 'autonomy'. However, it can plausibly be claimed that, on at least most of these understandings, recognising and respecting people's autonomy is a necessary part of treating them as ends-in-themselves. Hence, denial of autonomy would be forbidden by the first Kantian principle.

If *inertness* is understood as the absence of agency, then it also falls foul of the first Kantian principle, since seeing people as ends-in-themselves requires seeing them as agents – people who do, or at least could, act (with action being broadly understood so as not to exclude, say, people with severe physical disabilities).

Fungibility is also easy to deal with since this is exactly what is proscribed by the second Kantian principle. According to this principle, we should treat people as having 'dignity' rather than mere 'price'. What this means is that we should not treat persons as if they were *replaceable* or *interchangeable*. We should instead treat them as *irreplaceable* and *unique* – and perhaps even as *incommensurable* with respect to one another (which means that the value of each person is neither more than, nor less than, nor the same as the value of each other person). Nussbaum says that

> The connection between fungibility and instrumentality is loose and causal, rather than conceptual.[13]

About this, I would suggest, she is not quite right. For there does seem to be at least one *a priori* connection. The link is that anyone who adopts an entirely instrumental attitude towards X, in so doing, regards X as fungible. This is because to have a fully instrumental attitude to X is to value X only for its relevant causal powers – only for how effective it is as a means of achieving one's own ends. So if I value X in this way, I am indifferent as to whether I have X, or have a replacement, Y – provided that Y has the very same relevant causal powers as X.[14] Indeed, not to be indifferent as to whether I have X or have Y in such a situation would suggest strongly that I had not *fully* 'instrumentalised' X. A fairly trivial example should illustrate the point. Some people have fully instrumental attitudes to their cars. Others are emotionally attached to their cars, perhaps because they are sentimental about experiences that they've had in them. People of the first type also regard their cars as fungible. Because they only care about the car's ability to get them 'from A to B', they don't mind its being replaced with any other equally effective vehicle. People in the second category, however, don't regard their cars as fungible – and this is precisely because they don't regard them as mere instruments. Rather, they are emotionally attached to them and would be upset if their car were replaced by another, even if it were the same make, model, colour, etc. They (rightly or wrongly) regard their vehicles as unique and irreplaceable.

For completeness, I should add that although regarding something as purely instrumental necessitates regarding it as fungible, it *may* be possible to view something as fungible without also viewing it as merely instrumental. Aesthetic value is a leading example here. Someone may not care which of two equally beautiful paintings she owns and yet still regard the aesthetic value of each as intrinsic rather than instrumental. Cases like this are tricky because it's possible to redescribe them in ways which make it sound as if the viewer is 'instrumentalising' the paintings – for example, we can say that she uses the paintings as *means* of experiencing beauty (or pleasure). But they do at the very least show that viewing-as-fungible doesn't *obviously* entail viewing-as-merely-instrumental. Perhaps a better (though rather theoretical) example of viewing something as fungible without also viewing it as merely instrumental is classical utilitarianism.[15] This theory sees human happiness as the one and only *intrinsic* (non-instrumental) good. However, it also see happiness as a *fungible* good. For classical utilitarians don't (from a moral point of view) care *who* is happy, or which particular 'bits of happiness' exist, so long as overall happiness is maximised. People often attack utilitarianism on precisely this point, arguing that it wrongly obliges us to 'trade off' (in a thoroughly impersonal, 'agent-neutral' way) the welfare of one person against others, or even against the welfare of possible people.

The fifth item on Nussbaum's list is *violability*: failing to recognise and/or respect the person's right to bodily integrity. The right to bodily integrity is a limited right not to have one's body non-consensually damaged, invaded, touched, viewed, etc. It is typically invoked to explain such things as the wrongness of non-consensual medical treatment and rape. A commonplace view in ethics is that this right to bodily integrity follows from the principle of respect for autonomy, although saying why this is so is far from simple. In brief, one argument would be that an important part of being self-determining (autonomous) is having substantial control over one's own body – and, in order to have such control, one's body must be free from non-consensual interference by others. If this line of reasoning is correct (as appears plausible), then the wrongness of treating people as violable follows from the first Kantian principle. For the right to bodily integrity follows from the principle of respect for autonomy, which in turn follows from the idea that we should treat persons as 'ends'.

Ownership, the penultimate category, is not entirely straightforward since 'owning a person' can mean a variety of things. More specifically, to own someone is to have certain rights over her, and so there will be different sorts of ownership corresponding to different sets of rights. An extreme example of ownership would be a system of slavery under which slave owners were legally permitted to kill and otherwise physically violate their slaves. Under such a system, the slave owners would have what we might call *fully-fledged* or *unrestricted* property rights in their slaves – meaning that they're allowed to do whatever they like with and to them, including destroying them. Clearly, ownership of this kind is wrong. Not only is it cruel and harmful, but it also very obviously falls foul of Kantian principles because the slave's autonomy is not respected and it is highly likely that such slaves will be regarded as fungible. As Anderson puts it:

> In Kantian theory, the problem with slavery is that it treats beings worthy of *respect* as if they were worthy merely of *use*.[16]

However, not all ownership is like this, as Nussbaum reminds us:

> Slaves are not necessarily regarded as violable; there may even be laws against the rape and/or bodily abuse of slaves.[17]

So someone could have a much more limited set of property rights over another person. For example, there could be a *relatively* humane system of slavery under which, although the slave owners had complete control over their slaves' labour, they were nonetheless obliged not physically to hurt them, and to provide them with health care, adequate food and shelter, and rest days and holidays. We can construct a series of progressively more 'humane' examples like this and, if we keep going, we'll eventually reach a point at which the 'owned' person starts to look more like a well-treated employee than a slave – though at that point we may start to wonder if the person is really owned. This raises the following (closely connected) questions. First, what kind of rights over B (a person) must A have in order to count as *owning* B? Second, does A's owning B *necessarily* involve A's wrongfully objectifying B? I won't attempt to answer these here, since such difficult questions are the concern of the entire book. I'll simply note for the present that, although almost everyone is agreed that owning persons is wrong – since it amounts to or is like slavery – it's rather hard to say how we should distinguish between those clusters of rights which constitute owning *a part or aspect of a person (or of her life)* (for example, employers' contractual rights) and those which constitute *owning a ('whole') person* (for example, slavery). This issue will arise in various different forms throughout the book.

The final item on Nussbaum's list, *denial of subjectivity*, again follows pretty directly from the first Kantian principle. For, it can be argued, part of treating people as ends-in-themselves is recognising the existence and importance of their mental states and especially of the fact that they are subjects.

So to sum up, the view that each of Nussbaum's seven types of object-ification is (*prima facie*) wrong can be justified by reference to two Kantian principles. The first says that we must always treat people as ends-in-themselves and respect their autonomy. The second says that we must recognise and respect people's dignity and not treat them as fungible.

3.3 Wrongful use exploitation

The fundamental synonym for the verb 'exploit' is 'use'.[18]

When market norms are applied to the ways we treat and under-stand women's reproductive labor, women are reduced from sub-jects of respect and consideration to objects of use.[19]

With an analysis of objectification and its Kantian underpinnings in place, we're now in a position to say what wrongful use exploitation is. Wrong-ful use exploitation is identical with Nussbaum's first kind of objectifica-tion, instrumentality. A exploits B (in this sense) if A treats B merely as a tool for, or a means of, achieving A's goals.

What's the status of this claim, and what are the arguments for it? As regards its status, it is meant to be a rational reconstruction of what people in fact mean when they use the word 'exploitation' in this way – i.e. what really concerns them morally is that one person is *using another person as a (mere) means*. As regards arguments for it, these take two forms. First, if we analyse academic and non-academic ethical discourse we'll find that this is one of the ways in which 'exploitation' is actually used. The same goes for the analysis of case studies involving alleged exploitation. Many of these centre around the question of whether the putative exploitee has been used as a mere means or not. Second – and here we move into more normative territory, as opposed to simply attempting to capture the facts of ordinary moral language – there are some theoretical advantages (coherence, explanation, justification, neat-ness, etc.) to defining wrongful use exploitation in this way. One is that (provided we accept Kant's 'treat people always as ends' principle) it's easy to see what's wrong with wrongful use exploitation. For, by definition, this involves failing to treat people as ends and so always falls foul of the first Kantian principle. A second is that, on the definition offered, it's possible to fit wrongful use exploitation neatly into a family of moral concepts including commodification and objectification. Or, at least, that's what I aim to show in this chapter.

A question that we touched on during Chapter 2 and to which we can now return is: how exactly are the two exploitations ('disparity of value' and 'wrongful use') related to one another? Are they merely unrelated things which just happen to be referred to by the same word or do they have important features in common? Even though the analysis of exploitation isn't finished, it should already be clear, in general terms, what the main similarities and differences are. Their foremost shared feature is that, in all cases of exploitation, the exploitee (and/or one or more of her attributes) is used by the exploiter. This point is expressed in what I earlier called the use condition: the view that A exploits B only if A uses B in order to foster the achievement of A's goals. Where the two exploitations differ is in what's wrong (or thought to be wrong) with the use in question. In wrongful use exploitation, the exploitee is wronged by being *used solely as a means*, whereas in 'disparity of value' exploitation, the exploitee is wronged because she is *unfairly used* – with the unfairness typically consisting of being under-rewarded and of having her vulnerabilities taken advantage of (what Wood calls 'advantage-exploitation').

So although both exploitations involve using persons, they are really very different moral concepts. One is grounded in the Kantian 'treat people always as ends' principle and has nothing whatever to do with the unfair distribution of goods, or with taking advantage of the vulnerable; the other is all about the latter and nothing to do with the former. In practice, of course, both exploitations are often present together. This is no accident. If A subjects B to wrongful use exploitation, the fact that A also subjects B to 'disparity of value' exploitation shouldn't surprise us. For if A doesn't respect B as an 'end', A is not likely to be too concerned about treating B fairly or about not taking advantage of B.

This substantial difference between the two exploitations, combined with the facts that (a) they 'share' the same name and (b) they often occur together, helps to create a good deal of moral confusion. For example, it's sometimes hard for people to tell whether it's the *unfairness* of a particular using or *the plain fact that it's a using* (or both) that they find objectionable. For this reason and for stylistic reasons, I shall in subsequent chapters change my own terminology as follows. I'll reserve the word 'exploitation' for what I've so far been calling 'disparity of value' exploitation and I'll use the word 'instrumentalisation' for what I've so far been calling wrongful use exploitation. Does this mean that I think that wrongful use exploitation isn't *really* exploitation? It's not clear to me that asking this question is terribly helpful. I have said what, in my view, wrongful use exploitation is. I have said what it has in common with 'disparity of value' exploitation and what it does not. And I have said that people *call* wrongful use exploitation 'exploitation'. Beyond that, it's not clear to me that asking whether or not it's *really* exploitation has much point. Why, then, have I chosen to allocate the 'exploitation' label to 'disparity of value' rather than to 'wrongful use'? My reasons for doing so are linguistic rather than philosophical: it seems to me that using the word 'exploitation' to refer to 'disparity of value' exploitation is simply *more common* than using it to refer to wrongful use exploitation. Furthermore, it is harder to find a suitable alternative word for 'disparity of value' exploitation than it is to find one for wrongful use exploitation.

The next two sections explore instrumentalisation (wrongful use exploitation) further by (in 3.4) revisiting the idea of treating persons as ends-in-themselves and (in 3.5) looking at its relationship with treating people as means.

3.4 Treating people as ends-in-themselves

> That people should treat others as a means to their own ends, however desirable the consequences, must always be liable to moral objection. Such treatment of one person by another becomes positively exploitative when financial interests are involved.[20]

As we've seen, Kant's idea that we must always treat persons as ends-in-themselves and never as 'means only' plays a crucial role in explaining both what objectification is and why objectifying persons is *prima facie* wrong.

One feature of this principle which is sometimes overlooked (and which seems, incidentally, to be overlooked in the passage from the Warnock Report quoted above) is that it doesn't in fact prohibit treating people as means. Rather, it asserts that we've a positive obligation always to treat them as ends. So treating people as means may be permissible (according to the principle) so long as we *also* treat them as ends. That this is the meaning of the Kantian principle should be unsurprising, because if it ruled out treating people as means altogether, it would be wildly implausible. John Harris, commenting on the passage from the Warnock Report quoted earlier, makes the point as follows:

> it by no means follows, as Warnock claims, that where people treat others as means to their own ends there is automatically exploitation. We all do this perfectly innocuously much of the

time. In medical contexts, anyone who receives a blood transfusion has used the blood donor as a means to their own ends.[21]

So, to reiterate, the Kantian principle should be understood as a requirement always to treat people as ends – even if, at the same time, we treat them as means. One thing that follows from this is that there may be ways of breaching the principle which don't involve instrumentalising persons. In other words, there may be cases of wrongfully failing to treat people as ends which aren't also cases where those wronged are treated as means. That this is so can be shown by thinking back to Nussbaum's seven types of objectification. Some of these breach the Kantian principle not because people are treated as means, but just because they are (for other reasons) not treated as ends-in-themselves. *Denial of subjectivity* and *violability* are perhaps the clearest examples of this. Now, of course *often* it's the case that when people have their 'subjectivity denied' and/or their rights to bodily integrity ignored, it's because someone else is using them as a mere instrument. But this isn't the only reason why these kinds of objectification can occur.

At this point, it's helpful to draw a (probably not very sharp) distinction, within objectification, between regarding a person as a *useful object* and regarding a person as a *useless object*. Most discussions of objectification focus on people who are wrongfully *used* and hence on those who are, in one way or another, viewed as useful. However, there is another way of being objectified: to be viewed as an object in which the objectifier has no interest and to which she assigns not even instrumental value. Totally ignoring people who sleep rough on the streets is a possible example of this phenomenon. Sometimes, people on their way to work, or on the way home after a night out, regard these 'street people' as like objects, not in the sense of being objects of use, but on the contrary as being a bit like bags of rubbish which are inconvenient and/or aesthetically displeasing. The personhood of 'street people' is often ignored and, even when they actively approach passers-by, they are more likely to be blanked than argued with. Indeed, one common complaint made by 'street people' is that they are treated as if they don't exist, as if their voices can't be heard, as if they're invisible. Their subjectivity is denied or ignored. They are treated as mere irritations rather than as people with intrinsic value and are at risk of being treated as (in Nussbaum's terms) 'violable'. This seems clearly to be objectification (treating as a mere object), though not a kind that involves use.

We've seen, then that treating a person instrumentally, as a means, is not *necessary* for breaching Kant's 'treat people as ends' principle. This is because it's possible to fail to treat persons as ends-in-themselves without also treating them as means (the leading examples here being those where the objectifier treats people as 'useless' objects). We've also seen that treating someone instrumentally is not *sufficient* for breaching the Kantian principle, because it is possible to treat people *both* instrumentally *and* as ends-in-themselves. Given this, the obvious question to ask is: what exactly is the relationship between breaching Kant's principle and treating persons as means? This is the subject of the next section.

3.5 What's wrong with using people as means?

To answer this, let's first return to Nussbaum's article on objectification and, in particular, to what she has to say about Kant's views on sex and marriage:

> Central to Kant's analysis ... is the idea that sexual desire is a very powerful force that conduces to the thinglike treatment of persons ... above all, the treatment of persons not as ends in themselves, but as means or tools for the satisfaction of one's own desires. That kind of instrumentalizing of persons was very closely linked, in his view, to both a denial of autonomy – one wishes to dictate how the other person will behave, so as to secure one's own satisfaction – and also to denial of subjectivity – one stops asking how the other person is thinking or feeling, bent on securing one's own satisfaction.[22]

Kant may or may not be right about the nature of sexual desire (and this isn't, sadly, something that there's space to explore further here). But even if we don't accept his views on sex, we can still learn something from the above passage about the way in which viewing persons instrumentally might lead us to deny their autonomy. For Kant's proposal seems in general terms a good idea, and – what's more – a remarkably 'common-sense' one. His thought is that when we become focussed on a person's instrumental value, on her usefulness to us, we have a tendency to disregard the fact that she is an autonomous being who deserves respect. In other words, thinking of a person in terms of use encourages us to overlook the fact that she's not *only* for our use, but is also an end-in-herself.

Some ways of focussing on a person's instrumental value seem more dangerous in this regard than others, with the risk varying depending both on the type and on the extent of any use involved. Some people would, for example, say that sexual use of other human beings is especially morally hazardous – meaning that there's a considerable risk of the sexually used person's autonomy being ignored by the sexual user (who may be overwhelmed by desires, feelings, etc. and, in some sense, forget that the sexually used body 'belongs' to another person and/or that the other person deserves respect and consideration). By contrast, most of us would regard using someone as a teacher in order to learn as generally unproblematic. Because of the nature of teaching and of the teacher–student relationship, the use involved is not normally of a kind which encourages students to overlook the teacher's autonomy or personhood. Lying behind these views are, I suspect, a conception of sex which views the sexually used body as a passive and impersonal object, and a model of teaching which regards it as active, autonomous, and expressive of the teacher's personality. From this we might generalise as follows (without necessarily endorsing these particular views of sex or of teaching). When people (or people's bodies) are used as passive and impersonal objects, the risk of objectification is greater than when they're used in ways which are somehow expressive of their personalities.

Thoughts like these raise questions about the status of both (a) the general claim that when we think of people instrumentally we tend to disregard the fact that they're also 'ends', and (b) more specific claims about use, such as that using people for sexual gratification is more likely to make us overlook their personhood than using people as teachers. Are such claims just empirical psychological generalisations? Or are they 'deeper' conceptual truths? The word 'treat' – in the expression 'treat as an object' – is a useful shorthand for both the *attitudes* and the *behaviour* of the objectifier. And in order to answer this 'status question', we need to appeal to this kind of distinction, since we may need to give different answers depending on whether we're looking at how we *think of* people or how we *act towards* them.

Let's start with attitudes. It's clear that there's no reason in principle why valuing a person instrumentally must conflict with also valuing the same person as an 'end'. That this is so can be seen from our everyday lives. We all know individuals to whom we attach both instrumental and intrinsic value (such as those who are both treasured friends and proficient colleagues). Furthermore, not only *can* we attach both kinds of value, but often we *ought* to do so because the people in question really are *both* ends-in-themselves *and* undeniably useful. It would be bizarre to claim, surely, that in order to recognise and respect such people as persons, we need somehow to deny or ignore their usefulness.

In fact, this is just a particular application of a more general truth: that there's no reason in principle why one can't value something (or someone) instrumentally while at the same time recognising its other kinds of (intrinsic) value. We can use aesthetic value as an example here. Let's say that I own a beautiful figurine which I keep on my desk to look at and use as a paperweight. What's to stop me from *both* regarding it as useful *and* regarding it as an object of great beauty? Obviously, nothing. Indeed, assigning both kinds of value would be the rational thing to do, on the assumption that it really is both beautiful and useful, and doing so needn't involve any sort of conflict or contradiction. Or consider a similar case – architecture. Many buildings can be, should be, and are designed to be appreciated both for their aesthetic merits and for their utility. In such cases, what's clear is that recognising something's instrumental value doesn't *need to* displace our appreciation and regard for other kinds of value. This is as true of persons as it is for works of art, or for buildings.

3.6 The displacement thesis

As we've seen, there's no conceptual or logical conflict between thinking of something instrumentally and valuing it in other ways too. However, there is instead what I'll term the *displacement thesis*. This says that, even though different modes of valuation don't logically contradict one another, they nonetheless conflict *psychologically*: that, as a matter of fact, instrumental valuation tends to *displace* other important modes of valuation in the human mind. Consider, as an example, Elizabeth Anderson's assertion that

> The commodification of sexual 'services' destroys the kind of reciprocity required to realise human sexuality as a shared good. Each party values the other only instrumentally, not intrinsically.[23]

According to the displacement thesis, this claim should be understood as follows. For *psychological* reasons (which may be construed broadly) each party is very likely to neglect the other's personhood, intrinsic value, etc. This is because one party is interested primarily in using the other person as a *means of achieving sexual satisfaction*, while the other party is interested mainly in using the other person as a *means of obtaining money*. Both parties, though, are subject to broadly the same psychological phenomenon: the 'personhood perspective' on the other is *displaced* by a 'use perspective'.

Since my main aims are philosophical rather than psychological, I can't address in any detail the question of whether the displacement thesis is a good piece of psychology. However, before we move on, two further things can be said about it.

First, the fact that the displacement thesis is an empirical generalisation doesn't make it any less ethically significant (although it does, of course, raise the question of how good the empirical evidence for it is). Indeed, the displacement thesis is an important part of the answer to the question I posed earlier: what exactly is the relationship between treating people as means and the Kantian requirement that we must always treat people as 'ends'? There are two things to say in response to this question. One is to make a point about *action*, which we'll be looking at in the next section.

The other is to appeal to the displacement thesis and to say that what's wrong with thinking of people instrumentally (at least in certain ways or in certain circumstances) is that it encourages us to disregard their moral status as ends-in-themselves.

The second thing to note about the displacement thesis is that there are actually many different possible displacement *theses*. More specifically, some versions of the thesis are more or less *global*, whereas others are *local* – focussing specifically on *particular kinds* of use-valuation and/or on *particular kinds* of context or relationship. Clearly, a totally global displacement thesis – i.e. the view that instrumentally valuing x *always* increases the risk of failing to value x in other ways – would be implausible. This is because there are some cases of regarding-as-useful (such as the case of the teacher) in which valuing the person instrumentally doesn't appear to have any negative impact whatsoever on our appreciation of the person as an end-in-herself. Indeed, there are cases in which thinking that someone is good at something (and hence useful in that respect) *enhances* one's appreciation of 'the whole person'. What seem much more plausible are various local displacement theses. Sex is a leading example here and, as we've already seen, many people (including Kant) appear to believe in a local displacement thesis concerning sexual use – the idea being (roughly) that regarding people as sex objects encourages us to view them as *mere* sex objects. Another interesting example – one which seems to me to be more convincing than the sex case (not least because sexual relations can take so many different forms) – is cannibalism. Most people would find it hard simultaneously to regard someone as a person and as a tasty piece of meat. Thus, given this psychological incompatibility, one might argue persuasively that seeing people as succulent roast dinners is indeed likely to encourage us to ignore their moral status as persons.

One fascinating question (again, one which can't be addressed here) is: *why* are some kinds of instrumental valuation better than others at co-existing with respect for personhood? In fact there's really more than one question here. There's a question about causation. What are the *origins* of various attitudes to use? Are their causes mainly biological or are they 'social constructs'? And to what extent do these attitudes vary according to culture, ethnicity, gender, sex, etc.? There's also a structural question: is there anything about the *nature* of certain kinds of use that makes them more likely to displace respect for personhood?

3.7 Using persons, contexts, and relationships

[I]nstrumentalization does not seem problematic in all contexts. If I am lying around with my lover on the bed, and use his stomach as a pillow there seems to be nothing at all baneful about this, provided that I do so with his consent (or, if he is asleep, with a reasonable belief that he would not mind), and without causing him pain, provided, as well, that I do so in the context of a relationship in which he is generally treated as more than a pillow. This suggests that what is problematic is not instrumentalization *per se*, but treating someone *primarily* or *merely* as an instrument. The overall context of the relationship thus becomes fundamental.[24]

Let's turn now to the other sense of 'treat', *acting towards*. The position here is a little more complex, chiefly because it can be argued that some ways of using things are incompatible with recognising and respecting their intrinsic value. Let's go back to the case where I own a beautiful figurine which I also use as a paperweight. We can change the example slightly and say that not only is it beautiful, but it can also be used as a high-density projectile, although if I ever used it in this way it would be destroyed. First let's ask: is valuing it as a thing of beauty incompatible with recognising its value as a projectile? The answer is *no*. A rational person could (and maybe should) simultaneously acknowledge the existence of both kinds of value. But now let's ask a different question, one about action rather than attitude: is *actually using it* as a projectile incompatible with recognising and respecting its aesthetic value? Arguably, yes. For by using it as a projectile, I destroy it. And destroying a thing of great beauty is usually symptomatic of a failure to recognise and respect its aesthetic value. So we appear to have a case which shows that some ways of using things are incompatible with recognising and respecting their intrinsic value (although, of course, in extreme circumstances, even someone who respects its aesthetic value might destroy it, for example, to save a hundred human lives).

It's not hard to see how this might apply, and in a very direct way, to persons. Consider, for example, the case of Manuel Wackenheim. Wackenheim is a (so-called) dwarf who (until a ban was imposed by the local mayor) made a living from being 'tossed' by customers in bars and nightclubs. This 'tossing' formed part of a *dwarf-throwing competition* – a sport 'in which the aim of the competitors is to fling a dwarf over the furthest distance possible'.[25] (Apparently, the French record for dwarf throwing is 3.3 metres.)[26] Wackenheim appeared keen to pursue his chosen career and didn't welcome the ban on dwarf throwing, saying 'this spectacle is my life; I want to be allowed to do what I want'.

Wackenheim, rather like the figurine/paperweight, can be *regarded* both as intrinsically valuable (*qua* person) and as instrumentally valuable (*qua* projectile). That is, there's no reason in principle why a friend of his couldn't both respect him as an 'end' and recognise the fact that his body is formed in a way which makes it instrumentally valuable to dwarf throwers. But could Wackenheim's friend *actually use him* as a projectile while at the same time respecting the fact that he's an 'end'? The passage quoted at the start of this section (from Nussbaum) gives the key to answering this: it is the overall context of the relationship, along with other structural features of the situation, which determines whether he is appropriately respected. Surely this must be right, for it would be extraordinarily hard to argue plausibly that it's *impossible*, in *all* contexts, to use Wackenheim as a projectile while at the same time respecting his personhood. For what if he enjoys being thrown, gets paid for it, and freely and knowingly consents to it? If for these reasons – i.e. because I want to ensure that he derives pleasure and money, and am certain that it's what he really wants, etc. – I throw him, then there seems no basis whatsoever for saying that I'm failing to respect his personhood. For in such a case, I'm (let's assume) deliberately giving him what he wants (and wants in a free, informed, and otherwise autonomous way) and deliberately benefiting him. How can this be a failure to recognise his status as an 'end'?

It can't be. Although I should straight away add two qualifications. First, this doesn't rule out the existence of other separate moral objections to dwarf throwing. Second, there certainly are contexts in which dwarf throwing would constitute wrongful instrumentalisation. These may include cases in which the dwarves are substantially harmed and cases in which the dwarves don't consent or in which their consent is invalid. Indeed, this is my main point. What does all the ethical work here is context: in particular, issues relating to the existence and quality of the dwarf's consent – and, for the more paternalistically inclined, those relating to harm and welfare.

Lying behind this way of thinking is one of the following principles (which differ just in that the second, more cautious, principle includes a 'substantial harm' constraint).

> If A seeks and obtains from B valid consent to do x to B, that is sufficient to guarantee that B's status as an end-in-herself is respected by A (other things being equal).[27]

> If A seeks and obtains from B valid consent to do x to B, and x is not substantially harmful to B, that is sufficient to guarantee that B's status as an end-in-herself is respected by A (other things being equal).

These principles are driven by the view that: (a) respect for autonomy is either identical with, or is the most important part of, Kant's 'treat people always as ends' doctrine, and (b) the relationship between autonomy and consent is of the first importance. On this view A, just by seeking and obtaining valid consent, has respected B's autonomy and status as an 'end' – though I should add that it must also be the case that *A wouldn't have gone ahead and done x to B if B hadn't consented*. In other words, what matters isn't so much the *existence* of consent as the fact that A *requires* it. It is by *requiring* consent (i.e. by not being willing to act without B's consent) that A respects B's autonomy.

We'll be looking at valid consent again later. So, for now, I'll just restrict myself to making two observations. First, we should remember that the word 'valid' is doing a lot of work here. Consent *per se* is relatively insignificant, since an invalid consent, in ethical terms, is often no better than no consent. It is *valid* consent which matters most morally. Indeed, what 'valid' *means* here is that the consent in question is morally significant, that it goes at least some way towards justifying A's actions. Second, the view that A treats B as an 'end' so long as A requires B's consent does *not* entail the view that there's nothing to which B couldn't validly consent – that is, it's entirely compatible with the view that in practice there are certain kinds of use to which no one could validly consent. One may think (for example) that selling parts of one's body or being used as a projectile can't be validly consented to, because only someone whose consent was invalidated by coercion, manipulation, insanity, desperation, or whatever would agree to be used in such awful ways.

The picture that I'm offering is one in which there are no (non-normatively categorised) types of use that by their very natures preclude respect for personhood. Everything depends on the context in which the use takes place, on the relationship between the user and the used, and (most importantly of all) on the quality of the used person's consent. Having said that, there may well be kinds of use which nearly always involve failing to treat the used person as an 'end', and, for applied ethics and policy formation purposes, this is often what matters. In other words, for these purposes, a reliable statistical connection (for example, 'in 99 per cent of cases, B's personhood isn't respected') is as important as a necessary and universal one. The sorts of use which are likely to fall into this category are ones which are substantially harmful and/or unpleasant to the user. There are two possible reasons for this. First, we might think that if A respects B as an 'end', A won't harm B and so won't subject B to harmful use. A difficulty with this view, however, is what to say about cases in which B autonomously *wants to be harmed* by A. In such cases do we disrespect B's autonomy more by harming B or by adopting a paternalistic stance towards B, depriving her – 'for her own good' – of what she wants? A second (and better) reason for thinking that harmful usings are liable to involve not treating the person as an 'end' is that, more often than not, when people knowingly consent to be harmed, their consent is defective. For most people simply don't want to be harmed – and so why on earth would they consent to be harmed unless they were subjected to some kind of consent-invalidating pressure or manipulation? This seems to provide a very good reason for at least being suspicious of and scrutinising carefully cases of harmful use, since there's a fair chance that any consent offered in such cases is invalid. We should, however, note that it is possible in principle to consent validly to be harmed, both because it's possible for people autonomously to desire self-harm and because there may be external reasons, should as wanting to help a third party, for subjecting oneself to harmful use. Living organ donors would be a good example of the latter. They typically consent to be harmed in order to benefit the recipient.

3.8 Commodification

[F]or some, any financial inducement to increase the supply of organs constitutes a 'commodification' of something that is essential to saving lives, and this is intrinsically objectionable. This position is typically an emotionally charged assertion and not a reasoned argument.[28]

In the next two sections, I aim to say what commodification is, to say how it relates to objectification and to instrumentalisation, and to assess Manga's claim (above) that appeals to commodification are typically no more than emotionally charged assertions.

Like 'exploitation', the word 'commodification' has both a non-moral and a moral sense. In the first of these, 'commodification' refers to a social practice and/or legal system under which the relevant class of things is (or is allowed to be) bought and sold:

Commodification is a *social practice* for treating things as commodities, ie as properties that can be bought, sold, or rented.[29]

To commodify something is to exchange it for money, to buy or sell it.[30]

Radin calls this the *narrow* construal of commodification:

Narrowly construed, commodification *describes actual buying and selling (or legally permitted buying and selling)* of something.[31]

Used in this way, 'commodification' is purely descriptive: i.e. to say of a practice that it's commodification (in this sense) isn't to criticise it. This idea can be contrasted with the second sense, in which 'commodification' is to be understood as a negative moral term. 'Commodification', in this sense, is supposed to denote a specific kind of wrong.

Our interest is mainly in the second sense of 'commodification'. This is because what we're looking for are possible objections to commercialising the body, and the idea of commodification can't (of course) provide an objection if 'commodification' is *just another word* for commercialisation.

As an illustration, consider the following criticisms of organ sale (along with various other commercial practices) from Bob Brecher:

> The point about buying a pint of blood, or a kidney [or] renting someone's body for an hour or two . . . is that all these are . . . based on making a commodity of human beings.
> . . . the possibility of people's buying a kidney represents the further commoditisation [commodification] of human beings, [and] to that extent the practice resembles prostitution, certain forms of surrogacy, and . . . page three of The Sun[32] in symbolising, partly constituting, and encouraging a moral climate within which the commoditisation of human beings proceeds apace.[33]

Brecher's point here is not merely that permitting commercial surrogacy, organ sale, and prostitution would constitute an extension of the *social practice* of commodification. That claim taken alone would be too obvious to be worth a mention and certainly wouldn't constitute an *argument* for prohibition, but would be more like a description of what's to be prohibited. Instead, his point (which is far from trivial) seems to be that we ought not to permit these practices because doing so will encourage people *wrongfully to treat other people 'as commodities'*.[34]

To sum up, there's an important distinction between a purely descriptive sense of 'commodification', in which commodification just equals actual buying and selling, and a normative sense. It is the second (normative) sense which concerns us here.

3.9 Commodification, fungibility, and dignity

> If poor people . . . find themselves seeking to enter into 'desperate exchanges', such as selling their kidneys or their sexual services, some people will be troubled by their willingness to commodify attributes of self that our culture . . . does not conceive of as fungible.[35]

I have some sympathy with Manga's 'emotionally charged assertion' point (quoted at the beginning of section 3.8) insofar as words like 'commodification' do tend to get overused and sloppily used. For this reason, it's impossible to provide a coherent account of the moral concept of commodification which isn't in some way revisionary. Nonetheless, I hope that what I'm about to say will at least capture the spirit of and count as no more than a refinement of what people mean when they object to things by appealing to the idea of commodification.

Before we turn to the substantive analysis, two preliminary points need to be made. First, for reasons that will become clear shortly, commodification (in the normative sense) is a type of objectification. So, just as it's not possible to object*ify* something which is really an object, it's not possible to commod*ify* something which is really a commodity. For example, if I were to regard baked beans or sugar as commodities, I wouldn't thereby be commodifying them, since they *are* commodities. So it's not the possession of the commodifying attitude *per se* which is wrong but the inappropriate application of it to entities which aren't (proper) commodities (notably persons). We should, however, keep in mind that some people think that nothing is really a commodity and/or that nothing should be treated as a commodity – and that, for them, anything could be commodified.

The second preliminary point is that, although I have suggested on occasion that our interest should be principally in commodificatory attitudes, this is actually slightly too narrow. We might instead usefully employ the word 'treat' here (which, as we saw earlier, covers both attitudes and actions) and say that what we're interested in is the idea of *treating persons as if* they were commodities. Nonetheless, it's still best to carry out the analysis of commodification mainly in terms of attitudes because whereas treating x as a commodity always involves the possession of commodificatory attitudes, it may or may not involve acting on or expressing those attitudes. In other words, having the attitude is a necessary part of commodifying; acting on the attitude is not.

To turn now to the analysis, what we have so far is that to commodify is to treat as a commodity something which is not a (proper) commodity. In order to make this less schematic, and to distinguish commodification from objectification-in-general, we need to look a little more closely at what exactly a commodity is. The word 'commodity' can be used in a broad sense to refer to all those things that are traded. However, it also has a narrower sense, and it is this which can help us to understand what commodification is and what's wrong with it. In this narrower sense, *commodities are fungibles*: things such as coffee beans, gold, and oil. All these things come in slightly different forms and at different levels of quality. But they are nonetheless fungibles in that the buyer normally just buys a certain amount of a certain good at a certain price per unit mass/volume without caring which particular (token) sack of coffee beans, or lump of gold, or tanker of oil she ends up with. Commodities, then, are fungibles, and to regard something as a commodity is to regard it as fungible. Hence, to commod*ify* (in the normative sense) is to treat as fungible something which isn't fungible and/or oughtn't to be viewed as such. Commodification then seems to be identical with Nussbaum's fourth kind of objectification (fungibility). And when applied to persons it breaches the second Kantian principle, since treating persons as fungible fails properly to respect their dignity; it is to regard them as having mere 'price'.

The overall picture which is emerging, then, is that we have a comparatively general moral concept, objectification, of which there are roughly seven varieties. (There is, I suspect, a lot of arbitrariness about how we carve up the territory here – but Nussbaum's list of seven seems to me to be as good as any of the alternatives.) That each of these seven ways of objectifying is *prima facie* wrong (when applied to persons) can be shown by appealing to two Kantian principles: (a) don't treat people solely as means, and (b) don't treat people as fungible. As well as objectification, there are two more specific concepts: instrumentalisation (wrongful use exploitation) and commodification. These are forms of objectification. Each is closely related to one of the Kantian principles. To exploit someone in the 'wrongful use' sense is to breach the first Kantian principle by treating her solely as a means. To commodify someone is to breach the second Kantian principle by regarding her as fungible. Although distinct, instrumentalisation and commodification are closely linked. Perhaps the strongest link is that (for reasons offered in section 3.2) anyone who adopts an entirely instrumental attitude towards X, in so doing, regards X as fungible. Hence, it would seem that wherever there is instrumentalisation there is also commodification.

The final claim in the previous paragraph – that wherever there's instrumentalisation there's also commodification – will appear false to many people. This is because it's clearly possible to instrumentalise someone without any money changing hands and without trading of any sort taking place. For example, people are sometimes used (instrumentalised) as 'sex objects' within personal relationships in entirely non-commercial ways. So, one might ask: given that there are cases of non-commercial instrumentalisation, how can instrumentalisation entail commodification, since surely treating someone as a commodity must involve commercial transactions of some sort? What I've suggested so far does, I admit, sound strange because of the close association between commodification and money. This association is so close that many writers on the subject (including Radin) use terms like 'commodify' and 'monetise' more or less interchangeably.[36] Elsewhere, I have dealt with this by arguing that something can be treated as a commodity without any sort of commercialisation being involved.[37] One argument for this is that people can treat gifts, things that they find or steal, or persons with whom they have no financial relationship as commodities (i.e. as fungible).

However, I am not quite so confident about this answer as I once was. The reason is that the core moral concept here isn't, perhaps, commodification, but what we might term *fungiblisation*: wrongfully treating as fungible that which is not fungible and/or oughtn't to be treated as fungible. What's the relationship then between commodification and fungiblisation? About this, we have a choice to make – though one which is more terminological than philosophical. One option is simply to *identify* commodification with fungiblisation. This is what I've been doing so far in this section and what I've argued for elsewhere.[38] The other is to reserve the word 'commodification' for those cases of fungiblisation which involve commerce, money, etc. – in which case commodification becomes *a particular kind of* fungiblisation (maybe the most prevalent one). It now seems to me that there's a lot to be said for this second option. It has two main advantages. First, it stops the account of commodification from clashing with ordinary language and with people's intuitions about cases: for example, on this view, people who are non-commercially instrumentalised as 'sex objects' *aren't* also commodified (though they are fungiblised). Second, it enables more conceptual-linguistic precision, because we now have not only the general term, 'fungiblisation', but also a more specific term ('commodification') which usefully picks out those cases of fungiblisation which are caused by or otherwise intimately related to commerce, money, the market, etc.

So the account of commodification (of persons) that I now support is as follows. Fungiblisation is a type of objectification which involves wrongfully treating persons as fungible. And commodification (in the normative sense) is a type of fungiblisation: more specifically, to commodify is to fungiblise through, or because of, commerce. Although we express ourselves in very different ways, this – it seems to me – makes my view of commodification a little like Radin's. According to her, there are

> four indicia of commodification in conceptualisation . . . (i) objectification, (ii) fungibility, (iii) commensurability, and (iv) money equivalence.[39]

By *commensurability*, she means

> that the value of things can be arrayed as a function of one continuous variable, or can be linearly ranked.[40]

And by *money equivalence* she means

> that the continuous variable in terms of which things can be ranked is dollar value.[41]

The ideas of *commensurability* and *money equivalence* are useful when it comes to thinking about commodification's role within fungiblisation-in-general and about how commercialisation generates fungiblisation. The explanation is as follows. When a thing is commercialised, it is (by definition) assigned a monetary value. This forces, or at least encourages, us to view it as commensurable both in relation to money itself and in relation to other things with the same monetary value. What commensurability means is that if I'm a purely 'rational economic agent' (and interacting with a perfectly fluid and otherwise 'ideal' marketplace) I'll be indifferent as to whether I have x (worth $1,000), y (worth $1,000), or $1,000. It's not hard to see, then, how we get from the commercialisation of persons to their fungiblisation. For commercialising persons encourages us to regard them as commensurable (i.e. not to care whether we 'have' A, B, or $n), and this is in turn liable to cause or constitute fungiblisation (and hence commodification).

3.10 Uniqueness

[P]art of me is only me and mine and part of you is only you and yours. No one has had my or your exact history.[42]

Up to now, the discussion of treating people as fungible has proceeded at a fairly high level of abstraction. So I'd like now to raise a question about how these ideas might be applied, one which leads me to be a bit sceptical about the moral force of claims about the uniqueness of persons.

A good place to start is this passage from Sandra Marshall's paper on prostitution:

it is not difficult to see how fungibility can be an aspect of a market relation. One well-trained waiter is just as good as another, one paying customer is just as good as another. There may be nothing wrong with this: to treat people as interchange-able within the market activity need not be in any way damaging. Indeed, it is perfectly possible to imagine that with developments in robotics we could do without waiters altogether without loss.[43]

Marshall's remarks remind us that, in many contexts, regarding people as fungible is morally unproblematic. For I'm not obliged to care which particular hairdresser, or taxi driver, or 'checkout operative' happens to service me – and while personal engagement with people in these roles may well be desirable for all sorts of reasons, it's surely not morally required. Radin tells us that 'the idea of fungibility ... undermines the notion of individual uniqueness'.[44] About this she is right. But, as we've just seen, the problem with applying this idea to persons is that, in many respects, people don't appear to be unique. At least as role occupants, one customer/hairdresser/waiter is much like another. Or, even if we don't want to go that far, it's clear that before applying the idea of uniqueness to persons we need to know much more about the kind of uniqueness that's at stake. That is, the uniqueness thesis stands in need of clarification, so that we can say what it is that we're supposed to be wrongfully disregarding when we treat people as fungible. All of which takes us to the question that I want to pose in this section. How exactly is the claim that each individual human being or person is unique be understood? And ought we to believe it?

There are three main interpretations of this uniqueness thesis. Under the first, it's an empirical claim about diversity. People (on this view) *needn't* be, but as a matter of fact *are*, unique – meaning just that they, as a matter of fact, differ from one another considerably (for example, supporters of this view sometimes claim that genetics is on their side, because each human being has its own 'unique' set of genes). There are at least two problems with this version of the uniqueness thesis. First, as Thomas Kuhn reminds us, 'it is a truism that anything is similar to, and also different from, anything else'. Or to put it another way, it's very hard non-arbitrarily to specify what should count as difference/diversity and what should count as sameness/similarity. For this reason, unqualified statements such as 'everyone's basically the same' and 'everyone's a unique individual – we're all different' are hopelessly vague and lacking in content. The second problem is that this version of the thesis makes people's moral status dependent on accidental and seemingly irrelevant differences between them and others. This seems (at best) odd. To see why, consider hypothetical identical twins who are exactly similar in all respects. These twins aren't (*ex hypothesi*) unique: i.e. they don't differ from one another significantly. Yet it would be bizarre to claim that they lack the same moral status as other people, or that it's OK to treat them – but not other people – as fungible, or that the moral status of one twin would be higher if the other twin died, or if the other twin had never been born. For these reasons, we must reject the first interpretation of the uniqueness thesis.

According to the second interpretation, the uniqueness thesis is supposed to be a necessary truth about persons, something along the following lines: *no two persons share all the same properties.* The problem with this interpretation is that it appears to be either false or what philosophers call *trivially true* (i.e. true, but lacking in content or importance). There's clearly a sense in which two people could have all the same (non-relational) properties. For example, I could (in theory) be replicated, or split into two persons. And surely it would then be at least possible for me and the replicant to have all the same properties, both mentally and physically. At this point, defenders of this version of the uniqueness thesis will have to resort to such things as *spatio-temporal properties.* For example, they might say that the replicant is 3.7 metres closer to Canada than I am and therefore different from me in this respect. Furthermore, they might say that we're *necessarily* different, because our spatio-temporal properties must *always* differ (since two different objects can't occupy the same space at the same time).[45] Hence, it can be argued, even the replicant and I are unique because we're never in exactly the same place at the same time; we never share all the same spatial properties. However, this renders the uniqueness thesis *trivially true*. Or at least it's far from clear why this is a morally significant kind of uniqueness, because fruit flies and stones are as unique in this sense as persons are (for example, no two stones occupy the same space).

The third interpretation of the uniqueness thesis says that what's unique about persons is consciousness or 'the self'. It is extraordinarily hard to know what to make of such claims – not least because, as I suggested earlier, it's very hard non-arbitrarily to specify what counts as being different or unique. Is my consciousness or 'self' unique? Well (leaving aside sceptical worries about knowledge of other minds), I can think of no reason to believe that my lived experiences are radically qualitatively different from anyone else's. This is not to deny that people have different experienced lives. As far as I can tell, they do. But this isn't going to be enough to ground a (non-trivial) *uniqueness* claim, because just as some people have very different experienced lives from mine, others may well have rather similar experienced lives to mine.

Perhaps, though, this misunderstands the point. Maybe the claim isn't so much that my 'self' is *qualitatively different* from others' 'selves' but rather that I am unique and irreplaceable in the sense that *there will only ever be one Stephen Wilkinson* (though there are, of course, other people *called* Stephen Wilkinson). There's certainly a sense in which this is true. Unfortunately for the uniqueness thesis, though, this has more to do with the way proper names work than with the existence of some more profound philosophical truth about uniqueness. In other words, the reason why 'there will only ever be one Stephen Wilkinson' is true is just that 'Stephen Wilkinson' is being used as a proper name. Proper names are what Saul Kripke famously calls *rigid designators*.[46] This means that they pick out the very same individual in all possible worlds and are to be contrasted with *definite descriptions* such as 'North Staffordshire's best-dressed philosopher', which, though it may (or may not) designate Stephen Wilkinson in the actual world, can designate other individuals in other possible worlds. So uniqueness of this sort seems to be just a function of naming which makes the uniqueness thesis look ethically insignificant. For I may as well give my PC a name (say, John) and claim that 'there will only ever be one John' and that John is irreplaceable and unique. This will be true so long as John is understood as a proper name and in spite of the fact that, in practical terms, John is eminently replaceable – just as (I suspect) Stephen Wilkinson is, though with a little more difficulty given the present state of our biotechnologies.

What can we conclude from all this? There appear to be two fundamental problems with using uniqueness in ethical arguments. The first is that it is hard to make sense of the claim that persons are unique.

Depending on how it's interpreted it seems to be false, trivially true, or morally insignificant. And (of course) if persons aren't really unique in any interesting sense, then it's not clear why we're obliged to regard them as unique. Indeed, doing so seems irrational. The second problem is that there are clearly lots of contexts in which treating people as fungible is ethically unproblematic. The most clear-cut cases are perhaps ones where someone is filling a particular social or economic role, for example, driver, teacher, waiter. Here, at least in uncomplicated cases, it's hard to see why we shouldn't regard individual role occupants as replaceable and non-unique, at least *qua* role occupant. These considerations lead me to believe that we should regard appeals to uniqueness with a fair degree of scepticism.

3.11 Bodies and persons

So far I've talked almost exclusively about the objectification of *persons* and have said very little about the objectification of *bodies*. This is perhaps surprising given the concerns of the book, but there are good reasons for it. One is that, as we'll see in a moment, the distinction between 'innocently' treating a body as an object and wrongfully object*ifying* it is itself based on the idea of objectifying persons. A second is that (as we've seen throughout this chapter) the moral concepts of objectification, instrumentalisation, and commodification are, we might say, almost *made for* the concept of personhood. In particular, these concepts are linked directly to personhood via the two Kantian principles: (a) don't treat persons solely as means, and (b) don't treat persons as fungible. Furthermore (because of this conceptual closeness), it's fairly easy to show why the objectification of persons might be thought to be wrong. Things are not so straightforward, however, when it comes to bodies. And they are even less straightforward when it comes to bodily parts, products, and services. For, even if the objectification of persons is wrong, it doesn't follow from this (or, at least, it doesn't follow obviously or directly) that there's something wrong with treating body parts as (mere) objects.

Some readers may find it strange that I'm distinguishing between persons and bodies in this way, and it may appear to them as if I'm advocating Cartesian Dualism and suggesting that persons are disembodied souls.[47] I don't mean to suggest anything so metaphysically extravagant. Nor do I need to, because fortunately the relationship between mind and body, or persons and bodies, is not an issue in which we need become embroiled. For it can be shown that, regardless of what one thinks about the metaphysics of mind, most (if not all) of our ethical concerns about treating bodies as objects are really concerns about the treatment of persons.

To see why, let's start by reminding ourselves of something which is

obvious and yet sometimes overlooked by writers on the commercialisation of the body. Bodies and body parts are physical objects. Hence, any
ethical concerns that we have about the objectification of bodies can't be
about whether bodies are treated as objects – since they are objects.
Rather, our concerns (insofar as they're rational) must be about whether
bodies are treated as mere objects. But what does 'mere' mean here? Or, to
put it another way, what might bodies be over and above physical
objects? What is treating a body as a *mere* object to be contrasted with?

Some people think that bodies are nothing over and above physical
objects. For these people, it's impossible to objec*tify* bodies, since (mere)
objects can't be objectified. If, however, we reject this 'objectification-
sceptical' view, then there seems to be only one remotely plausible
answer to the question just posed. *Bodies are more than mere objects insofar
as they are intimately related to persons.* This is why, in the main, people
attach much less moral importance to dead bodies than to living ones. It
is because dead bodies aren't connected to the person in the way that live
bodies are. That's not to say, of course, that people don't attach *any*
importance to the bodies of the dead. They often do, though when they
do it's normally because they view the dead body as somehow significantly related to the person who used to exist – or, for those who believe
in 'life after death', still exists in a non-bodily form.

To objec*tify* the body, then, is to treat it as a *mere* object. This means
treating it as if it weren't *intimately related to a person*. This raises two
further questions. What is the nature of the intimate relationship between
body and person? And what counts as treating a body as if it's not intimately related to a person? The first question is essentially about the relationship between body, mind, and personhood, and it is at this point that
we can opt out of the metaphysics of mind by simply not answering it.
This is possible because (a) it's the second question which is *ethically* significant, not the first, and (b) provided that we're working within a
framework which accepts a few basic assumptions, such as that there are
such things as persons which are somehow related to bodies, then the
answer that we give to the second question needn't depend on the
answer that we give to the first. Thus, Cartesian Dualists, functionalists,
and physicalists (in other words, people with a wide range of different
views about the relationship between body, mind, and personhood)
might all agree that if A removes B's vital organs to feed to A's dog, then
A is treating B's body as if isn't intimately related to a person (either that
or A is deliberately harming B, in which case our moral objection to A's
behaviour is likely to be something other than objectification). Ethical
views like this don't depend on one's particular views in the philosophy
of mind.

What about the second question? What counts as treating a body as if
it's not intimately related to a person? A general answer is that treating a

body as if it's not *a person's* body is one common way of objectifying a person; when we treat a person's body as if it's not the body of that person, we thereby objectify not only the body, but the person too. Thus, what Nussbaum terms *denial of autonomy, inertness*, and *denial of subjectivity* will all often involve treating a person's body as if it's not the body of a person (as if it's a mere thing). In practical terms, consent and context will again be vitally important in every case. For example, if I act on another person's body without requiring and obtaining her consent this may amount, in a sense, to treating her body as if it's not 'hers' (as if it's a mere body). Conversely, if I require and obtain valid consent before acting on her body then (arguably) I'm not treating her body as a mere body, *no matter what I do to it*. What is clear, then, is that the idea of body-objectification is very much parasitic on the idea of person-objectification.

3.12 Summary and conclusions

This chapter doesn't have a great deal to say about the body. Its relation to the body commodification debate is that it aims to make sense in general terms of a certain sort of objection to commercialising the body. Objections of this kind focus principally on the idea that we shouldn't treat people solely as objects, or as means (instruments), or as commodities – and on the corresponding moral concepts of objectification, instrumentalisation (wrongful use exploitation), and commodification. All such arguments have a strongly Kantian flavour and are often based on Kant's view that we should treat people always as ends-in-themselves and never as fungible. Objectification (of which instrumentalisation and commodification are types) is supposed to be wrong in that it involves breaching these Kantian principles.

A lot of objectification arguments against commercialising the body do little more than draw attention to the fact that a person, or her body, is used as a means. We've seen, however, in Chapter 3 that such objections, if they're to work, need to say a lot more, since the relationship between using someone as a means and failing to respect her as an end is not straightforward. In particular, it's possible to use someone as a means while at the same time respecting her status as an end; using someone as a means doesn't entail a failure to respect personhood. Rather, everything depends on the overall context of the relationship and on the quality of the used person's consent.

That said, we've also seen that there may well be important links, albeit indirect ones, between treating people as means and failing to treat them as ends. One of these is (what I earlier called) the displacement thesis. This says that, even though different ways of valuing people don't logically contradict one another, they nonetheless clash psychologically in that instrumental valuation tends to displace other important modes of valuation in the human mind.

Turning now to commodification and fungiblisation, we've seen that the main problem with deploying these concepts it that it's hard to make sense of the claim that persons (and *a fortiori* their bodies) are unique. For, depending on how it's interpreted, it is false, or trivially true, or ethically insignificant. We're left wondering therefore whether commodification and fungiblisation are really independent wrongs or whether, instead, regarding persons as commodities is perturbing just because it's symptomatic of instrumentalisation, of regarding them solely as means.

4

HARM

> Exploitation is an evil that is not typically free-floating. More
> often than not, perhaps, it is harmful to the interests of the
> exploitee . . . But a little noticed feature of exploitation is that
> it *can* occur in morally unsavory forms without harming the
> exploitee's interests.[1]

Accusing commercial practices of being exploitative and accusing them
of being harmful are common moves in the body commodification
debate. This chapter aims to improve our understanding of such assertions by exploring the connection between exploitation and harm and by
looking at the nature of harm. The question of whether the commercial
utilisation of the body is harmful is vitally important, especially given the
widespread acceptance of Mill's *harm principle*. According to this,

> The only purpose for which power can rightfully be exercised
> over any member of a civilised community against his will is to
> prevent harm to others.[2]

In other words, only harmful practices should be prohibited. So while
showing the commercialisation of the body to be harm*ful* would provide
a powerful argument against it, showing it to be harm*less* would (if we
accept the harm principle) give us a powerful argument for not prohibiting it (even if it's morally wrong for other reasons). The same goes for
exploitation in general: i.e. supporters of Mill's harm principle should
only want to ban harmful exploitation, not harmless exploitation (if there
is such a thing).

The chapter starts by looking at the harm condition, the view that
exploitation is necessarily harmful to the exploitee (the exploited person).
It then attempts to say what harm is. The conclusion is that, properly
understood, the concept of harm is messy and moralised and that, for this
reason, moral principles such as *nonmaleficence* ('do no harm') and Mill's

harm principle aren't as useful (or, at least, aren't as straightforward) as many people think that they are.

4.1 Mutually advantageous exploitation?

Not surprisingly, philosophers disagree about whether the harm condition is true and about whether or not there can be such a thing as mutually advantageous exploitation. Buchanan, for example, supports the harm condition, saying that

> To exploit a person involves the harmful, merely instrumental utilization of him or his capacities, for one's own advantage or for the sake of one's own ends.[3]

Against, this Wertheimer offers the following perceptive remark, which constitutes an argument against the harm condition:[4]

> exploitation would be of much less theoretical interest on a 'no harm, no exploitation' rule. We do not need to be moral rocket scientists to know that it is wrong for A to gain from an action that unjustifiably harms or coerces B . . . By contrast, it is more difficult to explain when and why it might be wrong for A to gain from an action that benefits B and to which B voluntarily consents.[5]

The intuition Wertheimer appeals to here is that exploitation is a somewhat mysterious, or at least complex, moral concept, whereas harm appears not to be. Later on, we'll see that the concept of harm is not quite as straightforward as it at first seems. Nonetheless, we do normally feel that we know what harm is, and that we know that (in the absence of some special justification) harming others is wrong. Therefore, if exploitation were necessarily harmful, or a 'harm concept', we would expect it to seem more straightforward than it does – not least because the wrongness of exploitation could then be grounded in the idea of *non-maleficence* (roughly, the principle that inflicting harm on persons is wrong, other things being equal). Furthermore, although some exploitation claims are closely connected to associated harms, their content clearly goes beyond the fact that harm has been caused.

A more tangible way of making the same point is to look at some examples of exploitation in which the exploitee appears to benefit. Consider, for example, the following hypothetical:

Andrew and Brian

Brian is unemployed and has no food. If he doesn't get food soon, he will die. There are no welfare agencies, charities, or benevolent individuals around to help him, and turning to crime is unlikely to succeed, because Brian lives in a police state. His only way to survive, therefore, is to get a job. Andrew, a local factory owner, knows what position Brian is in and knows that there are plenty more like him in the local economy. With this in mind, Andrew (for purely selfish reasons) offers Brian a job in his factory. However, he requires Brian to do 50 per cent more work than existing staff and to accept 70 per cent less pay than the going rate. Brian is glad of the job, which pays him enough to survive, and enthusiastically accepts Andrew's offer. However, Brian later complains to his co-workers and friends that he is being exploited.

Andrew and Brian looks like a classic case of exploitation. Our intuitive concern is that Brian is overworked and underpaid (and also that his labour is, in some sense, forced). However, he appears not to be harmed, but rather to benefit overall, since his only alternative to taking the job was death by starvation. Indeed, as Wertheimer suggests, there's a good chance that Brian stands to gain much more than Andrew and that that's why Brian is keen to accept the job:

> I suspect that the exploit*ee* often gets much more utility from a transaction than the exploit*er*. It is precisely because the exploitee stands to gain so much from the transaction (relative to the exploiter) that his bargaining position is comparatively weak.[6]

We appear, then, to have a counter-example to the harm condition (the view that exploitees are necessarily harmed by exploitation) since Brian seems both to benefit and to be exploited.

How might defenders of the harm condition respond to the existence of cases like this? One option is to insist that Brian is not really exploited. Someone might, for example, argue that 'market forces' always generate just pay levels and, hence, that he isn't really underpaid. Or someone might argue that fully consensual arrangements can't be exploitative and that, since Brian consents, he's not exploited (even if he is underpaid). The first of these arguments – in particular, the assertion that 'market forces' alone always generate just pay levels – is implausible. For we can simply change our case, bit by bit, gradually making Brian's pay and conditions worse and Andrew's behaviour more repulsive. At some point, most reasonable people will concede that Brian is underpaid. And those who won't make this concession needn't be considered here, because their claim that 'the market' always generates fair pay is either a mere stipulation, or driven by a theory which is likely to be 'exploitation sceptical': i.e. one in which the moral concept of exploitation does not have a place. The consent argument is perhaps more promising. The difficulty in Andrew and Brian, though, is that the status of Brian's consent is unclear. Of course, he consents in *some* sense. But is his consent valid? Is it of a high enough quality to render the arrangement non-exploitative? We'll be returning to questions about consent in the next chapter.

4.2 Harm to interests

Another way of trying to reconcile the harm condition with cases like Andrew and Brian is to appeal to a more complicated understanding of harm. Wolff, for example, would concede that Brian is better off with the job than without it, but nevertheless wants to retain something like the harm condition:

> while exploitation involves making someone worse off, it cannot be defined in terms of making someone worse off than they would have been without the exploitative arrangement. But worse off than what? The best alternative is the view that the person is made worse off than they ought to be.[7]

In order to make sense of such claims, we need to look more carefully at the concept of harm. Feinberg's work is a good place to start.[8] He usefully distinguishes three different senses of 'harm'. First, 'harm' can be used in an extended sense to apply to inanimate objects. In this sense, it means pretty much the same as 'damage' or 'destroy':

> By smashing windows, vandals are said to harm people's property; neglect can harm one's garden; frost does harm to crops. Quite clearly this is harm in only a transferred sense; we don't feel aggrieved on behalf of the windows or the tomatoes, nor are they the objects of our sympathies.[9]

The word 'harm', used in this sense, is both non-moral and unconnected (or, at least, not directly connected) to the welfare of persons, or other sentient beings. For these reasons, we can disregard this first sense.

The second sense of 'harm' is *harm-to-interests*. Feinberg defines this as 'the thwarting, setting back, or defeating of an interest'.[10] Interests can be set back by a wide variety of things, including accidents, 'acts of God', illness, malicious attacks by persons, and others' (or one's own) negligence. Hence, to say that someone has been subjected to harm-to-interests isn't necessarily to make a moral judgement, because people can be harmed in this sense (by a falling tree or a virus, for example) without being in any way wronged. Feinberg does, however, talk of being harmed 'in the legal sense'. This kind of harm (which falls within the more general category, harm-to-interests) occurs when one's interests are 'invaded' by another person:

> One person harms another in . . . [this] sense then by invading, and thereby thwarting or setting back, his interest. The test . . . of whether . . . an invasion has in fact set back an interest is whether the interest is in a worse condition than it would have been in had the invasion not occurred at all.[11]

For all kinds of harm-to-interests the criterion is the same. As Feinberg suggests above, X has harmed me *if and only if one or more of my interests are in a worse condition than they would have been if it weren't for X.*

4.3 Relevant baselines

Harm, then, is a *comparative* concept. Judgements about harm compare someone's *relative* levels of welfare in two actual or possible situations. Where these two comparators are actual, we are looking at a welfare differential *over time.* For example, we might say that someone has been harmed by an event, meaning that she is worse off *after* the event (and because of it) than she was *before* it. However, more often than not, statements about harm involve comparing the actual world with a *merely possible* world: the idea being that someone is harmed by X (an event, say) if *she would have been better off if X hadn't happened.* Often, disputes about whether a thing is harmful, or about how harmful it is, centre on the question of which alternative possible world should be used as a comparator. Wertheimer offers us a good example of this. What if a psychotherapist sexually exploits a patient, but that patient (all things considered) is better off within this exploitative relationship than she would have been if she'd never had a psychotherapist at all? Has the patient been harmed? Wertheimer writes:

> it is not clear against what baseline we should evaluate the claim that the patient has been harmed by her psychotherapist. If we adopt a *pre-treatment* baseline, we say the patient is harmed only if she leaves the therapeutic encounter worse off than when she entered therapy. If we adopt a *normative* baseline, we say that the patient is harmed if she leaves the therapeutic encounter less well off than she could otherwise have reasonably expected.[12]

Clearly the use of pre-treatment baselines (to generalise, *pre-interaction* baselines) is unsatisfactory in such cases. There are two main reasons for this. First, thinking of benefits and harms in this way encourages too much *aggregation*, leading to counter-intuitive results. For example: what if S, a technically excellent surgeon, uses her skills to take P's (a patient's) welfare up from level 1 to level 9 but then, through sexual (or other) abuse, takes P's welfare back down to level 3? Should we say that S has harmed P? Use of the pre-treatment baseline suggests *no* because P used to be at welfare level 1 and now she is at level 3, which is an improvement, not a reduction. But surely this is the wrong description, and what we should say instead is that S has benefited P in one way, but harmed P in another. In other words, we should *disaggregate* the benefits and harms and insist on seeing the surgery and the abuse as two independently evaluable actions. For although S has benefited P by the use of surgical skills, S has *also* harmed P by abusing her. A second reason for rejecting the pre-treatment baseline is that there is a range of counter-examples based around such things as P's improving naturally, or P's improving because of third-party intervention, which render the pre-interaction baseline understanding of harm implausible. For example: P is unwell and at welfare level 2, but will if left untreated get better naturally, rising back to level 10 within a year. P goes to D (a doctor) seeking treatment. D intervenes and the effect of D's intervention is that P's rate of improvement is made slower, so that after one year P is only at level 5. Has D harmed P? Obviously *yes*! But again, use of the pre-treatment baseline gives the wrong answer (in this case, *no*) on the grounds that P ends up better off (level 5) than she was when she met D (level 2).

The use of pre-interaction baselines does seem in some cases to yield intuitive results. I would suggest, however, that all of these cases are ones where the pre-interaction baseline happens to coincide with one or both of the other two sorts of baseline: *closest possible world* baselines and *normative* baselines.

When we use a closest possible world (henceforth, CPW) baseline to assess whether harm has been caused, we are comparing B's *actual* level of welfare with the level of welfare that B *would have had if A hadn't acted, or hadn't occupied the role that she did, or hadn't existed at all.*[13] Whether the pre-interaction baseline coincides with the CPW baseline often depends on what would have happened if (for example) A hadn't been born. In many cases what would have happened is that B's level of welfare would have stayed at its pre-interaction level, in which case the two baselines (CPW and pre-interaction) coincide. For example, if a stranger assaults me there's a fair chance that, *had she not existed at all,* my level of welfare would have remained more or less 'flat': i.e. at roughly its pre-interaction level. Pre-interaction and CPW baselines are much less likely to coincide where A interacts with B mainly because A occupies a particular social role, such as being a member of a profession. For in these cases, the relevant possible worlds in which A does not exist will probably be ones in which A's role is not empty, but occupied by another role occupant, A*. Hence, pre-interaction baselines and the CPW baselines often come apart, since (if we use the latter) we assess whether or not B has been harmed by comparing her actual level of welfare with the level of welfare that she would have had if she'd interacted with A* instead of with A. And since there's not usually any reason to suppose that A*'s treatment will have no net effects on B's welfare, there's usually no reason to suppose that the pre-interaction baseline will be the same as the CPW baseline.

In order to see better how this idea works, let's turn back to Wertheimer's psychotherapist case. In this case, use of the pre-interaction baseline indicates that the patient has not been harmed, because she is better off after 'treatment-plus-sexual-exploitation' than she was beforehand. She is also, we can assume, better off relative to *some* possible worlds, because she is better off than she would have been if she'd never had a psychotherapist at all. So we *could* say that she's not harmed because treatment-plus-sexual-exploitation is better for her than *neither*-treatment-*nor*-sexual-exploitation. However, to use comparators like this is to invoke the wrong alternative possible worlds. For surely, it is (at least in the standard case) plausible to say that if the patient hadn't had psychotherapist A (for example if A had never been born) then she would instead have had psychotherapist A*. Hence, in assessing harm here, we should be comparing A's performance with that of A*, not with a world in which A's role is unoccupied. And, on the assumption that A* is competent and is not a sexual exploiter, this means comparing treatment-plus-sexual-exploitation (the actual world) with treatment-without-sexual-exploitation (the possible world in which A* is the therapist). This will, presumably, yield the conclusion that the patient really is harmed, since A is worse for her than A*.

CPW baselines, then, are generally preferable to pre-interaction ones for the purposes of assessing harm claims. However, there is a problem with CPW baselines, one which – at the very least – shows that we can't use them uncritically, or in every case. Consider, for example, the following:

Ian is treated at Stokehampton Hospital by Dr Van Zyl. Dr Van Zyl is seriously incompetent and his incompetence causes Ian to become moderately disabled. Subsequently, Dr Van Zyl is struck off, is forced to leave his job and never practises again. When Dr Van Zyl was interviewed for his post at Stokehampton he narrowly beat another candidate, Dr Trawlerman, who is (unbeknown to the authorities) not only less competent even than Dr Van Zyl, but also a serial killer who routinely murders his patients. So (let's say) the following conditionals are true. First, if it weren't for the presence of Dr Van Zyl, Dr Trawlerman would have treated Ian. Second, if Dr Trawlerman had treated Ian, Ian would have been murdered. (And, for completeness, let's specify that Ian has a 'life worth living', despite his disability.)

Cases like this reveal a problem with using CPW baselines in certain cases. For if we make a harm assessment here by comparing the actual world with the closest possible world, we must conclude that Ian is *not* harmed by Dr Van Zyl. On the contrary, he is benefited, because if it weren't for the existence of Dr Van Zyl, Ian would have been killed by Dr Trawlerman. This analysis is wildly counter-intuitive. For what we want to say is that Dr Van Zyl clearly harms Ian, regardless of the fact that he is, in a sense, 'shielding' Ian from Dr Trawlerman. Furthermore, this case reveals a structural feature which makes the use of CPW baselines problematic (at least in certain types of case). The problem is that using a CPW baseline in cases like Van Zyl and Trawlerman makes the question of whether or not Ian is harmed rest on a seemingly irrelevant and overly distant factor: namely, who would have got Dr Van Zyl's job if he hadn't got it. This is problematic in at least two ways. First, it just seems not to be a relevant consideration; in order to know whether or not Dr Van Zyl has harmed a particular patient we do not need to know who came second at the interviews. Second, allowing the alternative candidate to count as the comparator, for the purposes of harm assessment, can either generate impossibly high standards or let incompetents off the hook far too easily. For say that Trawlerman is the comparator and is both a spectacularly incompetent physician and a serial killer. If this is the case, then it will be almost impossible for Van Zyl to harm *any* of his patients, since it's almost impossible for him to be even worse than Trawlerman. Conversely, if the situation is reversed and Trawlerman is a sort of 'wonder-doctor', the best in the world, then it will be almost impossible for Van Zyl to avoid harming his patients – since, even if he does his best, he will be worse than (and hence harm them relative to) Trawlerman.

Faced with these problems, the attractions of using a *normative* baseline seem compelling.[14] Put in its most stark form, the normative construal of harm says that *A harms B if and only if A causes B to be worse off than she ought to be*, with the normative baseline being the *level of welfare which B ought to have had*. Both 'cause' and 'ought' hide a multitude of sins here. Many of these will have to be ignored, although some of the ones relating to causation will be picked up on later: for example, the question of whether omissions can cause harm. Normative baselines often coincide with one or both of the other types of baseline. Take a case in which A's harming of B violates one of B's negative rights: for example, where A wrongfully assaults B. Here the normative baseline coincides (in the standard case) with the pre-interaction baseline. This is because the normative baseline is B's level of welfare in a world in which A acts in accordance with his relevant duties. And since this is a world in which A refrains from interacting (so as to affect B adversely) the normative and pre-interaction welfare levels turn out to be the same. Or take a case in which A's harming of B breaches one of B's positive rights: for example, B is entitled to competent treatment from A, but A fails to be competent. Here, the normative baseline will often coincide with the CPW baseline, because it's often true that if B hadn't been treated by A, she would have been treated by a competent person instead: i.e. by someone who would have given B the level of welfare that she ought to have had.

Ought we to conclude, then, that normative baselines are always to be preferred and that the apparent appropriateness of other kinds of baseline is entirely parasitic on the fact that they coincide with the normative baseline in all those cases for which they look plausible? Unfortunately, things are not quite that straightforward. For there are at least two kinds of case in which we can't or shouldn't use normative baselines.

One is where harm is justly inflicted on B by A. In such cases (by definition) A does not make B worse off than she ought to be. One could, of course, deny that there are any cases in which harm is justly inflicted, by denying either that the standard counter-examples involve real harm or that they involve real justice. But such a view seems counter-intuitive and unmotivated. The other type of problem case (a very common one) is where the harm in question is not caused by a moral agent. As was noted earlier, interests can be set back by a wide variety of things, including accidents, natural disasters, and illness. In these cases, using a normative baseline to assess the harm claim makes no sense. For how can, say, a virus make someone worse off than she ought to be (leaving aside biological weapons and such things)? Here, we have to fall back on the use of CPW or sometimes even pre-interaction baselines.

So my conclusion is that things are somewhat messy. Usually, the claim that one person has harmed another should be assessed by reference to a normative baseline. However, sometimes, such claims (for example, about 'just harm') must be assessed instead by reference either to pre-interaction or to CPW baselines. The same goes for claims that a non-person has harmed a person. These must be assessed by reference to pre-interaction, or to CPW baselines, because there is quite simply no normative baseline available in such cases (since there are no relevant duties).

4.4 Omissive harm

The idea that if we are able to change things, to elect not to do so is also to determine what will happen in the world, is very old indeed ... In such cases, many men have found it natural not only to blame those who could have prevented the harm, but did not do so, but also to think of such men as having brought the harm about, as being its cause.[15]

As we have seen, assessing harm claims is less straightforward than it at first appears, because of the difficulties associated with selecting an appropriate welfare baseline as a comparator. Things are even more difficult when it comes to the claim that someone is harmed by an omission. Consider the following example:

Lawrence and Miss Ellis

Lawrence's school music teacher, Miss Ellis, is moderately incompetent. What she does, she does just about satisfactorily, but she completely fails to teach him anything about music history before 1900, or to develop his aural skills. When Lawrence takes his exams, he becomes aware of Miss Ellis's inadequacies. For he fails his history exam and his aural tests. He had been planning to apply to music college, but is now too demoralised to retake his school exams. He never gets to music college and his parents are dismayed about the fact that his promising career as a musician has been destroyed by what they regard as Miss Ellis's gross negligence.

What should we say about harm in this case? On the assumption that Lawrence would have been better off if he'd been a successful musician, and that he had enough 'potential' to become one, the intuitive answer is that he has indeed been harmed by Miss Ellis's inadequacies. In order to explain why, we need to think about relevant comparators. One comparator, the pre-interaction one, is *not having a music teacher*. If we use this one then Miss Ellis hasn't harmed him at all, as she's certainly better than nothing. Better comparators, though, would be possible worlds in which Miss Ellis is *non-negligent*, or *competent*, or *does what she ought*. And this is because we want to use a normative baseline and say that Miss Ellis has harmed Lawrence by *failing to do her duty*.

Miss Ellis harms Lawrence *without* exploiting him, whereas Andrew (in our earlier case) is an exploiter. In other important respects, though, the case of Lawrence and Miss Ellis is similar to that of Andrew and Brian. In particular, we can say of both cases that the question of whether harm has been inflicted depends crucially on whether we take as our relevant comparator (a) a possible world in which the putative harmer does nothing, or is simply non-existent, or (b) a possible world in which the putative harmer does more, or performs better, than she does in the actual world. In each case, if we take the first kind of comparator to be the relevant one, then the putative harmer turns out not really to have caused harm at all. For Brian would be *even worse off* if it weren't for Andrew's job offer and

Lawrence would be *even worse off* if he didn't have a music teacher at all. However, if we use the second kind of comparator, we get a different result. We've already seen how this works in the case of Lawrence and Miss Ellis: Lawrence is harmed in that he is worse off than he would have been if she had taught him competently (which she should have done). How this might apply in Andrew and Brian is more contentious. However, on the assumption that Brian is underpaid (an assumption we've been making thus far) we might say that Brian is harmed in the following sense: he is worse off than he would have been if Andrew had paid him a *fair* wage and demanded *fair* hours.

We can, then, distinguish, *within* harm-to-interests, between *active* and *omissive* harm. To be actively harmed is to be harmed by someone's actions and is what we were discussing in the previous section. To be omissively harmed, on the other hand, is to be harmed by someone's omissions.[16] An omission, here, is not a mere non-doing. Otherwise, I would count as being omissively harmed every time someone didn't benefit me. Rather, 'omission' is a moral(ised) term referring to someone's failure to comply with a duty to act, or to perform at or above a certain level.[17] Professional negligence, underpayment (for example, by employers), and failing to rescue can all be examples of omissive harm. For, in each case, the 'victim' might reasonably say that she has been harmed by others' failure to do what they ought.

The extent to which one deploys the concept of omissive harm will depend on how many, and what, positive duties one thinks there are. This is especially clear in the 'good (or bad) Samaritan' cases, frequently discussed by moral philosophers: cases in which a passer-by decides to rescue ('good Samaritan') or not ('bad Samaritan') a stranger who is drowning or who is injured at the side of the road. One of the main questions about such cases is: does the bad Samaritan, by not saving the stranger's life, *harm* the stranger, or does she merely *not benefit* him? If we apply what I have said so far about omissions and omissive harm, we get the following (admittedly schematic) answer. The bad Samaritan *omits* to save and therefore *omissively harms* the stranger only if she has a duty to save her. Otherwise, the bad Samaritan's not acting is a *mere non-acting*, rather than an *omission*, and so she merely fails to benefit the stranger. Hence, one could (and, on my view, should) think one of two things. Either one could believe that there is a duty to rescue, an omission and omissive harm. Or alternatively

> One might be tempted to argue that bad samaritans are not omitters at all, but only nondoers . . . On this account, an omission is the nondoing of an act one had a duty to do, and duties come only from special relations to the endangered party. The bad Samaritan, having no such relationship to the endangered party, had no

duty to assist him. Therefore, although he did not assist him, it is false that he *omitted* to do so.[18]

I can't hope to settle the issue of whether there is or is not a general duty to rescue here. My point, rather, is that those of us who see the moral landscape as densely populated by positive duties will and should – on the view presented – be much more inclined to ascribe omissive harm than those 'minimalists' who think that positive duties only arise within a very narrow range of special relationships.

Turning our attention back to exploitation, we can now see how Wolff's suggestion that 'exploitation involves making someone worse off than they ought to be', combined with the idea of omissive harm-to-interests, might be used to rescue a version of the harm condition.[19] The argument goes as follows. It was initially suggested that, necessarily, exploitees are harmed by exploitation (the harm condition). A counter-example to this, Andrew and Brian, was then provided in which Brian (the exploitee) appeared to be better off exploited than not. However, we are now in a position to argue that, even if Brian has not been *actively* harmed, he has nonetheless been *omissively* harmed, because he is worse off than he would have been if Andrew had paid him a fair wage. (Alternatively, by describing the situation in an appropriate way, it might be possible to argue that he has been actively harmed relative to a comparator baseline in which he is – for example – not made to work excessive hours.)

Importantly, this manoeuvre is not just a way of neutralising one particular counter-example. For it can also be a general strategy for establishing the existence of a necessary connection between exploitation and harm, by generalising the following argument:

1 Andrew only counts as an exploiter because there is *disparity of value*.

2 What disparity of value means (or, at least, entails) in this case is that Andrew breaches his duties towards Brian (for example, by not paying him enough or making him work too much). If there were no breaches of duty, there would be no disparity of value.

3 Therefore, given that, because of Andrew's actions or omissions, Brian is *worse off than he ought to be*, Andrew must have harmed Brian.

So the idea is, in brief, that exploitation entails disparity of value, which entails a breach of duty, which entails harm (relative to a normative baseline) and that, therefore, the occurrence of harm is a necessary condition for the existence of exploitation.

Even if the validity of this argument is established, the version of the harm condition that it saves only applies to disparity of value exploitation. So if a link between harm and the other kind of exploitation, instrumentalisation, is to be established, a quite separate argument will be required. (One such argument, concerning 'moral harm', is considered in the following section.) Furthermore, by broadening the notion of harm to include omissive harms and harms judged against normative base-lines, this (modified) harm condition states something less controversial and remarkable than did the original version. In other words, the modi-fied harm condition is relatively 'weak', because it still allows that there are cases of 'mutually beneficial exploitation', if by this we mean cases in which both the exploiter and the exploitee are better off than they would have been if there had been no exploitation. In these cases, the exploitee is not harmed relative to pre-interaction or closest possible world baselines and is only harmed (actively or omissively) relative to a normative baseline.

4.5 Moral harm

[I]t may be argued that the[re is] a deeper – Kantian – way in which what I have called mutually advantageous exploitation is actually harmful to B [the exploitee], namely, that A treats B merely as a means to be utilized to his own advantage rather than an end in herself. *And so treating a person is a harm to her.*[20]

In Chapter 3, I introduced the case of Manuel Wackenheim, a (so-called) dwarf who earned a living by being 'tossed' by customers in bars and nightclubs. This 'tossing' formed part of a *dwarf-throwing competition* – a sport 'in which the aim of the competitors is to fling a dwarf over the furthest distance possible'.[21]

One view of dwarf throwing is that it is not wrong provided that it is consensual and harmless, in the harm-to-interests sense. Another is that it is a case of harmless wrongdoing; for example, one might concede that dwarf throwing is harmless but nonetheless invoke the idea of instru-mentalisation, along with related notions such as degradation and (in)dignity. A third view is that dwarf throwing is harmful in the third sense of 'harm' noted by Feinberg:

To say that A has harmed B in this sense is to say much the same thing as that A has wronged B, or treated him unjustly. One per-son *wrongs* another when his indefensible (unjustifiable and inexcusable) conduct violates the other's rights.[22]

So someone might say that Manuel Wackenheim has been harmed, in this third sense, meaning that his rights (which will need, for this to work, to be *inalienable*, given that he seems to want to waive them) have been violated. Such (supposed) rights could include his right to dignity and his right to respect as a person.

At this point, though, we should ask: even if his rights have been violated, what is the point of calling any violations *harm*? If the rights in question exist and have been violated, then, of course, Wackenheim has been *wronged*. But using 'harm' to refer to wrongs which are not harmful in the standard (harm-to-interests) sense seems counter-intuitive and not to add anything to our understanding of these cases. Furthermore, and more importantly, using 'harm' in this expanded way is potentially very confusing, obfuscating as it does the distinction between wronging people by harming them (in the standard harm-to-interests sense) and wronging them in other ways. It would be much better, I suggest, to leave open the possibility that these cases are cases of harmless wrongdoing, reserving the word 'harm' for harm-to-interests, and rejecting talk of purely moral harm.[23]

4.6 Summary and conclusions

Practices involving the commercialisation of the body are frequently accused of being exploitative and of being harmful and, more often than not, these exploitation and harm claims accompany one another. With this in mind, Chapter 4 aimed to improve our understanding both of the nature of harm and of the relationship between harm and exploitation.

The discussion of the relationship between harm and exploitation centred around the harm condition, which states that exploitation necessarily involves harm to the exploitee. Evaluating the harm condition meant engaging in a deeper analysis of the concept of harm. The analysis started by drawing on Feinberg's tripartite division of harm into (a) the extended sense (under which *harm* means simply *damage*), (b) harm-to-interests, and (c) moral harm. The extended sense was deemed largely irrelevant, while the idea of purely moral harm was rejected on the grounds that using 'harm' in this way is confusing, as it obscures an important distinction between wronging people by harming them and wronging them in other ways. The focus for the remainder of the analysis therefore was harm-to-interests, which Feinberg defines as 'the thwarting, setting back, or defeating of an interest'.[24] People are harmed, in the harm-to-interests sense, if they are made worse off. However, lurking behind this seemingly simple idea are two thorny questions. What counts as *being* worse off? And what counts as *making someone* worse off?

The first of these questions could be restated as: worse off *than what*? For harm-to-interests is a comparative concept and, in order to know whether or not someone has been harmed, we need to know what to compare her actual level of welfare to; we need a welfare baseline to use as a comparator. Three types of baseline – pre-interaction, closest possible world, and normative – were discussed in some detail. It was concluded that things are 'messy'. More specifically, while *usually* the claim that one person has harmed another should be assessed by reference to a normative baseline, *sometimes* such claims should be assessed instead by reference either to pre-interaction or to closest possible world baselines.

The second question – what counts as *making someone* worse off? – is principally about whether we should allow both actions and omissions to count as harmful, or whether we should say instead that only actions can be harmful. Our conclusion was that there *is* such a thing as omissive harm, being harmed by someone's omissions. Omissions, however, are not mere non-doings, otherwise I'd be omissively harmed every time you decided not to benefit me. An omission is, rather, a failure to comply with a relevant ('positive') duty to do something, or a duty to do something at or above a certain level (for example, of competence).

The idea of omissive harm-to-interests can be used to rescue a version of the harm condition. According to this version, the following necessary connection between (disparity of value) exploitation and harm exists. In order for there to be a disparity of value, the exploiter must (a) *actively harm* the exploitee *and/or* (b) fail to give the exploitee something which she ought to give her (for example, by underpaying her). Obviously (a) involves harm, but (b) also involves *omissive harm* as defined above. Hence, one way or the other, exploitation always involves harm.

There is, then, a version of the harm condition which appears plausible. However, the plausible version seems 'weaker' and a good deal less interesting than what we started out with. For it relies on the acceptance of a fairly broad notion of harm – in particular, one which uses normative baselines and allows omissions to count as harmful. As was argued earlier, there are good reasons for having such an understanding of harm, and so these points are not objections to the 'weakened' harm condition. However, we should bear in mind that, even with this 'weakened' harm condition in place, there is still an important distinction to be made (within exploitation) between *exploitation which makes the exploitee worse off than she would have been if she hadn't been exploited* and *exploitation which makes the exploitee better off than she would have been if she hadn't been exploited*. It is tempting to call the former *harmful* exploitation and the latter *mutually advantageous* exploitation (assuming that the exploiter also gains). But this may be misleading, given that cases in the latter category will also turn out to be harmful if normative baselines are used.

I'd suggest, however, that we can still legitimately use the expression *mutually advantageous exploitation* to refer to cases of the second kind, even though such cases are harmful to the exploitee when measured against a normative baseline. It's important for us explicitly to recognise this category for two reasons. First, the fact that an instance of exploitation is mutually advantageous (in this sense) is often morally relevant, especially in the context of arguments about legal prohibition. For what we might sensibly say about some such cases is that the exploitation should be allowed because the exploitees are *better off with it than without it*. (Another, forceful, way of making the same point is to say that to ban it would harm the exploitees, relative to a pre-interaction or CPW baseline.) Second, the fact that some instances of exploitation are mutually advantageous plays an important role in the minds of prospective exploitees, for they will often have strong prudential reasons for subjecting themselves to exploitative arrangements of this kind. And this may itself have moral significance, for it is at least worth taking seriously the possibility that exploitation which is rationally consented to and desired by the exploitee is morally preferable to exploitation which is forced and unwanted. These matters, including the issue of consent, will be looked at in the next chapter.

So to sum up, the relationship between exploitation and harm is as follows. It is right to classify *all* (disparity of value) exploiters as harmers. This follows from the broad understanding of harm which I have argued for in this chapter – an understanding which includes omissive harm and harm measured against normative baselines. I take this to be not merely a trivial or linguistic claim but – especially given the importance of harm in our moral–conceptual landscape – an interesting and substantive moral truth, grounded in proper understandings of exploitation and of harm. For example, it has practical implications, such as that exploiters cannot (or should not) defend themselves by claiming that what they are doing is entirely harmless. We should keep in mind, though, that, while all exploitation is harmful, there is an important distinction to be drawn between what I earlier called 'mutually advantageous exploitation' and other forms of exploitation, and that mutually advantageous exploitation (for reasons explained above) will often be less morally objectionable than other forms.

5

CONSENT

> When exploiting friends or lovers, we are not *forcing* them to
> do anything whatsoever. They do what they do happily,
> willingly, voluntarily.[1]

The idea of consent, or valid consent, has both a primary and a secondary
role within the body commodification debate. The primary role is that it's
thought by many to explain directly the wrongness of certain commercial
practices. For example, it has been argued both that surrogate mothers
and that people who sell parts of their bodies (for example, kidneys)
don't, or can't, validly consent. For this reason (so the argument goes)
such practices are wrong, since interactions that are as intimate, or as
dangerous, as these ought to be properly consensual. Consent's secondary role is the contribution that it makes to the justification of exploitation
claims. For, as we've already seen, most (maybe even all) instances of
exploitation appear to involve a consent that is somehow defective or
inadequate.

This chapter addresses the following questions. First, what is valid
consent? Second, what factors can invalidate a consent? And third,
what is the relationship between consent and exploitation? Specifically,
is genuinely consensual exploitation a possibility, and (conversely), is
defective (or absent) consent a necessary condition for a transaction's
being exploitative?

5.1 Absent consent and defective consent

I've already suggested that there's an important link between defective
consent and exploitation. However, one puzzle is that we don't normally
want to describe those wrongs which involve the *complete absence* of consent as exploitation.[2] Consent to sexual intercourse is an interesting case
in point. It would be extremely odd to say (at least of relatively straightforward cases) that what's bad about rape is that it's exploitative; to do so

would both understate and misidentify the wrong involved. By contrast, though, the claim that prostitution is exploitative is commonplace. What's more, the rationale for accepting this exploitation claim is that (many) prostitutes are, in effect, *forced* into prostitution by poverty, social exclusion, etc. So the puzzle is that, although (arguably) both rape and prostitution are wrong because they involve forced sex, we want to describe only the latter as exploitation. Why could this be?

What we have here is an awkward intuition about how the word 'exploitation' should be applied. We have a choice about how to handle this intuition. Either we can get our account of exploitation to accommodate it (or, even better, show that it already accommodates it). Or we can try to show that the intuition is somehow flawed or misleading.

Perhaps the best answer of the second kind appeals to Wertheimer's idea of moral occlusion.[3] Rape, we might say, really is exploitative, but the exploitation involved is *occluded* by more serious and tangible wrongs, such as bodily violation and mental and physical harm. In other words, the reason why it would be peculiar to say that what's bad about rape is that it's exploitative is not that rape isn't exploitative, but rather that its being exploitative is a relatively minor evil compared to the others involved. So it's the decision to *foreground* exploitation and the suggestion that exploitation is the main evil which are strange, rather than the claim that it is exploitative *per se*. An analogous case here is murder. Often, this will involve lesser occluded evils, such as violation of bodily integrity and physical injury. These occluded evils exist. But it would strike us as odd if they were foregrounded, or if someone argued that what's wrong with murder is that it involves violation of bodily integrity, since the main evil is obviously death.

In general, the idea of moral occlusion is an interesting and useful one. However, it does seem to me that the answer it delivers here is unsatisfying. There are two reasons for this. First, other things being equal, we should prefer accounts which save the appearances, those which trust our intuitions, to those which view our intuitions as defective or misleading. Of course, other things are not always equal, and there are often good theoretical (or other) reasons for holding that things are not as they seem. However, here (as we'll see in a minute) there does seem to be a plausible appearance-saving account available. The second reason is that it's not clear that appealing to occlusion really does explain why we view rape and prostitution differently. In the case of rape, the claim is that the exploitation involved is occluded by the other more serious evils. But it is tempting to ask why the same isn't true of prostitution. For many people believe that the most serious evils involved in prostitution are similar to those involved in rape – for example, bodily violation and mental and physical harm – and that its being exploitative is a *relatively* minor matter. Nonetheless, we don't regard the claim that prostitution is exploitative as odd and, perhaps more importantly, don't seem to have a problem with believing (even pre-analytically) *both* that it is exploitative *and* that exploitation is not the main evil involved.

Let's turn now to the other kind of answer, the one which takes our intuition at face value and attempts to explain why rape is not normally exploitative, while prostitution often is. Allen Wood suggests (below) that there is a sense in which typical victims of exploitation (such as the starving person and the indebted gambler) are likely to be all *too* willing to be exploited, all *too* willing to give their consent, owing to the absence of less bad alternatives. Hence, according to Wood, 'exploitation is often voluntary' and consensual:

> Someone who is propertyless and starving has a lot to gain by striking a deal with an employer who is willing to offer bare subsistence in exchange for long, hard labour under dangerous conditions – and a lot to lose (namely, life itself) if no such exploitative bargain is in the offing ... A gambler who owes a large amount of money to ruthless and violent characters will be in desperate need of the loan shark who offers the needed funds at a usurious rate of interest; such a person will be more than willing under these conditions to consent to virtually any terms of payment.[4]

These do seem to be classic cases of exploitation and are structurally identical to the case of the prostitute who may be keen to take on sex work given her poverty and lack of preferable alternatives. I would suggest, then, that Wood is at least partially right, and that the following is true of exploitation: *it takes place only where there is (at least) 'minimal consent' from the exploitee.* What I mean by this is that, although the exploitee need not (and normally does not) provide *valid* consent (a concept that we'll be looking at in more detail shortly), she does consciously *choose* the exploitative arrangement rather than some other (even worse) alternative.

To draw on Wood again, a plausible explanation of why this is so can be found in the model of exploitative use suggested in section 2.4. According to that model, exploitation necessarily involves (what Wood calls) *advantage-exploitation*, making use of 'someone's weakness or vulnerability' – such as her desires and needs – in order to gain 'a hold over the person'.[5] This is played out in practice by A using B's vulnerability to get B 'minimally' to consent. Entirely non-consensual uses of persons, by contrast, fail to involve advantage-exploitation, for they bypass the will, or conscious choice, altogether. For example, to rape someone does not (or need not, except in the crudely physical sense) depend on using the victim's weaknesses or vulnerabilities to gain 'a hold over' her. The reason for this is simply that no 'hold' is required, since there is no need to make the victim choose sex and no need for her minimal consent. Rather, rape is a physical violation. Similar things can be said of burglary (which isn't normally exploitative), and this can be usefully contrasted with the actions of, say, confidence tricksters (who normally do exploit). Burglary doesn't involve advantage-exploitation. On the contrary, its victims don't even need to be present. So burglary isn't normally exploitation. Confidence tricksters, on the other hand, do rely on getting 'minimal' consent from their victims. The victim needs actually to *hand over* the cash or to *sign* the contract. Hence, the victim does need to be advantage-exploited. That is, a psychological weakness – such as fear, greed, impatience, or ignorance – is taken advantage of.

For completeness, I should add that things look very different when we turn to instrumentalisation ('wrongful use' exploitation). This is mainly because, as we saw in section 2.4, instrumentalisation needn't involve advantage-exploitation. Take, for example, the kind of objectification claims that people make about prostitution. The leading idea behind these claims is that *it is wrong to treat another person as a mere sex object* and that treating people in this way constitutes instrumentalisation. Treating another person as a mere sex object, though, doesn't require even minimal consent and can entirely 'bypass the will'. Rape, for example, does (or can) involve the victim being treated as a mere sex object and so would seem to be a case of instrumentalisation. But rape doesn't (or needn't) involve 'minimal' consent and so doesn't (or needn't) involve advantage-exploitation.

5.2 Valid consent

We've already seen that, as well as the distinction between consensual and non-consensual transactions, there is a further distinction – *within* the consensual – between *valid* and *invalid* consent. Whereas the distinction between consensual and non-consensual is essentially psychological or social, the valid/invalid distinction is moral. Invalid consents are perfectly *real*: for example, if I hand over my money in response to a 'Your money or your life!' threat, then I really have agreed to give you the money. But such consents don't have the same moral significance as valid consents. In particular, valid consents (for example, to sexual intercourse, surgery, or the taking of property) can morally justify acts in ways that invalid consents can't. Indeed, as I suggested in section 3.7, what it means to say that a consent is valid is precisely that it provides a justification for certain action(s) (sometimes on its own, sometimes in conjunction with other facts). For example, to say that I have *validly* consented to having my tooth removed is to say that my consent is of a sufficiently high quality (in conjunction with other facts) to *justify* my dentist's (tooth-removing) actions.

Cases like this aren't quite the whole story, though, because one other morally significant thing that valid consents sometimes do is to create additional duties for the consenter. What I have in mind here are things like contracts and promises which involve someone's agreeing (consenting) to take on particular moral and/or legal duties, normally in exchange for something. In such cases, the consent offered must be valid in order for the additional moral duties to be generated. For example, if a promiser only makes her promise because she is lied to by the promisee, most of us would say that she has no moral duty to keep it. This is because, although we wouldn't usually put it in quite these terms, her consent (her agreeing to take on the obligation) is invalid.

So valid consents are morally significant in one or both of two ways. *Either* they justify (partly or wholly) the interventions of third parties, such as dentists and doctors; *or* they generate additional obligations for the consenter if, for example, she agrees to enter into a contract. The aim of the next few pages is to say what valid consent is. In areas like medical ethics valid consent is normally called *informed consent*. The expression *valid consent* is preferable, however, because, as we'll see, adequate information is only one part of validity, and consent can be invalidated by factors other than lack of information.

The concept of consent is widely used both in everyday contexts and by moral and political philosophers. One of the places where it has been most heavily employed and analysed in recent times is within healthcare ethics. Consider, for example, these two definitions of 'consent', both provided by bioethicists (Gillon, and Faden and Beauchamp respectively):

> consent means a voluntary, uncoerced decision, made by a suf-
> ficiently competent or autonomous person on the basis of
> adequate information and deliberation, to accept rather than
> reject some proposed course of action.[6]

> an informed consent is an autonomous action by . . . a patient that
> authorises a professional . . . to initiate a medical plan for the
> patient . . . an informed consent is given if a patient or subject
> with (1) substantial understanding and (2) in substantial absence
> of control by others (3) intentionally (4) authorises a professional.[7]

Plausibly, both definitions suggest that in order for a consent to be valid, three main elements must be present (or present in sufficient quantities): information, competence, and voluntariness.

Let's now take a look at these three main elements, starting with information. Medical ethicists have spent a great deal of time on attempts to construct a substantive account of how much information a patient or research subject needs in order for her consent to be valid. I'll not try anything that ambitious here, not least because my concerns are rather more general than theirs. It is, however, worth saying something about why information matters and, schematically, about what sort of information matters and how much there should be. The reason why information matters is simply that in order for A to consent to X, A needs to know what X is and what the likely consequences of X are. Exactly how much A needs to know about X is not something that I'll investigate here. However, it seems fair to say that, at least in the standard case, A needs to know about X's main benefits and drawbacks and about any other factors which one would reasonably expect to affect A's decision about whether or not to accept X.

Two further points about information need to be made before we proceed. Both are fairly obvious but nonetheless important, not least because they are sometimes overlooked in the body commodification debate. The first is that *full* or *complete* knowledge is not required for validity. The main reason for this is that even if we allow that such a complete knowledge state is a theoretical possibility, it is certainly not a state in which humans very often (if ever) find themselves in practice. Hence, if we decided to make full knowledge a requirement, that would commit us to the (absurd) view that there are virtually no cases of valid consent. The second point (which is in many respects similar) is that *experiential* knowledge is not generally required for validity. Experiential knowledge of X is knowing what it is like to experience X, which normally means having experienced X and being able to remember experiencing X. Experiential knowledge – for example, of the pains or pleasures associated with certain things – can be very important and may well help to validate consents and, more generally, help people to make good decisions. However, it can't be a general requirement because otherwise it would be, at best, difficult for people to consent to things for the first time. Again, sexual consent provides a pretty clear case in point. If experiential knowledge were required then it would be almost impossible for virgins to consent validly to their first sexual encounters. And depending on how finely we individuate items of experiential knowledge it may, similarly, be impossible even for non-virgins validly to consent to their first sexual experience with A, with B, with C, of X, and so on. We'll be returning to the idea of experiential knowledge and consent during the discussion of surrogacy, because some people have objected to surrogacy on the grounds that the surrogate's consent is rendered invalid by her lack of experiential knowledge.

To turn now to *competence*, this term refers to the consenter's mental capacities. Is she capable of making reasonable decisions? Can she understand relevant information and issues and rationally assess the pros and cons of what is proposed? Examples of consents being invalid because of lack of competence include consents given by young children, consents given by people suffering from mental disabilities or illnesses, and consents given by people whose minds are under the influence of alcohol or other mind-affecting drugs. As I've suggested, people in all three categories can validly consent to *some* things, depending on the degree of mental incapacity. For example, we'd view most contracts between drunks and taxi drivers or bartenders as valid, and many drunken consents to sexual intercourse as valid (except, perhaps, in very extreme cases of intoxication, or where the intoxication is itself involuntary).[8] Given their mental limitations, though, people in the categories just mentioned do, in general, run a substantial risk of providing invalid consent, especially for complex and/or important decisions. After all, we wouldn't, for example, take seriously an extremely drunken consent to organ donation from a prospective live donor.

As I suggested earlier, the third element of valid consent is *voluntariness*. This is not to be confused with what philosophers call *free will*. That is, you don't need to be completely free from all causal determinants in order to act voluntarily. Rather, to act voluntarily is just to be free from certain specific types of influence, notably coercion. Because coercion is such a difficult, important, and highly relevant concept, it merits a chapter of its own (Chapter 6).[9]

5.3 Consensual exploitation?

The idea of exploitation usually implies that the exploiter is able to apply some coercive pressure that those whom she exploits are unable, or ill equipped, to resist.[10]

So far in this chapter we've seen that, in order for exploitation to occur, the exploitee must provide at least 'minimal' consent. This is one of the main differences between exploitation and theft; theft needn't be even minimally consensual. In this section, I'd like to ask whether it's possible for an exploitee's consent to be valid or whether instead what I'll term the consent condition – the view that A exploits B only if B's consent to the arrangement is invalid – is true. I'll contend that it is, that exploitation always involves 'defective' consent from the exploitee.

Why would anyone believe the consent condition? Perhaps the best reason for doing so is suggested by this passage from Schwartz:

If I am entitled to a coat because I made it, you may still receive it justly, not because you are entitled to it, but because I give it to you. That isn't theft, nor do you exploit me in receiving the coat. The reason is that the transfer is free and unforced ... The problem with surplus transfer in class societies is that in general it is arguably not free and unforced. In slave and feudal societies that is clear ·enough. Producers hand over the surplus *or else*. Marx argues that this is true, despite appearances, in capitalism.[11]

For Schwartz, what differentiates the exploitative economic transactions that are endemic within capitalist societies from (say) genuine gifts is that the latter are 'free and unforced' – or, we might say, validly consensual – whereas the former are not. It seems to me not only that Schwartz is right about this, but also that we can generalise this insight and say that the presence or absence of valid consent is what distinguishes exploitation from gifts, and being exploited from being generous.

As we've seen, people who are exploited suffer some (negative) 'disparity in the value of an exchange of goods and services'.[12] They are (for example) under-rewarded for something which they provide for the person or institution which exploits them. However, not all cases of under-reward are cases of exploitation. If someone very poor is forced to work in a factory for $1 per day in order to avoid starvation for her family, then she is probably being both under-rewarded and exploited by her employer. But if, on the other hand, a wealthy professional person agrees, entirely voluntarily, to spend a day working for charity for a 'token' $1 per day, then she is (probably) being under-rewarded but *not* exploited. The key difference between these two cases is the nature of the consent that each person gives. In the former case, the validity of the consent is questionable, but in the latter case, the consent to underpayment is unproblematic. This is the thinking underpinning the *consent condition*, according to which A exploits B only if B's consent to the arrangement is invalid. In short, what the consent condition does is to allow us to distinguish cases of exploitation from non-exploitative cases in which an individual waives her rights to a fair share of the burdens/benefits. The consent condition is neutral with respect to particular conceptions of valid consent and furthermore is compatible with the view that different standards of consent are applicable in different types of case. Hence, the consent condition will only yield substantive results when allied with a particular account of valid consent.

Both Wertheimer and Wood argue against my view that exploitation necessarily involves defective consent. Consider again Wood's starving person and indebted gambler (cited above).[13] As we've seen, Wood says that these victims of exploitation are likely to be all *too* willing to be exploited, because of the absence of less bad alternatives, and hence 'exploitation is often voluntary' and we oughtn't to make defective consent part of our definition of exploitation.[14] This does seem to present a problem for the consent condition, since both of Wood's cases look like fully voluntary cases of exploitation. We should, however, bear in mind that the proposed criterion is not *mere voluntariness*, but *valid consent*, which is a more demanding and more 'moralised' standard.

One way of dealing with Wood's cases, then, is to argue that neither the starving person nor the gambler validly consents, because of their lack of acceptable alternatives. Although this seems initially intuitive, I'd be reluctant to put too much weight on the idea that lack of acceptable alternatives is in and of itself sufficient to invalidate a consent. There are two main reasons for this. The first, a very general worry, is that it will be difficult, if not impossible, to specify non-arbitrarily what counts as a sufficient number of sufficiently good alternatives. Second, it would seem strange to say (as this proposal implies) that if someone were faced with an entirely free choice between X, which is extremely good, and Y, which is extremely bad, that that person could not validly consent to X because of the lack of acceptable alternatives. Consider, for example, this case provided by Wertheimer:

> If A (a physician) should say to B (a patient), 'You can choose to have this leg amputated or you will die', we don't say that B's decision to have his leg amputated is coerced because death is an unacceptable alternative. Rather, we seek B's informed consent to the procedure.[15]

It would be quite bizarre to rule out the possibility of valid consent here just because of the lack of acceptable alternatives.

Much more promising is the idea that it is *coercion* which invalidates consent in Wood's cases. This looks straightforwardly plausible in the case of the gambler who is being threatened by 'ruthless and violent characters'. He is, we might say, coerced into taking the loan from the loan shark since the ruthless and violent characters will harm him if he doesn't pay them and (let's assume) getting money from the loan shark is his only means of doing so. So *de facto* they are coercing him into taking out the loan. Wood's other case, the starving person, is one which we might naturally talk about in terms of the person's being forced by poverty or by starvation. But is this really coercion, or is it merely a lack of options, or some other sort of non-coercive forcing? This isn't an easy question and, in order to deal with it, we'll need to tackle directly the question of what exactly coercion is. This is one of the main aims in the next chapter.

5.4 Summary and conclusions

Valid consent has both a primary and a secondary role in the body commodification debate. The primary role is that it's thought by many to explain directly the wrongness of certain commercial practices, while the secondary role is its contribution to the justification of exploitation claims. It has this secondary role in virtue of its relationship with exploitation. I've suggested that this relationship's key elements are (i) that A exploits B only if B minimally consents, and (ii) that A exploits B only if B's consent is somehow defective. Element (ii) is what I earlier termed the consent condition.

Valid consents are morally significant in one or both of two ways. Either they justify (partly or wholly) the interventions of third parties, such as healthcare professionals, or they produce obligations for the consenter, if, for example, she agrees to enter into a contract. In order for a consent to be valid, three main elements must be present in sufficient quantities: information, competence, and voluntariness. Occasionally (and notably in the debate about commercial surrogacy) consent objections to body commodification are based on concerns about (the absence of) competence or information. However, more often than not, they're based on concerns about voluntariness, especially coercion. For this reason, and because coercion is conceptually difficult, Chapter 6 will investigate coercion in more detail.

6

COERCION

Both coercion and deception infringe upon the voluntary
character of the agent's actions. In both cases a person will
feel used, will see herself as the instrument of another's will.[1]

Whenever coercion takes place one will is subordinated to
another. The coerced is no longer a completely independent
agent. If my will is overborne by yours I serve your ends and
not mine. I am motivated by your interests and not mine. I
do what you want, not what I want.[2]

This chapter aims to provide an analysis of the concept of coercion.
Accusations of coercion often underpin attempts to show that particular
commercial practices involve the wrongful use of people, or the violation
of their autonomy, or that any consent given is invalid. More specifically,
it's sometimes said that only people who were coerced would 'volunteer'
to sell a body part, or to provide 'sexual services', or to be surrogate
mothers. For, as Kligman and Culver put it,

an offer of payment can take on some of the qualities of manipulation, or even coercion; for example, if the offer is grossly unfair, or
one party has no way of accurately assessing the value of his
services, or one's need for the offered sum is so pressing that one
is not genuinely free to refuse the offer.[3]

6.1 Introducing coercion

Unfortunately, confusion over what the term 'coercion' stands for
has not stopped people from using it.[4]

Coercion is ethically significant in a number of different ways.[5] First,
'coercion', more often than not, is used as a negative moral term.[6] It suggests a particular kind of moral criticism, and coercion's *victims* regularly

complain, in moral terms, about having been coerced. Second, being the victim of coercion normally 'serves to nullify or mitigate one's legal or moral responsibility for one's actions'.[7] We regard coerced actions as forced and involuntary. Hence, someone who is coerced into breaking a moral or legal rule can, in her defence, reasonably say something like 'I couldn't help it – I had no real choice'. The actions of the person who is coerced are, as Dworkin puts it,

> in one sense hers because she did them [but] . . . in another sense attributable to another. It is because of this that such infringements may excuse or (partially) relieve a person of responsibility for what she has done.[8]

Finally, the use of coercion to gain consent typically renders any resultant consent invalid, usually with important ethical implications.

Let's start our analysis by considering the following example.

> An armed woman breaks into my house and threatens to kill my beloved cat, Tiddles, if I don't give her $5,000. I decide to give her $5,000, since I would undoubtedly prefer to be $5,000 worse off than to watch poor Tiddles be murdered.

In this case, there clearly *is* a sense in which I freely decide to pay $5,000 rather than watch Tiddles die. I do, after all, act on a genuine preference and could have decided to keep the money instead. However, we probably *would* want to say of the Tiddles case that my decision to hand over the cash wasn't truly voluntary because I was coerced, and that (a) the cat killer's actions made me less free than I otherwise would have been, and (b) I was not fully responsible for my actions, so that even if giving the cat killer money were wrong (for example, because she would spend it on weapons, or on 'hard' drugs for children) I shouldn't be held (fully) responsible.[9] We would also probably want to say that any consent given by me under such coercive conditions was invalid. This can be seen clearly in our intuitive responses to the following questions. First, if I took the cat killer to an ATM to get the $5,000 that I 'promised' her and got a chance to escape without paying up, would I be morally obliged to refrain from escaping and to give her the money? Second, does my coerced 'consent' to her taking the $5,000 in any way justify her taking it? In both cases, we would (rightly) say *no*. This is because of the invalidity of my consent – a 'minimal' consent which neither justifies the cat killer's actions nor morally constrains mine.

So what exactly is coercion? In fact there are two different, though intimately related, questions here. One concerns the coer*cer* and is about what counts as coerc*ing* or, more accurately, as *acting coercively*; the other concerns the coerc*ee* and is about what counts as having been successfully coerced (which is typically contrasted with being free or acting freely).

The most plausible answer to the first question (though one that will have to be refined later) is that A coerces B when A threatens to harm B if B doesn't do what A wants. As Wertheimer puts it,

> In general, A coerces B to do X if A proposes (threatens) to make B worse off with reference to some baseline condition unless B does X.[10]

Hence, we can say that the cat killer coerces me because she threatens to harm me (by killing my cat) if I don't do what she wants (hand over the cash). On this view, which I regard as fundamentally correct, the account of coercion is based principally on a distinction between threats and offers, with coercion being equated with threatening. We'll look soon at whether *all* threats are coercive, or whether instead threatening is merely a necessary condition for coercing, while, in section 6.3, we'll be taking a closer look at how to draw the required distinction between offers and threats.

A plausible answer to the second question (the one about the coercee) is offered by Gerald Dworkin. A puzzle which concerns Dworkin is

> why coercion is thought of as a way of getting someone to do what he doesn't want to do rather than a way of getting someone to want to do something else.[11]

This relates to the idea (mentioned above) that when I hand over the $5,000 I do so because I *prefer* life without the $5,000 to life without the beloved Tiddles. This is clearly true, for I *could* have chosen Tiddles's death instead if, say, I valued her life at only $3,000. Nonetheless, the intuition that the cat killer is making me hand over the money *against my will* remains strong.

What Dworkin (and I) think this shows is not that all actions (even coerced ones) are voluntary but rather that our account of being coerced cannot depend on a distinction between acting on one's own desires and acting on something other than one's own desires – because even if my desires are caused by coercion, they are still *mine*. In 'Acting freely' (1970), quoted above, Dworkin's alternative account of coercion is based on the negative attitudes of the coercee to the desires on which she acts. More specifically, the account is 'in terms of the resentment or aversion men have to acting for certain reasons'.[12] So, of the cat killer case, we could (employing Dworkin's view) say that I am successfully coerced because I am caused to act on reasons which I *resent* having to act on (for example, that I prefer preventing Tiddles's murder to saving $5,000).

In Dworkin's later work, notably *The Theory and Practice of Autonomy* (1988), this account of coercion is made more general and fitted into a wide-ranging theory of autonomy. On this later view, coercion is one of a number of ways in which someone's autonomy can be disrespected or undermined. Coercion does this in one or both of two ways. It may cause the coercee to act on desires which she does not reflectively endorse (at the level of her 'second-order' desires). Alternatively, it may lead to 'failure of procedural independence', which Dworkin describes in general terms as follows:

> Spelling out the conditions of procedural independence involves distinguishing those ways of influencing people's reflective and critical faculties which subvert them from those which promote and improve them. It involves distinguishing those influences such as hypnotic suggestion, manipulation, coercive persuasion, subliminal influence, and so forth, and doing so in a non ad hoc fashion. Philosophers interested in the relationships between education and indoctrination, advertising and consumer behaviour, and behaviour control have explored these matters in some detail, but with no finality.[13]

Since autonomy, coercion, and Dworkin are not the principal concerns of this book, there won't (sadly) be space here to explore in detail these important and interesting matters (although coercion is explored a little more in the next few sections). I can, however, briefly make the following points. First (as Dworkin admits), although resenting (or otherwise not reflectively endorsing) the reasons on which I 'have to act' is probably a *necessary* part of having been coerced, it's certainly not *sufficient* for having been coerced – since one may resent 'having to act' on an addictive desire, or on a deeply held moral conviction, without being in any way coerced into acting on them. Second, it seems to me likely (though this is not the place to argue the point) both that the correct account of being coerced will be built around the idea of autonomy and that something like Dworkin's account of autonomy – which sees being autonomous as 'having the capacity to raise the question of whether I will identify with or reject the reasons for which I now act' – is correct.[14]

6.2 Descriptive or normative?

At the most general level, there are two views about coercion. One view holds that coercion claims are essentially value-free, that whether one *is* coerced into doing something is an ordinary empirical question. Another view holds that coercion claims are moralized, that they involve moral judgements at their core.[15]

In this section, and indirectly in the next, I want to consider further coercion's role in ethics, in particular the debate between those who regard it as 'value-free' or 'descriptive' and those who regard it as 'moralised' or 'normative'.

Coercion could be 'moralised' without always being wrong. Nonetheless, it's useful to start by asking whether coercion is ever permissible. Cheyney Ryan argues that it's sometimes permissible as follows:

> Janet has a highly contagious disease, which would have disastrous consequences if allowed to spread. The government orders her to stay in the house, but Janet's disease makes her irascible and she refuses to comply. The government seal her house and threaten her with reprisals if she attempts to leave. Janet acquiesces. There is little doubt that . . . the threats of the government have coerced her into staying put, despite her own wishes. But clearly she has no right to leave the house and contaminate the society around her, and the government has the right to keep her quarantined.[16]

This and similar cases seem decisive. The government's actions are both clearly coercive and clearly not wrong. Hence, coercion is not always wrong.

Not everyone agrees, however. Some writers maintain that the concept of coercion is normative in the strongest possible sense, and that actions don't even count as coercive unless they're wrong. Jennifer Greene's paper, 'Coercion: description or evaluation', illustrates this. She asks us to think of threats in terms of loss of *conjunctive options*:

> every time an agent faces a demand accompanied by a threat, she loses what I shall call a *conjunctive option*. Although the victim of coercion can still choose between complying and refusing to do so, the conjunctive option of *both* refusing to comply *and* avoiding the threatened penalty has been made impossible.[17]

She then goes on to claim that A coerces B *only* *if* 'A's intervention *illegitimately* closes off a conjunctive option to which B is entitled' – and (conversely) that those threats which *justifiably* remove conjunctive options aren't cases of coercion.[18] What, then, should Greene say of Ryan's Janet case (above)? She'll have to choose between saying that the government's actions are wrong, or denying that Janet is really coerced.

And, of these, one would think that the latter is preferable, although it does seem at odds with ordinary usage of the term 'coercion'.

Greene, however – and about this much she's right – doesn't take the fact that her theory departs from everyday language to be a decisive objection. On the contrary, her theory of coercion is unashamedly *revisionist*, as the following passages demonstrate:

> confusion over the meaning of 'coercion' ... is in large part responsible for the ubiquitousness of the term. Charging someone or something with 'coercion' seems to be a national pastime. But ... the charges would not come up so frequently if we did not ultimately consider coercion to be a very serious form of injustice.[19]

> those who cry 'coercion' at every turn often seem to want to take advantage of the implicit wrongfulness of the act of coercion and yet make it impossible for the term to designate any particular wrong-doing. Sloppy overuse of the concept has led to its complete impoverishment.[20]

So there may be grounds for taking a revisionist line about the Janet case. This would involve admitting that many users of the word 'coercion' in fact view Janet as *both* coerced *and* fairly treated, but also claiming that these 'coercion' users are mistaken and ought not to be classifying this as a case of coercion (*precisely because* Janet has not been treated unjustly).

As we'll see shortly, I have a certain amount of sympathy with this sort of revisionism. Furthermore, the strategy outlined above for dealing with the Janet case and, more generally, Greene's view are not incoherent. There do, however, seem to be two things which count against her position. The first is that she presents us with a false dichotomy: *either* we must believe that coercion is not a normative concept at all, *or* we must believe that coercion is always wrong. This stark choice is what leads her to be such a radical revisionist. But these are not the only options, and it's possible to maintain that coercion is essentially normative without adopting Greene's style of absolutism about coercion. Her highly counter-intuitive position is therefore unfounded, since it's possible to get what she wants (a normative account of coercion) without departing so extremely from standard intuitions.

The second problem with her position is that it forces us to say odd things about Janet-type cases. Janet has 'a *highly* contagious disease, which would have *disastrous* consequences if allowed to spread'. But what if her disease were only *fairly* contagious, with *quite bad* consequences if allowed to spread? Or *a little bit* contagious, with a threat of *mild inconvenience* if allowed to spread? What I'm getting at here is that there is a set of cases ranging from 'catastrophic/extremely contagious' through to 'mildly inconvenient/hard to catch'. At some point on the continuum, the risk to public health becomes so great that threatening Janet becomes justified. Greene's view is that, at the very same point on the continuum, threatening Janet ceases to become coercion. Consider, for example, the following case:

> An excessively cautious government agency uses threats to make Janice, who poses a low–moderate risk to public health, stay indoors. The risk to public health is (*ex hypothesi*) not great enough morally to justify the agency's actions. However, Janice's infectiousness unpredictably rises to a moderate–high level and, on Tuesday, her condition becomes so contagious that the agency's ongoing detention strategy becomes fully justified. Given, however, that no one could have predicted her post-Tuesday state in advance, the fact that she is now a moderate–high risk does not retrospectively justify the agency's pre-Tuesday actions.

What I am trying to bring out in this case is the peculiarity of saying that the agency coerced Janice until Tuesday, but on Tuesday it stopped coercing her and instead justifiably threatened her. Of course, one *could* say this, and Greene would have to. But this is a major drawback for her position. When it comes to conceptual and linguistic questions like this, occupying a highly counter-intuitive position isn't ruled out in advance, but it's best to steer clear of such positions unless there is a compelling reason to adopt them.

The next question I want to look at is whether, on the assumption that coercion is not always wrong, coercive*ness* might nonetheless always be wrong-*making*. This question probably sounds a bit odd to non-philosophers (and perhaps to some philosophers too). What it means is: is coerciveness the sort of property which always counts as a moral reason not to perform those actions which have it? Or if we prefer to talk in terms of value, we could ask instead whether coerciveness is the sort of property in virtue of which actions are always morally 'more bad' and/or 'less good'. Even if coerciveness were universally wrong-making, there would (or could) be some cases of permissible coercion. In such cases, the fact that the action in question was coercive would count as a moral reason not to perform it, but this 'anti' reason would be *outweighed* by some other 'pro' reason, such as the fact that it would save many lives. This is how, in Chapter 2, I suggested that we should think of exploitation. What I said there was that exploiting persons is always wrong, provided that other (sufficiently strong) countervailing moral considerations are absent. But another equally good way of making the same point would have been to say that the property *being exploitative* is universally wrong-making (in the sense just outlined).[21]

The view that coerciveness is always wrong-making is compatible with Ryan's Janet example. This is because the best analysis of this case is that sealing Janet's house and threatening her is *prima facie* wrong (partly because it's coercive and partly for other reasons). However, sealing the house, etc. is not wrong *all things considered* because the 'anti' considerations, such as coerciveness, are *outweighed* by countervailing 'pro' considerations – in particular, the fact that Janet has a communicable disease, one which would have catastrophic consequences if spread. That this is the best analysis is confirmed by modifying the case slightly and thinking about what we would say (a) if she didn't have a communicable disease, or (b) if a less coercive way of stopping her from spreading the disease were available. In (a) we would say that sealing her house, etc. is wrong because of the *prima facie* wrongness of acting coercively and because of the absence of any countervailing 'pro' considerations (i.e. there is no contagious disease to justify the coercion). In (b), on the other hand, we would regard less coercive ways of ensuring her compliance as morally better than more coercive ways, provided that all the ways were roughly equal in terms of their effectiveness.

A trickier case, also from Ryan, is the following:

> You arrive home one evening to find that an intruder has broken into your house and is assaulting your wife. Before you are noticed, you grab your pistol from the desk drawer and threaten to shoot him if he does not immediately leave. He leaves.[22]

In this case, thoughts such as 'the intruder *deserves* to be threatened' and 'the householder was *acting within his rights*' do a lot of intuitive work. If they are to be believed, and I don't see any reason why they shouldn't be, then arguably what's shown is not merely that threatening the intruder wasn't wrong, but that any coerciveness involved in the householder's actions was *not even wrong-making*. But why should we take this extra step? Why not just use the same analysis as in the Janet case and say that the coerciveness is wrong-making, but is simply outweighed by much weightier 'pro' considerations such as the fact that the householder's wife is in danger and the fact that the intruder has already violated the couple's rights?

One way of answering this is to think, as we did in the Janet case, about varying the case slightly and asking: if a less coercive but equally effective (and otherwise relevantly similar) method of making the intruder leave had been available, would this have been morally preferable? If we answer yes, then it looks as if the coerciveness involved is seen as a bad feature of the action, because an action with less of it would have been better. But if we answer no, then the coerciveness is not viewed as bad. Unfortunately for our purposes, people's intuitions about this case vary substantially. To a great extent, this depends on what they think justifies the use of a threat in the first place. People who think that the justification is self-defence tend also to think that the less coercive option is preferable, because self-defence only justifies *necessary* levels of coercion and force; for these people, the coercion is a necessary evil. Other people think instead in terms of the householder's rights, or in terms of the intruder's deserving to be threatened. These people don't think of coercion here as an evil at all because the householder *has every right to* coerce, or the intruder *deserves* to be on the receiving end of coercion. Finally, some people don't even regard this as a case of coercion. For example, Ryan (who provided the example) uses it as a counter-example to the non-normative view of coercion. He says that the non-normative view would make us describe the householder's threat to the intruder as having '*coerced* him into not raping your wife', which is 'absurd'.[23]

This takes us back to the question of whether *all* threats are coercive. Greene would say no because, for her, only wrongful threats are coercive. Ryan, whose 'normativist' view is more complex, would also say no; whereas someone who regards coercion as 'value-free' would say yes, because there's no more to coercing than threatening. My own view, which I shall develop in the next section, is that things are not quite as straightforward as these answers suggest and that we need both to look more carefully at the distinction between threats and offers and to return to the idea of welfare baselines in order to answer this question properly.

6.3 Threats and offers

> When are proposals coercive? The intuitive answer is that threats are coercive whereas offers are not . . . The crux of the distinction between threats and offers is quite simple: A *threatens* B by proposing to make B *worse* off relative to some baseline; A makes an *offer* to B by proposing to make B *better* off relative to some baseline. More precisely, A makes a threat when, if B does *not* accept A's proposal, B will be worse off than in the relevant baseline position. A makes an offer when, if B does *not* accept A's proposal, he will be *no* worse off than in the relevant baseline position. A's proposal may include both a threat and an offer (what Michael Taylor calls a 'throffer').[24]

Wertheimer's answer to the coercion question (above) is fundamentally correct, but more needs to be said. Take, for example, a case which is slightly different from the Tiddles case discussed earlier. In this new case, Tiddles is suffering from a life-threatening illness and is taken to the vet, who says that Tiddles's life can be saved, but only if I'm willing to hand over $5,000 in vet's fees. Structurally, this seems just like the case in which my home is invaded by a hostile cat killer. For, in both cases, the choice is between being $5,000 worse off or losing Tiddles. But in the second (vet) case, we probably don't want to say that the vet is threatening me, provided that her fees are not exorbitant and that she is behaving otherwise reasonably.[25] Why do we feel inclined to draw this distinction?

The key to understanding the distinction between offers and threats is contained in our earlier discussion of harm: in particular, the discussion of harm and relevant baselines. Coercing always involves making a threat. And to threaten someone is to tell her (though not necessarily directly or explicitly) that you will harm her if she doesn't (or does) do X. This is to be contrasted with making someone an offer, which means telling her that you will benefit her (or, in cases where people's desires are not self-interested, that you will provide something that they want) if she does (or doesn't) do X. Finally, for completeness, a *throffer* is a proposal which contains both a threat and an offer (for example, 'sell me your car for $1,000,000, otherwise I'll kill you').

This explains why we want to (and should) view the cat killer and the vet differently. The would-be cat killer acts coercively because (given a few plausible assumptions) she threatens to harm me, relative to all three possible baselines. She threatens harm relative to a *pre-interaction* baseline because she proposes to take me from a state with Tiddles to a state without Tiddles. She threatens harm relative to a *closest possible world* baseline on the (plausible) assumption that the relevant possible world is not one that contains an even worse incident (for example, a cat killer who proposes also to assassinate my goldfish). And she threatens harm relative to a *normative* baseline on the assumption that she ought not to kill Tiddles.

To turn now to the vet, why should we say that she is offering rather than threatening? The reason is that (again, given a few plausible assumptions) she is not proposing to harm me if I don't hand over the cash, but rather offering to benefit me if I do hand it over. If we use a normative baseline here, what's doing the work is the thought that, unless she is paid, the vet has no obligation to treat Tiddles. If she did have such an obligation and proposed not to act on it, then I could rightly view her proposed behaviour (in this case, an omission) as harmful and her proposal to do nothing as a threat. Then her position would be rather like that of a public servant who, despite being paid an adequate salary by the state to provide its citizens with a free service, insists also on receiving bribes from individual service users.[26] Such a public servant would be threatening to harm service users relative to a normative baseline, since she proposes to withhold from them something to which they have a right, and which she has a duty to provide.

In the vet case, we assume that the vet has no positive obligation to provide free treatment. Hence, it looks as if saying that she won't treat Tiddles unless she's paid is an offer, not a threat (so long as the amount of money requested is reasonable). To put it in a slightly different way, the normative baseline is a possible world in which the vet acts in accordance with all of her *freestanding* (which, here, means something like *pre-contractual*) obligations to Tiddles. That world is (let's assume) a world in which the vet does nothing to help Tiddles. What the vet proposes then is, in return for money, to bring about a future in which Tiddles and I are *better off* than we would be in this ('pre-contractual') normative baseline world. So she is *offering* (to benefit us) rather than *threatening* (to harm us). We can then track our intuitions about coercion by understanding the distinction between offers and threats in terms of *harm relative to a normative baseline*. As just suggested, if the vet has no freestanding obligation to treat Tiddles for free, then her proposal is an offer (and not a threat) because she proposes to *benefit* me, relative to the normative baseline, in return for money. If, on the other hand, the vet *does* have a freestanding obligation to treat Tiddles for nothing, then her proposal is a threat (and hence coercive) because she proposes to *harm* me, relative to the normative baseline, if I don't give her money.

This (like public servants demanding bribes) would be a case of *omissive coercion*, because the vet would be threatening me with *omissive harm* (see section 4.4). Generalising, we can say that A omissively coerces B to do X if and only if

1 A has a duty to do Y for B and A's failing to do Y would cause or constitute omissive harm to B; and
2 A proposes (threatens) *not* to do Y for B unless B does X; and
3 the existence of A's duty to do Y for B does not depend on B's doing X (i.e. it is 'freestanding').

Omissive coercion is presumably quite a widespread phenomenon. Imagine, for example, that an employee already deserves a pay-rise (based on past performance) but that the employer says that she won't get it unless she does extra work. Surely, this is omissive coercion – a threat not to give her that to which she already has a right. And, as we have already seen, corrupt public servants who demand bribes are often guilty of omissively coercing (amongst other things).

However, saying whether (and why) someone's behaviour counts as *omissively coercing* X rather than merely *not offering to benefit* X can be far from straightforward. One of the most interesting discussions of this problem (and, more generally, of the threat–offer distinction) is Robert Nozick's paper 'Coercion'. Consider, for example, what he has to say about his widely discussed *drowning case*:

Q is in the water far from shore, nearing the end of his energy, and P comes close by in his boat. Both know there is no other hope of Q's rescue around, and P knows that Q is the soul of honesty and that if Q makes a promise he will keep it. P says to Q 'I will take you in my boat and bring you to shore if and only if you first promise to pay me $10,000 within three days of reaching shore with my aid.' *Is P offering to take Q to shore if he makes the promise, or is he threatening to let Q drown if Q doesn't make the promise?*[27]

In many respects, Nozick's view of this and similar cases is like the account sketched so far here:

whether someone makes a threat against Q's doing an action or an offer to Q to do the action depends on how the consequence he says he will bring about changes the consequences of Q's action from what they would have been in the normal or natural or expected course of events. If it makes the consequences of Q's action worse than they would have been in the normal or expected course of events, it is a threat; if it makes the consequences better, it is an offer. The term 'expected' is meant to straddle *predicted* and *morally required*.[28]

If I say 'I *expect* all of my students to turn in their assignments on time', that can mean two entirely different things. *Either* they are fantastically hardworking, reliable, etc., and so I *believe that they will* turn in their assignments on time. *Or* they are (morally, or according to the regulations, or whatever) *obliged to* turn in their assignments on time. Nozick's view is that there are two usable baselines, corresponding to these two different senses of 'expect': one *predictive*, the other *normative*. If this is applied to the drowning case, there are on his view two plausible answers to the 'offer or threat' question. One involves asking what Q can rationally expect of P in the predictive sense. Hence, we might ask what a (statistically) normal person from P's (or Q's) society would do in these circumstances. The other involves asking what P's moral duties are.

Unless one adopts a very crude form of moral relativism (such as the view that P's duties are necessarily the same as what a normal person from P's society would do), it's obvious that these two baselines can generate different results. For example, it might be true both that P has a freestanding duty to rescue Q *and* that members of P's society are incredibly reluctant to allow strangers onto their boats and would only do so for a handsome reward. If so, then use of the normative baseline generates the conclusion that P threatens Q, while use of the predictive baseline generates the view that P makes Q an offer.

My own view is that the predictive baseline looks rather implausible in the drowning man case and that the normative one is to be preferred. The reason for this is rather like the reason why one might want to reject crude forms of moral relativism. The objection to moral relativism that I have in mind is that whether A's actions are right or wrong ought not to depend (directly) on whether or not A's actions conform to the norms of A's society. For it's possible in principle for *all* members of A's society to have false moral beliefs and/or to behave very badly from an objective moral point of view. Much the same can be said of the 'offer or threat' question (which I take to be a morally significant question, at least sometimes). That is, whether or not P is threatening Q ought not to depend (directly) on what other members of P's society would have done in similar circumstances. To see this point more clearly, think back to the cat killer example. Would her 'offer' be any less of a threat, or any less coercive, if we both lived in a society full of cat killers? Obviously not – for what we should say of such a society is just that it contains *lots of* coercion and *lots of* felicide (cat murder). Yet assessing her 'offer' relative to a predictive expectation baseline gives the conclusion that she really is offering, not threatening – since behaviour like that is only to be expected (in the predictive sense) in a society of cat killers.

Interestingly, this also suggests a 'knock-down' argument against the *universal* use of predictive expectation baselines. Such use would – absurdly – rule out *a priori* the existence of societies which were *both predictably and extremely coercive*. For in order to count as coercive, what's 'threatened' would always have to be worse than the norm. Hence, even if everyone in an alternative society (S) acts 'coercively' (i.e. in ways which *we* would regard as coercive) S won't count as a more coercive society than ours because the behaviour of its members isn't worse than what one would rationally expect.

So given these problems, why not just use normative baselines? Nozick considers and rejects this possibility:

> One might think that in deciding whether something is a threat or an offer, the (morally) expected course of events always takes precedence over the normal or usual course of events, where these diverge. It is not obvious that this is so. I have in mind particularly the example . . . where your normal supplier of dope says that he will continue to supply you if and only if you beat up a certain person. Here, let us suppose, the morally expected course of events is that he doesn't supply you with drugs, but the course of events which forms the background for deciding whether he has threatened you or made you an offer is the normal though not morally expected course of events (in which he supplies you with drugs for money); it is against this

background that we can obtain the consequence that he has threatened you.[29]

Wertheimer rightly suggests that Nozick's analysis of this case may not be right because even if the drug relationship is 'immoral from an external perspective, it is arguable that *within* that relationship, A is morally required to continue to supply B with drugs'.[30] Nonetheless, I think that we can find cases that will do what Nozick wants, such as the following:

The laundry case

A is a 40-year-old bachelor. He lives with his mother, B. B does all of A's laundry and has done so throughout his life. A makes only a modest financial contribution to the household despite now having a well-paid job. B asks A if he would be willing to increase his contribution to the household budget by 20 per cent. A says no, because he is saving money for a new sports car. After persuasion and reasoned argument fail, B *threatens* to stop doing A's laundry if he doesn't pay the extra money.

This is clearly a threat. But, equally clearly, B doesn't have a duty to carry on doing the laundry. So this must be a case where the predictive baseline takes precedence. We are happy to call this a threat because a strong *predictive expectation* has been established by B's behaviour towards A during the last forty years.

The concepts of threat and coercion, then, are rather like the concept of harm. All three are *multiple baseline* concepts. What I mean by this is that while, in some (most) cases, we have to work out whether behaviour is threatening, or coercive, or harmful, by comparing what *is* proposed or done to what *ought to be* proposed or done, in other cases such assessments have to be carried out using other comparators, such as *the way things were* ('pre-interaction'), or the way things *would have been* if things had been relevantly different ('relevant possible world'), or the way we could *reasonably expect them to be* ('predictive expectation'). I would suggest that these complexities lead to a good deal of confusion about how exactly to define and apply the terms in question – and, in particular, that it's responsible for spawning the debate discussed in section 6.2 about whether coercion is a 'normative concept' or a 'descriptive concept'. In fact, this is the wrong question, or an overly simple or general question, because whether or not a particular coercion claim has normative significance depends principally upon which baseline is used.

For example, in the laundry case (above) the fact that the mother's proposal is a threat has no normative significance at all. It's not wrong to threaten her son in this way, and what's more, the fact that her proposal is a threat isn't even *wrong-making*. The main reason for this is that her proposal only counts as a threat if we use a predictive expectation baseline (i.e. she threatens to make him worse off than he could reasonably have predicted given her previous behaviour). If we'd used a normative baseline (i.e. compared what she proposed to what she ought to do), then her proposal would have turned out not to be a threat, on the plausible assumption that she has no open-ended obligation to provide domestic services. There's nothing wrong with using the predictive expectation baseline in cases like this. On the contrary, it fits very well indeed. But, under this interpretation, the assertion that the mother's proposal is a threat is without intrinsic normative significance. By contrast, in the cat killer case (discussed earlier) the fact that the cat killer's proposal ('pay me or I kill Tiddles') is a threat *does* have normative significance – the reason for this being that her proposal is a threat relative to a normative baseline. In short, she ought not to slay Tiddles but nonetheless proposes to (if I don't comply).

So is coercion a normative concept? The answer is that those coercion claims which make use of normative baselines have intrinsic moral significance, whereas those which use other baselines do not. More specifically, in all cases of the first kind, the coerciveness in question is wrong-making – although the act of coercion need not be wrong because of the possibility of countervailing moral considerations. That coercion relative to a normative baseline should always be *prima facie* wrong should hardly be surprising given that, when such baselines are used, the threatener is necessarily threatening *either* to do what she ought not to do *or* not to do what she ought.

Finally, what about the relationship between coercion and threatening? It seems to me – and this is just a 'linguistic intuition' – that we use these two terms a little differently. We are more willing to use the word 'threat' non-morally than we are the word 'coercion', and conversely 'coercion' has stronger negative moral connotations than does 'threatening'. Unfortunately – and about this Greene is quite right – our ordinary linguistic practices are neither clear nor consistent, and there's no doubt that 'coercion' can be used non-morally and that 'threatening' often does have negative moral overtones. However, one can envisage an only slightly revisionary account of coercion according to which coercing is a subset of threatening. More specifically, coercion claims would be those threat claims which utilised moral baselines, with other threats – like the one in the laundry case – being classed as non-coercive threats. In substance, this position is exactly the one I have defended thus far, the only difference being the addition of a linguistic change. On this view, which I support, coerciveness (in the sense just specified) is necessarily wrong-making, but threatening(ness) isn't.

6.4 Summary and conclusions

The concept of coercion is ethically significant in a number of ways. 'Coercion' is routinely used to express moral disapproval. Coerced actions tend to be thought of as forced and involuntary in ways which can relieve coerced actors of legal and/or moral responsibility. And the use of coercion to gain consent typically renders any resultant consent invalid. Furthermore, concerns about coercion often underlie people's opposition to controversial practices including the sale of body parts, prostitution, and commercial surrogacy. This chapter has aimed to give an account of coercion which will help us to understand these concerns. The (slightly revisionary) view argued for here is that we should reserve the word 'coercion' for a particular kind of threat: those cases in which (1) A proposes (threatens) to harm B if B doesn't comply with A's wishes, and (2) the proposed harm to B is harm *relative to a relevant normative baseline*. (See Chapter 4, especially section 4.3, for an explanation of harm and relevant baselines.)

Part II

PRACTICES

7

ORGANS FOR SALE

The subject of this chapter is the sale of human organs for transplantation. Many of the arguments it addresses apply equally to all body parts and, indeed, to all body products. The chapter, however, will focus almost exclusively on the sale of kidneys. There are a number of practical reasons for this, including the fact that, in the ethics literature, kidney sale is very extensively discussed, and the fact that (as we'll see in a moment) illicit kidney trading appears to be practised on a large scale:

> Thousands of [Chinese] prisoners are executed every year in order to provide fresh organs for transplantation in the times and places where they are most needed. First prisoners are shot through the back of their heads, but drugged, IV'd, and occasionally even respirated so that their hearts will keep beating until they are adjacent to the organ recipients. Then the doctors cut the functioning organs out of the prisoners and transplant them to the waiting patients – often either high-paying foreigners or members of the communist elite. Since brain death is not recognised in China, prisoners' organs are usually removed while they are technically alive, and there is no concern for the pain or death which this causes the prisoners.[1]

Organ sale, as it's popularly known, can occur in a number of very different forms. The most troubling is where living people have their organs stolen for their cash value or, even worse, are killed so that their organs can be 'harvested' and sold. Becker's disturbing account of the execution of Chinese prisoners (above) appears to fit into this category.[2] There have also been worrying reports (from several countries including Brazil, India, Israel, and the Philippines) of body parts being stolen both from cadavers and from living hospital patients. These parts are said to include whole eyes (not just the cornea), bone, skin, pituitary glands, and heart valves.[3]

A less disturbing – but still, some would argue, unethical – practice would be for us to use a commercial market to distribute the, organs usable for transplantation from people who die 'naturally' from accidents, age, or disease.

A third practice is one in which living individuals volunteer to sell one of their own organs (one which they can live without, such as a kidney) in order to satisfy their need or desire for money. My main interest is in this category: cases in which an organ for sale comes from a paid living donor who, in some sense, volunteers. From an ethics point of view, these cases are much more interesting than those in which people are murdered so that their organs can be 'harvested'. For in 'harvesting' cases, it's pretty obvious what the moral objections are, as the opening quotation from Becker illustrates. Saying what exactly is wrong with voluntary paid donation, on the other hand, isn't easy despite the 'feelings of outrage and disgust' that it often arouses.[4] For organ sale of this sort appears to be both consensual and beneficial to the donor, once financial benefits are taken into account. So why would anyone object?

During the course of this chapter we'll see that there are a number of ethical arguments against this sort of commerce. Many utilise the moral concepts analysed in Part I. For example, people argue that paid organ donors would be harmed, or exploited, or commodified – and that organ vendors' consents would be invalid. Objections like these are the principal concern of this chapter. For this reason, there's a sense in which the chapter (and indeed the whole of Part II) is negative. What I mean by this is that it aims not to provide a comprehensive account of all the arguments for and against organ sale, but rather just to provide a critique of the case against. One reason for this narrow focus is simply lack of space. As always, it's not possible to cover everything that one might wish to cover. Another is that the arguments against organ sale tend to be more ethically interesting than those in favour. For the latter tend *either* to be practical and/or utilitarian arguments, focussing solely on the ability of a market in organs to save the lives of people on transplant waiting lists, *or* to be 'doctrinaire' libertarian arguments which have little to do with the specific moral standing of organ sale and a lot to do with an entirely general commitment to 'individual liberty' and the 'free market'. A third reason is that, given the very obvious advantages of permitting organ sale and the fact that it is illegal almost everywhere, it's important to scrutinise very carefully the moral arguments against the practice. For as Janet Radcliffe-Richards *et al.* remind us, banning the sale of kidneys is harmful and so there should only be a prohibition if there is a very convincing moral case against the practice:[5]

> The well-known shortage of kidneys for transplantation causes much suffering and death. Dialysis is a wretched experience for most patients, and is anyway rationed in most places and simply

unavailable to the majority of patients in most developing countries. Since most potential kidney vendors will never become
unpaid donors, either during life or posthumously, the prohibition of sales must be presumed to exclude kidneys that would
otherwise be available. It is therefore essential to make sure that
there is adequate justification for the resulting harm.[6]

This quotation from Radcliffe-Richards *et al.* leads us nicely onto
another preliminary distinction: between those arguments which purport
to show that trading in human organs is immoral and those which purport to show that it ought to be criminalised. In general – and especially
in such hotly contested areas as abortion, censorship, and euthanasia –
this law–morality distinction is important.[7] For there may, of course, be
moral arguments against *doing* x which, even if successful, don't justify
banning x. However, in the context of the present chapter, this is a distinction that, in practical terms, collapses. What I mean by this is that,
although I'll be concerning myself exclusively with moral arguments and
concepts, my findings will inevitably have implications for the law in this
area. This is because, given the very substantial practical benefits that a
commercial market in human organs would deliver, the case for legal
prohibition must inevitably be a moral one (and, almost certainly, a non-
utilitarian moral one).[8] Hence, by critically assessing the moral objections
to organ sale, I'll in so doing be assessing the case for legal prohibition (or
at least the most important part of that case). If these moral objections
turn out to be flawed, then not only is the case for legal prohibition
undermined, but – given the above-mentioned practical advantages – we
will have a strong *prima facie* case for allowing (encouraging even) a
commercial market.

To turn now to the substantive assessment of the arguments, Chapter 7
will proceed as follows. First, section 7.1 will give a brief overview of
contemporary regulation and practice. Then, five objections to organ sale
will be considered in turn. These are:

1   That it would cause harm (or excessive harm) to organ vendors.
2   That free donation expresses or promotes altruism and social solidar-
    ity, while (allowing) paid donation damages these things.
3   That organ vendors' consents would, in many cases, be invalid.
4   That (prospective) organ vendors would be coerced into selling their
    organs.
5   That organ vendors would be exploited.

These seem to me to be the best – and the most widely accepted – arguments against organ sale. However, this list isn't exhaustive and there are
further objections that I don't consider here. One notable omission is

what, in Chapter 3, I called commodification arguments. There certainly are commodification arguments against organ sale (indeed, I've published a paper on such arguments.)[9] However, I don't discuss them in this chapter, chiefly because they are dealt with both in Chapter 3 and in Chapters 8 and 9. While there are undoubtedly things to be said about commodification arguments against organ sale, to say them here would generate too much repetition. Also, it seems to me that commodification arguments (insofar as they work at all) work better against commercial surrogacy and DNA patenting than they do against organ sale and, hence, it's more sensible to consider them in these other contexts than to consider them here. (The fact that commodification claims about kidneys look less plausible than those about surrogacy and DNA patenting is, I suspect, attributable to the widespread belief that childbirth, gestation, reproduction, and all things genetic are intimately related to persons or 'to personhood' in ways that particular solid organs, such as kidneys, aren't.)

7.1 Contemporary regulation and practice

The buying and selling of human organs for transplantation purposes is a criminal offence in nearly all countries.[10] Furthermore, it has been rejected by most relevant professional organisations since the 1980s.[11] Interestingly, though, there's some Canadian evidence indicating that public attitudes to organ sale are much more 'permissive' than those of healthcare professionals and legislators, and a survey conducted by Guttmann and Guttmann in the early 1990s found that, in response to a particular case study, more than 70 per cent of the general public, but less than 30 per cent of healthcare professionals, said that they would support kidney sale.[12]

The World Medical Association issued the following *Statement on the Live Organ Trade* as far back as 1985:

> In due consideration of the fact that in the recent past a trade of considerable financial gain has developed with live kidneys from underdeveloped countries for transplantation in Europe and the United States of America. THE WORLD MEDICAL ASSOCIATION condemns the purchase and sale of human organs for transplantation. THE WORLD MEDICAL ASSOCIATION calls on the governments of all countries to take effective steps to prevent the commercial use of human organs.[13]

This policy was replaced in 2000 with the more wide-ranging *Statement on Human Organ and Tissue Donation and Transplantation*. Section 34 states:

Payment for organs and tissues for donation and transplantation should be prohibited. A financial incentive compromises the voluntariness of the choice and the altruistic basis for organ and tissue donation. Furthermore, access to needed medical treatment based on ability to pay is inconsistent with the principles of justice. Organs suspected to have been obtained through commercial transaction should not be accepted for transplantation. In addition, the advertisement of organs should be prohibited. However, reasonable reimbursement of expenses such as those incurred in procurement, transport, processing, preservation, and implantation is permissible.[14]

This more recent statement mentions what the WMA takes the main moral objections to be: that organ vendors' donations aren't truly voluntary, and that organ donation ought to be motivated only by altruism. We'll be assessing both of these arguments shortly.

Criminalisation and condemnation by professional associations notwithstanding, stories about the buying of kidneys from live donors continue to appear frequently in the news media and there is evidence that organ trafficking from 'developing' countries to 'developed' countries still goes on.[15] One notable example here is India, which, despite making organ sale illegal in 1995, remains one of the parts of the world where organ purchasing is rife.[16] A kidney from a live donor can be bought in India for less than $2,000 – a bargain for a rich American or European, but a sizeable sum considered from the perspective of a slum dweller living in poverty.[17] Amritsar in northern India is reported to be a major centre for the organ trade, and it is alleged that its local government and health authorities collude with traffickers.[18] Middlemen, who tell them that they will be given good jobs, bring many organ sellers to Amritsar under false pretences. Victims find themselves imprisoned in private houses and 'persuaded' to donate their kidneys, sometimes being subjected to torture if they don't 'consent'.[19] In other cases, moneylenders, who subsequently pocket most of the fee, force people who are heavily in debt into selling organs.[20] So there is – and this understates the point – a consent issue here. For many of these Indian donors are coerced, or misled, or under-informed, or forced by poverty to surrender their kidneys.[21]

Such practices aren't confined to India. A recent English newspaper report describes how organ trafficking from Moldova (in Eastern Europe) to Israel via Turkey is rife. The case of Sergei (a Moldovan man) is given as a graphic illustration:

an agent in the Moldovan capital, Chisinau, tricked him [Sergei] into surrendering a kidney . . . after luring him to Turkey with the promise of a job. When the job failed to materialise, the agent . . .

said Sergei would have to sell blood to raise the bus fare back home. She guided him to a private hospital on the outskirts of Istanbul and a jab in the arm followed . . . As the anaesthetic wore off . . . the agent simply walked into the room and said; 'We've taken your kidney. There's nothing you can do. I'll give you £1,800 for it.'[22]

Not all potential organ sellers come from comparatively poor countries, though, as an interesting story from the UK illustrates.[23] Early in 2000, Mick Taylor, a 26-year-old from Halifax (England) won £4,100,000 on the National Lottery. Mr Taylor was a kidney patient who had been suffering from kidney disease since the age of 11. He had already had two kidney transplants, but both had failed (one after a year, the other after three and a half years). At the time of winning the lottery, he had to attend St Luke's Hospital in Huddersfield three times a week for renal dialysis treatment. When interviewed about his lottery win by the press, Mr Taylor remarked, 'I'd exchange my millions for a new kidney. I was more excited when I got my transplant than when I won this money.' Subsequently, dozens of calls were made to English newspapers by people who wanted to sell Mr Taylor one of their kidneys in exchange for all or part of his lottery winnings. According to the *Guardian* newspaper, organisations dealing with dialysis patients were 'outraged' at the behaviour of these callers. Nick Turkentine, (then) head of charity affairs at the National Kidney Research Foundation, was quoted as saying:

I am speechless. I can't believe that people would offer to sell their organs for the chance of some lottery cash. What this man was trying to say was that he would give up everything to have his health – he wasn't saying he wanted to buy a new kidney. Words cannot express how we as a charity feel about people trafficking in human organs.[24]

This, of course, is no more than anecdotal evidence, but it does suggest that even in relatively affluent countries such as the UK, there are people who would be willing to part with one of their kidneys if the price were right.

Similarly anecdotal evidence from the US suggests that there are plenty of willing buyers around too, buyers who are willing to part with very substantial sums of money. In 1999, the world's largest internet auction house, *eBay*, discovered (and removed) the offer of a kidney for sale posted on its website.[25] The seller, known simply as *hchero* from Sunrise, Florida, offered a 'fully functional kidney for sale'. His (or her) advertisement read:

You can choose either kidney. Buyer pays all transplant and medical costs. Of course only one for sale, as I need the other one to
live. Serious bids only.[26]

By the time *eBay* intervened to stop the proceedings, bidding had already
started at $25,000 and risen dramatically to more than $5,700,000. *eBay*
representatives said afterwards that it wasn't possible to tell whether or
not the offer was genuine, or the bids serious.

We can, then, sum up the state of contemporary regulation and practice as follows. In spite of being almost universally criminalised and
condemned, a 'black market' in organs persists, particularly in 'developing' countries like India. That this is so should hardly be surprising
given the desperation which exists on both sides of the transaction: the
desperation of Americans and Europeans who urgently need (and can
afford to pay for) kidneys and that of the organ vendors who need the
money.

In the next few sections, we'll scrutinise the ethical arguments against
organ sale to see if any of them are successful.

7.2 Harm

The most straightforward way of objecting to organ sale is to say that it's
wrong because it involves unnecessarily subjecting organ vendors to pain
and risk. In other words, it's wrong because it's harmful. This argument
(the 'harm argument'), however, faces a number of obvious objections –
some of which, it seems to me, are decisive.

The first (an empirical point) is simply that kidney removal isn't terribly dangerous if performed in good conditions. Nicholson and Bradley,
for example, claim that 'donor nephrectomy [kidney removal] is generally very safe, with a perioperative mortality of about 0.03%' and that
with 'careful donor selection and rigorous prophylactic measures it
should be possible to reduce mortality further'.[27]

The second objection, which is directed specifically at the legal prohibition issue, says that, if our concern is exposing the organ vendor to risk,
then the last thing we should be doing is banning sale since, as Cameron
and Hoffenberg put it:

> If one accepts the practice, then well-organized programs in
> which the donor is properly apprised of risk, fully assessed and
> followed up, with results available for public audit, can and have
> been organized, for example, in India. It is the marginalization of
> paid organ donation that leads to its performance in less than
> ideal circumstances. Paid organ donations need be no more risky
> than unpaid.[28]

In other words, the best way of avoiding harm to organ vendors is not to criminalise and drive sale underground but rather to accept and regulate it. This style of argument is familiar from other contexts, notably debates about the legalisation of abortion, drugs, and prostitution.

The third objection goes as follows. No matter how dangerous paid donation is, it needn't (if carried out in the right conditions) be any *more* dangerous than unpaid donation, since the mere fact of payment doesn't *add* any danger. So if paid donation is wrong because of the danger to which the donor is subjected, then free donation must also be wrong on the very same grounds. Free donation, though, is not wrong; on the contrary, we tend to regard it as commendable, heroic even. Therefore, paid donation isn't wrong either – or, if it is wrong, it's wrong because of something other than the danger to which the donor is subjected.

At this point, it might be argued that what's wrong with organ sale isn't danger *per se* but rather the fact that someone is being *paid* to endanger herself. There are two readings of this argument. One is as a worry about consent, the idea being that payment somehow invalidates the vendor's consent. We'll be returning to this in section 7.4. The other is as an expression of a moral principle according to which (quite independently of concerns about consent) it's wrong to pay someone to endanger herself. Quite what the basis for such a principle might be is hard to see. Furthermore, the principle is almost certainly false. Or if it's not, then many different widely accepted occupations would fall foul of it. For, as Cameron and Hoffenberg put it,

> The actual risk of loss of life during donation of a kidney has been estimated to be approximately 0.03%, which is considerably less than the risk associated with some paid occupations, for example, deep sea diving, construction work, or mining, or even of dying in an automobile accident in many countries.[29]

Common forms of 'risky labour' are often *more* dangerous than organ sale, but are regarded as heroic, rather than condemned; it is seen as quite proper to reward those who undertake them. And this difference in attitude can't be justified in terms of the good consequences that 'risky labour' produces, since the consequences of an organ sale (often, saving a life) may be just as good or better.

The view that organ sale is wrong because it involves subjecting organ vendors to pain and risk, then, seems untenable. This is because organ sale is too similar in relevant respects to other widely accepted practices: in particular, unpaid donation by living donors and 'risky labour' of various kinds. So it's hard to see how we could, without inconsistency, condemn or ban organ sale, while at the same time *not* condemning or banning these other practices. There are also a number of less straightforward objections to the harm argument. One of these is that organ sale often isn't harmful *all things considered*; in particular, once we weigh the financial benefits that the vendor gains against the modest health disadvantages that she suffers. Another is that banning organ sale in order to protect the health of potential vendors is unduly paternalistic. However, there's no need to deploy such objections in order to show that the harm argument is flawed, so I won't be saying anything more about them here.

7.3 Altruism

The idea of altruism figures prominently in the debate about whether or not we should pay people for their renewable body products: especially blood, but also sperm and ova. John Keown, for example, in a paper arguing against paid blood donation, claims that

> A major argument for exclusive reliance on unpaid donation is that, unlike paid donation, it promotes altruism and social solidarity.[30]

And Brazier notes that the UK's HFEA (Human Fertilisation and Embryology Authority) issued a consultation paper on payment for gamete donations in 1998 in which they 'reiterated their support for a "culture of altruism"'.[31] Similarly, the HFEA's 1999 annual report stresses

> its commitment to altruistic donation and its belief that the donation of sperm or eggs to create new life should be *a gift, freely and voluntarily given*.[32]

When it comes to organ sale and the ethical debate surrounding it, the concept of altruism has a similar, if less foregrounded, role to play. Thus, Siminoff and Chillag describe for us an anti-market transplantation culture in which the organ is seen as 'the ultimate gift'. This 'dominant metaphor for organ transplantation', they tell us, 'directly reflects the ethic of voluntarism and altruism on which the entire donation system is predicated'.[33] Similarly, we find statements like the following in numerous places:

> Organs are priceless and should be donated for altruistic reasons . . . provision of an organ should be seen as a donation or gift . . . freely given in the spirit of altruism.[34]

This section critically assesses *altruism arguments* against organ sale (i.e. those arguments against organ sale that rely heavily on the idea of altruism). These arise in a number of different forms, but most of them have the following underlying structure:

1 Altruism is a good thing, either intrinsically or because of its positive effects (or both).
2 Permitting and/or practising organ sale would reduce the amount of altruism in the world.
3 *Therefore*, we oughtn't to permit and/or practise organ sale.

In what follows, I'll briefly assess each of this argument's premises (1 and 2) and then ask whether its conclusion (3) follows from these premises.

(A) Is altruism a good thing?

Altruism is usually defined as *acting out of disinterested concern for the well-being of others*. Why might one think that such actions are morally good? Two main answers are available. The first says that altruism, acting beneficently, acting so as to promote others' welfare, etc. are *intrinsically good* – and are to be contrasted with morally bad characteristics and motivations, in particular selfishness. The second answer (which isn't incompatible with the first) says that altruism is good because of its positive effects, not only its direct effects on the person to whom the altruism is directed (for example, an individual organ recipient), but also its indirect effects on wider society (for example, what Keown calls 'social solidarity'). Both of these answers have got a lot going for them. Many examples of acting out of disinterested concern for the well-being of others do seem to be paradigm cases of moral goodness, especially where there is substantial self-sacrifice on the part of the altruist. And it seems plausible to suppose that, other things being equal, a society with more altruistic acts would be better than one with fewer, both in terms of 'solidarity' and in other ways.

That said, two reservations about the claim that altruism is a good thing should be noted. First, altruistic acts aren't *always* morally good. Indeed, they're not even always *permissible*. Hugh McLachlan makes the point as follows:

> Actions can be altruistic and wrong and worthy of discouragement . . . Altruism can be good in some contexts and can be bad in others. It can have good effects as well as bad effects. It can be done for good motives as well as bad ones: altruistic motives are not always good; self-interested motives . . . are not always bad.[35]

How can an altruistic act be wrong? This is best answered by simply listing some types of case. Perhaps not all of these will be accepted as possibilities – but I think that it is pretty hard to maintain that all of the following are impossible.

1 The altruist is culpably mistaken about what's really in the interests of the person she's trying to help and ends up harming rather than helping.
2 The altruist benefits the person she's trying to help, but her intervention is wrongfully paternalistic.
3 The altruist benefits the person she's trying to help, but in so doing wrongfully harms innocent third parties.

McLachlan provides what seems to be a compelling example of (3) (or perhaps of something *even worse* than (3) if we think that these 'altruists' didn't even manage to benefit anyone):

> Often, altruism results in extremely wicked actions because people can, wrongly, be prepared to do for other people things which they would, rightly, be too ashamed to do solely for themselves. The recent suicide bombers in Israel, who killed over a dozen bystanders in a crowded marketplace and injured many more were not – or possibly were not – lacking in altruism.[36]

To generalise, it's easy to think of more everyday cases in which A loves B so much that A is prepared to do bad things to a third party, C, in order to benefit A. Such cases range from minor wrongdoing to serious evil. So, as McLachlan points out, while many acts of altruism are paradigm cases of moral goodness, it's clear that others can be 'extremely wicked'.

My second reservation about the claim that altruism is good is that, as it stands, it ignores an important distinction between cases in which altruism is *obligatory* (such as where there's a *duty* to rescue) and cases in which altruism is *supererogatory* (which means *morally good, but not morally required* – going 'above and beyond' one's duty). This distinction is important for the following reason. If (say) altruistic blood donation were morally obligatory, then to demand money for one's blood (and, arguably, to accede to such a demand) would be wrong. But if, on the other hand, altruistic blood donation were supererogatory, then to demand money for one's blood wouldn't be wrong. Rather, it would be merely non-supererogatory: not good, but not wrong. So, with this distinction in place, one might (at least of some cases) accept that altruistic donations are good while also saying that there's nothing *wrong* with non-altruistic donation – the point being that non-altruistic donation, while not *as good as* altruistic donation, is nonetheless permissible. This has implications for the sort of altruism argument which can be made against organ sale. If it could be shown that altruistic donation is *obligatory* then the argument would be stronger, or at least more straightforward, because it would follow that selling was wrong. But if all that could be shown was that altruistic donation is *good*, then it wouldn't follow from this, or at least wouldn't follow directly, that selling is wrong. For, as we've seen, it might be merely non-supererogatory.

(B) Would organ sale reduce the amount of altruism in the world?

[I]f to a voluntary blood donor system we add the possibility of selling blood, we have only expanded the individual's range of alternatives. If he derives satisfaction from giving . . . he can still give, and nothing has been done to impair that right.[37]

As the quotation from Arrow (above) suggests, there's a puzzle about why permitting payment for blood or organs should be thought to reduce the amount of altruism in the world. After all, it seems obvious that (at least in principle) paid and unpaid donation systems could peacefully coexist, with people who want to give freely continuing to do so. Furthermore, paid donations may even add to the amount of altruism in the world. For there can be cases in which a person sells an organ not for 'selfish' reasons, but in order to pay for someone else's medical care.[38] Such cases aren't merely a philosopher's thought experiment, but perfectly real. One example is England's 1989 'kidneys-for-sale' scandal, in which[39]

it was revealed that a human kidney transplanted into a private patient at the Humana Wellington Hospital in London had not been donated, but rather had been sold by an impecunious Turkish peasant.[40]

One of the less well-known facts of the case is that one of the Turkish organ vendors was offering his kidney for sale in order to be able to purchase lifesaving medication for his daughter, who was suffering from tuberculosis. Since this man had 'no employment and no other saleable assets', stopping him from selling his kidney prevented an act of altruism and deprived his daughter of her best chance of being saved.[41]

Given cases like these, we've every right to ask: how exactly will allowing organ sale lead to there being less altruism in the world? The main answer given is that it would (we're told) undermine the practice of free donation.[42] Abouna *et al.*, for example, claim that there's

considerable evidence to indicate that marketing in human organs will eventually deprecate [*sic*] and destroy the present willingness of members of the public to donate their organs out of altruism.[43]

But is it really true that kidney sale would undermine the practice of free donation? There are a number of reasons for answering *no* to this. The main one is that it's far from clear that there is a significant practice of free donation to be undermined. As Harvey points out,

> it is doubtful that there is a great number of willing, non-related potential organ-donors who will give without payment.[44]

Given the pain, risk, and inconvenience involved, free donation (except by relatives) is very unlikely to take place anyway. This is borne out by some of the available statistics. If we take a look, for example, at the UK regulatory body ULTRA (the Unrelated Live Transplant Regulatory Authority), which was established under the Human Organ Transplants Act 1989 to approve all transplant operations involving a living donor who is not a close 'blood' relative of the organ recipient, we'll see that throughout the whole period from 1990 to 1998 it approved only eighty-five kidney transplants from unrelated live donors.[45] This is a drop in the ocean compared to the 5,000 or so British patients who were waiting for transplants throughout that period, and it's clear that (as Cameron and Hoffenberg put it) 'the blunt fact is that altruism alone has failed to supply enough organs to meet demands'.[46]

(C) Is the altruism argument successful?

Earlier, I suggested that altruistic acts aren't always good, that they are sometimes wrong, and that sometimes altruistic motivations can lead people to do terrible things. These are potentially serious problems for the altruism argument. But, these reservations notwithstanding, let's grant for the present that there's something good about encouraging altruism and see where it takes us.

Can this assumption underpin an argument against organ sale? The answer to this depends partly on how we answer the question we've been addressing in the last couple of pages: would permitting sale reduce the amount of altruism in the world? Ultimately, this is an empirical question to which a definite answer can't be given here. That said, there do seem to be some pretty strong reasons for answering 'no' in the case of kidney sales from live donors. The most powerful of these is that there isn't a substantial pre-existing system of free donation to be undermined. In other words, allowing paid donation is hardly likely to reduce the number of altruistic donations, since these just aren't happening anyway. Another reason for answering 'no' is that allowing kidney sales may bring into existence opportunities to be altruistic which don't presently exist (or exist only outside the law). This was demonstrated by the case of the Turkish man who offered his kidney for sale in order to buy medicines for his daughter.

Kidneys may then be importantly different from (say) blood. For, as we've seen, if there's no substantial system of free donation in place, then (of course) free donation can't be undermined by permitting sale. But if a substantial system of free donation *does* exist (as, in most countries, it does with blood), then there is at least a possibility of its being undermined. Thus, the argument which says that what's wrong with sale is that free donation would be undermined might well work for blood, even if it doesn't for kidneys.

This difference between kidneys and blood reveals a general structural difficulty for altruism arguments against sale. For what we've seen is that altruism arguments (insofar as they work at all) work much better for those things which are already freely donated on a large scale than for those things which are hardly freely donated at all. Hence, they will tend to be most successful where they are needed least – because if there's already widespread free donation, then commercialisation will be simply unnecessary. This isn't a decisive objection, since there are (of course) things which are in short supply *in spite of* widespread free donation. But it is a problem for this style of argument because there will be a tendency for it to be least successful where it's most needed. Wilkinson and Moore make a similar point about paying biomedical research subjects:

> If hardly anyone would volunteer for research without pay, then refusing to allow inducements would not promote the gift relationship and it would, moreover, cause a shortage of research subjects. If, on the other hand, people would generally be willing to volunteer for free, even if inducements were allowed, then prohibiting inducements would be redundant; the desired attitude would already exist.[47]

I'll end this section by raising a pair of interrelated problems for the altruism argument. One is a concern about uncertainty; the other, a doubt about the value of encouraging altruism, relative to other goods. The following comment from Gillon provides a good way into these objections:

> When benefits in altruism and social solidarity can be obtained along with the maintenance of optimal health care we can all cheer. But should the pursuit of altruism and social solidarity impair the provision of health care many would give priority to

optimal health care even at the cost of more commerce and less altruism.[48]

Gillon's point, which seems to me to be a good one, is that while attempting to promote altruism and social solidarity may be all well and good, it's not clear that these laudable aims give us sufficient reason to deliver sub-optimal health care. Or to put it more starkly, it's far from clear that the pursuit of altruism and social solidarity justifies the implementation of anti-commerce laws and policies which (in effect) kill kidney patients who need transplants (those who may well get lifesaving transplants if organ sale were allowed) – not to mention the harm done to prospective organ vendors, some of whom will be deprived of money that they desperately need.

This point – which, in essence, boils down to 'even if promoting altruism is good, is it good *enough* to justify the loss of thousands of lives?' – is bolstered by what I just called a 'concern about uncertainty'. Proponents of the altruism objection often talk confidently about the positive social effects of the 'culture of voluntarism'. However, it's not obvious that voluntary donation really has these effects – or, if it has, that they are as positive as is assumed. As we saw earlier, these are complex and highly contested empirical matters. Altruism (or, at least, the altruism level of a whole population) is hard to measure accurately. One reason for this is that any downturn in observed 'public' altruism (blood donation, donations to charities, etc.) could be easily outweighed by an upturn in unobserved 'private' acts of altruism (for example, acts of generosity to friends or colleagues). Another reason is that altruism is fundamentally a matter of people's motivational states. Hence, we can't infer with certainty from (say) the mere fact that someone is giving something away for free that she is acting altruistically, for there may be other motives (for example, making herself appear and/or feel generous). Conversely, it would be naive to hold that just because someone asks for a fee, she is acting non-altruistically. (Think back again to the Turkish man who wanted to sell his kidney to save his daughter.)

What follows when we combine this point about uncertainty with Gillon's point about the price we sometimes pay when we ban commerce is a powerful objection to the altruism argument against organ sale. The objection goes as follows. Admittedly, many people believe that banning organ commerce encourages altruism and social solidarity. But this belief is shaky on a number of counts. There are doubts about whether altruism and social solidarity are as good as they're portrayed as being. But, more importantly, it's far from clear that there's firm empirical evidence for the view that banning organ commerce encourages altruism. So the altruism objection to sale is built on rather wobbly foundations. Against this uncertainty, we have to weigh a certainty: that thousands of people will die if they don't get transplant organs. In the US alone, 76,000 people were waiting for transplants in 2000 (up from 18,000 in 1989), but there were only 6,000 donated organs (including from cadavers). The figures indicate that 5 per cent of Americans need a transplant at some point in their lives and half of these die while on waiting lists. As Nancy Kay, executive director of the South Carolina Organ Procurement Agency, puts it: 'they are needlessly dying because we have the knowledge and ability to save them'.[49] So we've to choose between an 'anti-commerce' policy which *might* have some long-term social benefits but which *certainly* condemns thousands to die and a 'pro-commerce' policy which would *certainly* save thousands and *might* lead to the loss of some rather intangible social benefits. When it's put in these terms, it's hard to resist the conclusion that the altruism argument is inadequate.

7.4 Inducements and consent

This section considers the consent argument against organ sale: the claim that what's wrong with organ sale is that the vendor's consent (if she consents at all) is likely to be invalid. In Chapter 5, we saw that in order for a consent to be valid, three main elements must be present (and present in sufficient quantities): information, competence, and voluntariness. The consent argument against organ sale focusses mainly on the last of these, voluntariness. That's not to say that there are no instances in which lack of information and competence are at issue, for there clearly are such cases. Nonetheless, consent arguments against organ sale in general, against the whole practice, tend to focus almost exclusively on the voluntariness element and, in particular, on the relationship between voluntariness and financial incentives.

Before proceeding with an assessment of the consent argument, we should first note that there are obviously many particular cases in which organ donors (paid or otherwise) don't provide valid consent. Some examples were mentioned early on in the chapter: Chinese prisoners, Brazilian hospital patients who had parts of their bodies stolen, Indian organ sellers who were subjected to torture or forced to sell by money-lenders. Horrific though these cases are, they don't contribute much to the consent argument, because what makes them so objectionable (and non-consensual) isn't payment, but rather some other factor (for example, assault, coercion, murder, theft, torture). So to use cases like these in a general argument against organ sale would be rather like arguing against all employment on the grounds that there are some cases of slavery, or arguing against property because there are some cases of theft.

To turn now to our analysis of the argument, a good starting point is the World Medical Association's assertion that we should ban organ sale because 'a financial incentive compromises the voluntariness of the choice'.[50] Why might someone think this? And how exactly are monetary incentives supposed to reduce the extent to which a decision is voluntary? There are three main answers:

1 Financial incentives encourage ('make') people do things that they wouldn't otherwise do.
2 Financial incentives are (or can be) coercive.
3 Financial incentives, even if not coercive, can make people's actions and decisions less free and/or autonomous.

In what follows, I'll briefly dismiss (1), which is a very weak answer. The rest of section 7.4 will then analyse, and ultimately reject, (3). Argument (2) (coercion) receives a separate treatment in section 7.5. Both (2) and (3) are really about autonomy and could in principle be merged. I've kept them apart just because they give rather different accounts of the way in which commercialisation compromises autonomy. These accounts aren't, however, incompatible, and one could hold that financial incentives erode autonomy both by being coercive and in other ways.

To turn first to (1), the reason why this is inadequate is simple: the fact that payments encourage people to do things that they otherwise wouldn't clearly doesn't, in and of itself, generate any sort of consent problem. For, if it did, then consent problems would be endemic and would occur every time someone was 'encouraged' by payment to go to work for wages or to hand over property in return for a fair price. So while it's conceded on all that sides that most organ vendors wouldn't have given up their organ *if it weren't for the money* (indeed, the whole point of the market is that more people give up their organs than otherwise would!), this fact alone in no way invalidates their consent.

Answer (3) is more promising. As I've just suggested, the first problem that any answer must overcome is that there's a puzzle about why payment is held by many people to be incompatible with valid consent. Wilkinson and Moore (in a paper about paying research subjects) make the point well:

> the idea that inducement undermines consent is surprising. People receive inducements all the time to do things they otherwise would not do, such as parting with their goods or working under particular conditions for particular employers. There is no suggestion in the vast majority of these cases that their being paid undermines the voluntary nature of their actions.[51]

Clearly, then, neither the mere fact of payment nor the mere fact that someone is influenced by payment is enough to ground a consent argument against organ sale. The thought rather must be that *certain sorts* of payment, or payments *in certain circumstances*, exert '*undue* influence on a participant's decision'.[52] So what counts as *undue* influence? The central ideas here are autonomy and freedom. An influence is 'undue' insofar as it erodes or fails to respect the consenter's autonomy and/or freedom.[53]

It's no accident that accusations of undue inducement almost always occur in one of two different contexts. The first is where the 'victim' of the inducement is in desperate need of money because of poverty, or because she has some special need – such as to purchase costly medical treatment. The second is where the 'victim' isn't in desperate need of money, but is offered such a huge amount of money to do X that doing X becomes, in some sense, irresistible. (It's also possible for both these contexts to be present at the same time: i.e. for the 'offeree'[54] to be desperate *and* for the offer to be enormous, but such cases don't require special consideration.)

We've already seen plenty of examples of the first context: Indian organ sellers being forced into the sale by moneylenders or the like. Cases of the second are less common in real life, but we can nonetheless easily envisage top sports stars being offered multi-million-dollar deals to transfer from one team to another, or more generally employees being 'headhunted' by rival employers who offer to triple their salaries. A good fictional example is provided by the film *Indecent Proposal*,[55] in which David and Diana Murphy (Woody Harrelson and Demi Moore) do a deal with billionaire financier John Gage (Robert Redford) under which he pays them $1,000,000 in return for a one-night sexual encounter with Diana.[56] Here, one might argue that the amount of money offered by Gage is so great, compared to what is after all only one night of Diana's life, that the offer becomes irresistible to them. Incidentally, perhaps the *Indecent Proposal* scenario isn't as far-fetched as one might think. UK surveys have suggested that 65 per cent of people would sleep with a complete stranger for £1,000,000,[57] and furthermore that:

> 16% of men would sleep with someone for £100 or less. A quarter of men ... would have sex with someone for £1,000, 35% for £10,000 and 51% for £100,000. Of women interviewees asked the same question, 3% would do it for £100, 8% for £1,000, 16% for £10,000 and 29% for £100,000.[58]

We now need to ask what morally relevant features (if any) these two types of situation have in common. Let's, for convenience, call them *desperate offeree* cases and *enormous offer* cases. One notable thing that they have in common is that there's a huge gap between (a) the offeree's level of welfare if she *doesn't* accept the offer and (b) her level of welfare if she *does* accept the offer. In desperate offeree cases, this is because the offeree needs what's offered and will be substantially harmed if she doesn't get it, while in enormous offer cases, it's simply because of the offer's sheer size that the offeree stands to gain a lot by accepting. Of course (as viewers of *Indecent Proposal* will know) whether an enormous offer is worth accepting, *all things considered*, depends on what's demanded in return and on the side-effects of accepting the offer. But let's focus, for the time being, just on cases in which the *net* gains for the offeree are vast.

Is this, then, the morally relevant feature: that in both kinds of case the difference between accepting and not accepting is simply so great that it's psychologically impossible (or almost impossible) to resist? We should certainly concede immediately that, in both desperate offeree and enormous offer cases, it's tremendously hard for offerees to decline. Whether it's strictly *impossible* for them to do so raises difficult questions about free will and about the nature of temptation.[59] However, we don't need to tackle those questions here, because there are independent reasons for thinking that the consent worry in such cases can't be justified by reference simply to the size of the gap between the offeree's level of welfare if she doesn't accept and her level of welfare if she does. To see why, consider the following remark:

> If the sole alternative to death is some lifesaving treatment, then one is unfree to turn it down, but this does not rule out autonomous choice of the treatment. All the features of autonomous choice might be present: careful deliberation, correct understanding of the options, no manipulation, and so on. If informed consent is possible, despite the dire choice one faces, it cannot be because one is free to refuse the treatment. It must be because one can nonetheless act autonomously.[60]

Wilkinson and Moore (quoted above) are surely right about this. Even if we grant that there's a sense in which the recipients of enormous offers and desperate offerees aren't *free* to decline, this doesn't mean that they can't *autonomously* accept and (hence) validly consent. This must be so. Otherwise, it would be impossible for anyone ever to consent validly to lifesaving operations, not to mention lottery 'jackpot' wins or large salaries; the mere fact that a proposal is tremendously attractive clearly doesn't mean that it can't be validly and voluntarily accepted by the offeree.

This may, however, seem a bit swift, and a little more needs to be said about the distinction between freedom and autonomy. In particular, in what sense is a person offered lifesaving medical treatment 'unfree to turn it down' (as Wilkinson and Moore claim)? There clearly is a sense in which people are free to turn down these treatments, for there are plenty of cases in which people explicitly refuse life-prolonging therapy. It seems to me, though, that what Wilkinson and Moore have in mind here isn't freedom in that sense, but rather *lack of choice relative to one's funda-mental goals*. What does this mean? The thought is that A can be unfree to decline X (an offer) in that *in order to achieve A's fundamental goals* (which, typically, include or require staying alive) A *has to* accept X – A has, we might say, *no alternative* to X as a means of achieving her fundamental goals.[61] On this understanding of freedom, we can say that someone who wants to stay alive and is offered necessary lifesaving treatment isn't free to refuse it. She has no choice, unless she abandons her fundamental goals. But if someone who *doesn't* want to stay alive is offered the same treatment, she *is* free, because (let's assume) her fundamental goals don't include or require staying alive.

I've proposed so far (following Wilkinson and Moore) that one doesn't need to be free (in the sense just outlined) in order validly and voluntarily to consent, and that what matters as far as consent is concerned isn't free-dom but autonomy. So what exactly is autonomy? I suggested in Chapter 6 that something like Gerald Dworkin's account of autonomy is correct. According to this account, autonomous persons are those who have 'the capacity to raise the question of whether [they] will identify with or reject the reasons for which [they] now act', while autonomous choices are those which are made by autonomous persons who are (suf-ficiently) free from 'distorting' or 'controlling' influences.[62] So a person may autonomously consent to something, even in the absence of tolerable alternatives, provided that she has the capacity to reason and reflect, the capacity to make (many of) her desires 'line up' with the outcomes of her reflections, and freedom from distorting or controlling influences. One important implication of this is that while desperate offerees are almost by definition not free to decline an offer (by which I mean that they have no practicable alternative), they may still be capable of making a fully autonomous choice, provided that they meet the conditions just men-tioned. Hence, the Turkish man who wants to sell his kidney in order to buy medical treatment for his daughter, or the woman who wants to sell her kidney for £1,000,000 to a National Lottery winner may well be acting autonomously, particularly if they have deliberated rationally about the decision, and have reflectively endorsed the relevant desires ('to save my daughter'; 'to become a millionaire').

Does this mean that the consent argument against organ sale is unsuc-cessful? We've so far looked at the following possibilities for grounding the argument: (a) the fact that donors are influenced by payment, (b) the fact that payment makes accepting hugely attractive compared to declin-ing, and (c) the fact that 'desperate offerees' aren't free to decline (in the sense just discussed). And we've concluded that none of these will suffice. However, there may still be a version of the consent argument which is at least partially successful, one which focusses on the donor's non-autonomously held desires.

Desires can be more or less autonomously held. As a useful shorthand, we might say that some desires are more autonomous (more autonomously held) than others.[63] (Like most philosophers, I use 'desires' here as a general term covering not only what people ordinarily call 'desires' but also such things as aspirations, cravings, ends, goals, objectives, wants, wishes, etc.) What makes a desire autonomous? A full answer to this could occupy a whole book, but a reasonably accurate (if incomplete) answer is that a desire is autonomous insofar as it is susceptible to *elimination by reflection*.

The idea of elimination by reflection can be 'cashed out' as follows. Some desires, like wanting to go to the library on Tuesday afternoon to return a book, can be easily got rid of by rationally considering new evidence, or by reconsidering priorities. So if, say, I discover that there's a bus strike on Tuesday, or that the library is closed on Tuesday, or that my book isn't actually due back until Thursday, there's a good chance that – *just by thinking about this evidence* – I'll eliminate the original desire and replace it with another (say, wanting to go to the library on Wednesday morning). Alternatively, even if no new evidence comes in, I might – just by reflecting – eliminate the original desire by deciding that I don't care about returning my library books on time, or that I care about other things more (going on holiday, going to the pub, participating in 'anti-globalisation' protests, or whatever). My desire to go to the library on Tuesday afternoon, then, is easily eliminable by reflection, and as such is highly autonomous.

Wants of this sort should be contrasted with those which are hard, or impossible, to get rid of just through deliberation. Addictive desires (those which constitute addictions) are the most obvious candidates. For example, people who smoke cigarettes and want to give up, but can't because they are addicted, have a desire for cigarettes which they can't get rid of just by rationally reflecting. The smoking addict's position is often described in terms of first- and second-order desires. A first-order desire is a desire for something that is not itself a desire (for example, wanting chocolate cake), whereas a second-order desire is a 'wanting to want' or 'wanting not to want' (for example, 'I wish I didn't want chocolate cake'). Thus, the smoking addict may rationally reflect, decide (on some level) that she no longer wishes to smoke and, in the process, form a second-order desire – something along the lines of 'I want not to want cigarettes.' However, if she's an addict, then just doing this is unlikely to be enough, because her relevant first-order desires (for example, wanting a cigarette now) will be fairly unresponsive to what happens at the second order. The first-order desires are, we might say, immune to elimination by reflection, meaning that even if the smoking addict reflects and decides that smoking isn't a good policy, that won't be sufficient to rid her of these desires. And so the desire to smoke is, for this person at least, non-autonomous.

Before this is applied to the case at hand, several further clarificatory remarks need to be made. First, this is *not* an anti-smoking point; the idea *isn't* that the desire to smoke is non-autonomous because smoking itself is irrational (for example, because of its health effects). Indeed, it's undoubtedly possible in principle for the desire to smoke to be entirely autonomous (though only for people who aren't addicted). This is because what matters (for autonomy) isn't so much the nature of the object of desire as the relationship between the desirer and the desire – in particular, is the desire immune to elimination by reflection? So it's possible in principle for wanting to go to the library on Tuesday afternoon to be just as non-autonomous as wanting the next cigarette, or the next 'fix' (although, if the library-desire were non-autonomous to this extent, then we'd probably say that the person in question was afflicted by some kind of irrational, maybe even pathological, library-compulsion).

Second, we should remember that it's of course possible even for addicts to give up smoking and (eventually) to stop wanting cigarettes. So immunity to elimination by reflection needn't be total and, more generally, such immunity is a matter of degree. Some non-autonomous desires are harder to get rid of by reflection than others.

Third, while all addictive desires are to some extent non-autonomously held, not all non-autonomous desires are addictions – or, at least, not all non-autonomous desires would normally be *called* addictions. One reason for thinking this is that some non-autonomous desires simply aren't powerful enough to be termed addictions: for example, a desire for chocolate cake, which, although ineliminable by reflection, only has very mild effects on the desirer's behaviour. Another reason is that, as I've already hinted, there might be compulsions that aren't addictions, such as 'having to' go to the library on a Tuesday. That said, many people might consider labelling such a compulsion a 'library addiction', for people these days do tend to use the term 'addiction' quite loosely to cover a wide range of things (including exercise, gambling, internet usage, masturbation, overeating, pornography, 'relationships', sex, shopping, stealing, and work).[64] The most compelling reason for thinking that not all non-autonomous desires are addictions, though, is that many entirely normal 'bodily' desires (including sexual desire, the desire to avoid pain, wanting to sleep, and wanting to eat) are non-autonomous, since they can't generally be eliminated by reflection. Of course, such desires can be influenced both by social forces and by the will-power of individuals. Thus, I may (for example) be able to wean myself off hamburgers and fries and onto fresh fruit and vegetables in response to health information, or may manage to change my sexual behaviour after taking an ethics course. However (a small number of heroic exceptions notwithstanding), the extent to which individuals can modify (and, *a fortiori*, the extent to which they can eliminate) their bodily desires *just by thinking about them* is very limited indeed. Thus, people usually *can't help* desiring things like food, sex, and sleep, in one form or another. One interesting implication of this is that, insofar as these desires are an inevitable consequence of embodiment, embodiment itself is autonomy-limiting. (This, though, doesn't mean that embodiment is bad, since autonomy isn't the only thing we value.) Another implication is that normal bodily desires and addictions are, in some respects, very similar (and the same might be said about strong emotional attachments).

Having spent a while looking at the nature of autonomy and, in particular, at the concept of non-autonomous desire, we're now in a position to apply these ideas to the consent argument against organ sale. What they generate is a version of the argument which claims that we've reason to be suspicious about the quality of any consent given by organ vendors, because the financial incentive involved will, in many cases, incite them to act on non-autonomously held desires. It's my contention that this argument won't work, but, before saying why, it's worth first saying that there are particular contexts in which this *style* of argument seems to be at least partially successful. Consider, for example, those sex-workers who are driven into prostitution by drug addiction.[65] If such people also attempted to sell their kidneys, there would be an extremely serious autonomy worry about the quality of their consent, since they would be motivated by a highly non-autonomous desire (for drugs). Similar concerns would be raised if a so-called 'shopoholic' (shopping addict) tried to sell her kidney to fund her habit. Again, the objection would be that she was motivated by an addictive desire (for shopping). Whether these autonomy worries are sufficient to make buying an organ in such circumstances wrong remains an open question. Nonetheless, what is clear is that (in these cases) those propounding this autonomy argument have a point. The prostitutes and shopoholics, however, are special cases because they are addicts, and it's not so clear that the autonomy argument applies to organ sale in general, or even to its most prominent forms. As before, it will be useful to consider enormous offer cases separately from desperate offeree cases, since slightly different problems arise.

In enormous offer cases, the argument is that such sinister forces as greed and cash-lust will unduly influence prospective kidney vendors. So, for example, when people tried to sell their kidneys to Mick Taylor (the £4,100,000 lottery winner), many of them, it could be argued, weren't acting autonomously because they were overwhelmed by a non-autonomous lust for money. Whether this is true is really an empirical psychological question, not one to which I know the answer with any certainty. However, it does seem that there are some 'armchair' reasons for thinking that it isn't that likely to be true of these prospective vendors. The main one of these is that, even for an averagely well-off British person, desiring £4,000,000 seems eminently sensible, as does selling one's kidney for £4,000,000, especially given the data discussed in section 7.2, which suggest that the level of risk involved is quite low. Getting £4,000,000 for one of your kidneys is, basically, a very good deal compared to, say, working for a living – for (if we use UK figures as a reference) it would take someone with an average salary several lifetimes to earn such a sum. So while, of course, it's *possible* non-autonomously to desire something which it would be rational and sensible to desire, there seems not to be any reason for being especially suspicious about the motivations of people like those who tried to sell a kidney to Mick Taylor. And even if there are reasons for being suspicious, these will surely be equally applicable to (say) well-paid jobs.

To turn now to 'desperate offeree' cases, the concern here isn't so much about greed and cash-lust but about the desperation and poverty of prospective donors. Paul Hughes, for example, says:

> one common objection to allowing a market in organs is that the economically worst off members of society will be exploited, since they will be the least likely to *resist the temptation* to profit financially in this manner.[66]

It's notable that Hughes, like many who speak and write on this subject, thinks in terms of poor people succumbing to temptation – suggesting that their plight is rather like that of the addict or of the person overcome by cash-lust. But is this the correct model? And why should we think that desperation renders people's desires non-autonomous? Again, the problem for the anti-sale argument is that – given dire circumstances – wanting (say) to sell one of your kidneys for $2,000 seems very sensible. So why view such a want as non-autonomous? Furthermore, it seems fair to assume that most 'desperate' organs sellers' desires to sell and desires for money are in fact eliminable by reflection. For if the vendor discovered that she (miraculously) no longer needed the money, then (presumably) her desire for money would fade. Or if she found out about a more attractive way of earning the money, then (presumably) her desire to sell the organ would vanish. So the relevant desires (to sell, and for money) appear pretty autonomous, because they are vulnerable to elimination by reflection.

It may, though, be objected (understandably) that the relevant desires have been misidentified: that in the case of the sex-workers and the shopoholics, what was focussed on wasn't the desire for money but rather an *underlying* desire (drugs, shopping), so that's how we should view other organ sellers. At this point, generalising becomes hard because there are a wide variety of different reasons why one might want to sell an organ. Two common ones, though, are (a) to save one's own life and (b) to save the life of a close relative. So perhaps these are the kinds of desires on which we should be focussing. And they do indeed seem to occupy the same motivational position as do drugs and shopping in the other cases. So are desires like (a) and (b) autonomous or not? Whether they are depends on the individual concerned. However, to generalise, it does seem that such desires are likely not to be autonomous. This is because, for most people, desires like wanting to carry on living and wanting one's loved ones to carry on living have a high degree of immunity to elimination by reflection. Indeed, people often talk about such desires ('survival', 'protection of the young', etc.) as *instincts*, suggesting that they're innate and hard or impossible to get rid of just by reasoning. (Note, however, that I'm not suggesting here that wanting to survive and to protect one's offspring is *irrational*, or even *non-rational* – rather, the idea is just that such desires may be non-autonomous insofar as they're immune to elimination by reflection.)

If we grant, at least for the sake of argument, that desires like 'survival' are (for most of us at least) non-autonomous, what follows from this? One possibility – the one required by the argument against organ sale – is that organ vendors can't validly consent when they are motivated by such desires. Surely, though, this conclusion can't be right. For, if it were, we'd be left (again) with a position according to which it's almost impossible for anyone validly to consent to lifesaving medical treatments – since (bizarrely) one could only do so if not motivated by the desire to survive! It's clear, then, that *either* desires like 'survival' aren't really non-autonomous *or* it's possible for a person validly to consent even when she is motivated by such non-autonomous desires. Either way, this particular argument against organ sale fails.

Section 7.4 has assessed the claim that financial inducements, or *undue* financial inducements, compromise the voluntariness of people's choices and render their consents invalid. There appear to be two main reasons why one might believe this. The first is that an undue financial inducement works by making the offer it supports seem, as it were, too attractive – perhaps even irresistible. The second is that undue inducements incite people to act on non-autonomously held desires. However, as we've seen, both of these (putative) reasons are flawed – or, at least, neither is sufficient to ground a consent argument against organ sale. The problem with the first is that it's clearly possible for people validly to consent to extremely attractive offers – notably offers of lifesaving medical treatment. And it's hard to see what (in this respect) differentiates the 'desperate' organ seller from the 'desperate' patient who wants a lifesaving treatment. Given that desperation doesn't (I take it) invalidate consent in the latter case, why should it in the former? The problem with the second reason is a little more complex. We saw that inducements can sometimes incite people to act on non-autonomously held desires.

However, serious doubts were raised about whether the desires on which organ sellers normally act are non-autonomous and about whether, even if they are non-autonomous, they are the sort of motivations that should be counted as consent-invalidating. Leaving aside the coercion issue, which is to be dealt with in the next section, I conclude therefore that the arguments for the view that financial inducements compromise the voluntariness of organ sellers' choices and render their consents invalid are weak.

7.5 Coercion

If organ sale were permitted, would (prospective) organ vendors be at substantial risk of being coerced into selling their organs? If so, this may underpin an additional argument (the coercion argument) against the practice, as well as bolstering the consent worries discussed in the previous section.

As we've seen, there are undoubtedly particular cases in which people are coerced into selling their organs by threats of violence or death. Clearly, such coercion is wrong. But if accusations of coercion are to underpin a more general argument against organ sale, these accusations themselves need to be more general. They must also be capable of withstanding two immediate objections. The first is that coercion worries are by no means confined to *commercial* transplantation and so it may be hard to construct a coercion argument which doesn't 'prove too much' – i.e. one which doesn't entail the condemnation or prohibition of *both* free donation *and* sale. Harvey makes the point well:

> there is financial pressure when the potential [paid] donor is in poverty. And perhaps it may be argued that this alone is sufficient for banning all paid-for donations. But then, in consistency, the same reasoning should be applied to related donors: since *some* of them are open to heavy psychological and emotional pressure (for example, perhaps by being the submissive and 'guilt-ridden' offspring of an extremely domineering and now ailing parent).[67]

The second objection is that we could screen out most cases of coercion by decriminalising organ sale and using a regulatory body, perhaps rather like the UK'S ULTRA (the Unrelated Live Transplant Regulatory Authority). Part of ULTRA's remit is to ensure that

> a doctor has explained to the donor the nature of the procedure and the risks involved in the removal of the organ in question . . . the donor's consent was not obtained by coercion . . . the donor understands that his or her consent can be withdrawn at any time

... and the donor and the recipient have been interviewed separately by a suitably qualified independent person, who is not part of the transplant team, and that person is satisfied that the above conditions have been met.[68]

Of course, ULTRA exists partly to screen out cases in which there have been inducements, but there's no reason in principle why the checks outlined above couldn't be carried out within the context of a properly regulated commercial market in human organs (i.e. within a context in which inducement was permitted, but not coercion).

Let's turn now to the question of what a coercion argument against organ sale in general might look like. The standard opening move is to claim that poor people will be *forced by poverty* into selling their organs. But what does this mean? One interpretation is just that poor people are 'forced' insofar as they don't have any viable alternatives. But under this interpretation, the 'forced by poverty' claim just collapses into the kind of the things that were discussed in the previous section – the effect of lack of options on freedom, autonomy, and so on. How else, then, might 'forced by poverty' be understood? Perhaps the main difficulty with making sense of this, in relation to coercion, is that (on the account of coercion defended in Chapter 6) only agents can coerce. This is because to coerce is to threaten (more specifically, to threaten harm relative to a normative baseline), and obviously only agents can threaten. Given this, it's clear that poverty *per se* can't coerce, even though (like other deprivations) it can be used as a *method* of coercing. So in order to make sense of coercion arguments against organ sale we'll need to ask who is supposed to be doing the threatening.

As just suggested, poverty can be used as a method of coercing. What this means is that people can be *threatened with* poverty (including the continuation of existing poverty) if they don't comply with the coercer's demands. An obvious example of this is the behaviour of exploitative employers during times of high unemployment. They can threaten workers with unemployment – and, hence, poverty – if they don't comply with their demands. People can be made poor by action or by omission, actively or passively. If a person has all of her possessions stolen then she has been *actively* impoverished; while if a person isn't given assistance to which she has a right then she has been *passively* impoverished. This distinction corresponds to a distinction made in Chapter 6 between active and omissive coercion. To coerce actively is to threaten active harm, while to coerce omissively is to threaten omissive harm. More specifically, A omissively coerces B to do X when

1 A has a duty to do Y for B and A's failing to do Y would cause or constitute omissive harm (harm by omission) to B; and

2 A proposes (threatens) *not* to do Y for B unless B does X; and

3 the existence of A's duty to do Y for B does not depend on B's doing X (i.e. A's duty is freestanding).

In the light of these distinctions, it seems that the most plausible version of the coercion argument against organ sale is one which focusses on omissive coercion. But who is doing the omissive coercing? In order to answer this, we need to know who has a freestanding duty to alleviate the prospective organ seller's poverty, because having such a duty is a necessary condition for practising this particular form of omissive coercion. Moore and Wilkinson make the point as follows:

> it is a necessary condition of an offer's being coercive that the offerer is also responsible for the bad circumstances of the offeree. For example, if we poison you and then offer to provide the only available antidote in exchange for your stamp collection, that is coercive. If you are poisoned in a way for which we are not responsible, and we make the same offer, that is not coercive . . . as long as those making an offer are not responsible for the circumstances of the potential subjects, their offer is not coercive.[69]

Coercers are only coercers, then, insofar as they're responsible for the coercee's situation – although, as I've already suggested, this responsibility can include both negative and positive duties, and so coercers can be *responsible for* (alleviating) the coercee's situation even if they haven't themselves *caused* it.

Returning to the case in hand let's, as a shorthand, call people with a freestanding duty to alleviate the prospective organ seller's poverty 'rescuers'. If a rescuer proposes to alleviate the prospective organ seller's poverty *but only in return for an organ*, she is omissively coercing the organ seller (in accordance with the tripartite account of omissive coercion outlined above). Such a situation is comparable to Nozick's *drowning case* discussed in Chapter 6, in which P (the occupant of a boat) offers to save Q (who is drowning close to the boat), but only if Q promises to pay P $10,000 within three days of reaching shore. The view defended in Chapter 6 was that, in this case, P coerces Q if and only if P has a freestanding duty to save Q without remuneration – i.e. only if P is a rescuer.

It's not hard to see how, in principle, this style of coercion argument could work against organ sale. What's much harder is working out who the rescuers are. For, at the level of individuals, pinning down plausible candidates is tricky. The standard case about which accusations of coercion are made is one in which the purchaser is a rich Westerner and the vendor is someone desperately poor from the 'developing' world. The Westerner, it is said, uses poverty to 'force' (coerce) the poor person into giving up the organ. On the picture sketched so far, this coercion claim is true only if the Westerner in question is responsible for the vendor's poverty. But is she responsible? This question is simply too big to be taken on in any detail here, raising as it does fundamental issues in political philosophy about the distribution of goods and about the duties of the rich to the poor. However, what we can say is that this kind of argument seems to work much better at the level of groups than it does at the level of individuals. The problem with attributing responsibility to individual organ purchasers is that the extent to which they are rescuers may vary enormously depending on their own positions of wealth and power, and on the extent to which they have already done virtuous things in an attempt to act on their duties towards the poor. For example, a Western organ purchaser could have already devoted a large part of her income and time to charitable projects aimed at the alleviation of poverty and may herself have relatively little money – just enough to buy a kidney. Do we really want to say that such a person has a freestanding duty to give her money to the prospective organ vendor without receiving a kidney in return, and that she is responsible for the vendor's poverty? Maybe we do, but insofar as the answer to this question isn't *obviously* yes, the coercion argument against sale remains weak.

A more promising option is to focus on groups rather than individuals. One might argue, for example, that the rich nations have a duty to alleviate poverty in the poor nations. With this (plausible) assumption in place, it could then be argued that when the rich nations 'offer' the poor nations money for organs, this isn't really an offer, but rather an instance of coercion. This is because the rich nations should be giving the money anyway, not demanding organs in return for it. So what the rich nations are doing is threatening to withhold resources to which the poor nations have a moral right, unless the poor nations hand over organs: a classic case of omissive coercion.

As I've already mentioned, we face serious difficulties in making sense of group responsibility and of the way in which group-actors' responsibilities are connected to those of individuals. These theoretical problems left aside, though, much of the argument just outlined seems believable. However, there's a further serious problem with it – or, rather, there's a serious problem with attempting to use it specifically as an argument for the legal prohibition of organ sale. The problem is simply that the argument works equally well against *all* trade between the rich nations and the poor ones. For (in simplistic terms) if the rich nations have a duty to *give* resources to the poor nations, then any time that the rich nations insist on trading rather than donating, they will be practising omissive coercion – threatening to withhold money that they should be giving anyway, unless they're provided with goods of one sort or another. And, as far as the coercion argument is concerned, there's no reason to single out the trade in organs for special treatment. This is a decisive objection to the coercion argument. Either it doesn't work at all, or it works but 'proves too much' and gives us no reason to single out organ sale for condemnation and/or prohibition.

7.6 Exploitation

The last argument that we're going to look at in Chapter 7 is that, if allowed, organ sale would cause or constitute exploitation. This claim occurs frequently in the ethics literature, as the following examples illustrate:

> [One of the] compelling reasons to object to the sale of organs . . . is exploitation, that is, when one person takes advantage of the misfortune of another for his or her own benefit.[70]

> The paid donor in a developing country is usually poor and ignorant concerning the whole process of organ donation and transplantation, and may be open to both coercion and exploitation and thus loss of autonomy. The practice of the poor selling their organs to the rich tacitly endorses the inequality of society and represents the ultimate exploitation of the poor by the rich.[71]

> the poor will be exploited by a market for organs because their comparatively limited range of viable options (i.e. their limited real autonomy) is being taken advantage of.[72]

The first thing to note is that there's clearly a lot of overlap between the kind of exploitation arguments that people put forward in the literature and the arguments that we've been considering in the last few sections. In particular, it's common for writers to group together exploitation claims with what are distinct claims about defective consent and/or coercion. So, having already provided separate treatments of consent and coercion, in this section I'm going to focus narrowly on the idea that organ purchasers would wrongfully *take advantage of* organ sellers, since this is what seems to me to be the main thing which differentiates the exploitation argument from the arguments previously discussed.

People who put forward the exploitation argument against organ sale are usually thinking about the exploitation of the poor. Thus, Kahn (quoted above) talks about *taking advantage of others' misfortune*, while Hughes (also quoted above) talks of taking advantage of people's *comparatively limited range of viable options*. Although poverty isn't the only thing that can render someone vulnerable to exploitation, this concentration on economic disadvantage is probably right, just because in practice it is the lack of and need for money which are most likely to motivate people to sell parts of their bodies for relatively modest sums. The focus on economic disadvantage does, however, immediately present a difficulty for the exploitation argument. For if the main concern is that organ purchasers will take advantage of other people's economic misfortune, the obvious solution is not to ban organ sale altogether, but instead just to prohibit the purchase of organs from people below a certain level of wealth – thus precluding the possibility of exploiting the misfortunes of the poor. Under such a system, the poor would be treated in some respects as like children and mentally incompetent adults, as a vulnerable group which needs to be protected from exploitation.

Most readers will find this proposal preposterous. But while there may well be sound arguments against it, appealing to exploitation won't suffice. For the exploitation argument, as we've seen, is about the maltreatment of the poor and so, if the poor are excluded, our exploitation concerns should vanish. One practical objection to a system which excluded only the poor is that it would deliver no (or hardly any) organs, because only people who are desperately poor would be willing to sell a kidney. However (as we saw in section 7.1), this is probably false if the price is right, and a system which excluded only the poor would certainly deliver more organs than outright prohibition. One likely effect of excluding the poor is that organ prices would be much higher, since (for example) a middle-class American is unlikely to sell an organ for $1,000, but may well sell it for $100,000. In this respect, the exclusion of the poor would be rather like having a regulated labour market and strict immigration controls in order to stop wages from falling and unscrupulous employers from exploiting. This is perhaps why people feel so uncomfortable about allowing sale from the rich while banning sale from the poor. For it seems at best ironic and, more likely, patently unfair to exclude from an organ trading system the very people who most need the money it could provide and who would be the most willing participants. How will a poor person who is willing to sell a kidney for $2,000 to buy medical treatment for her daughter feel when she's told that (to protect her from exploitation) *she* isn't allowed to sell – while, at the same time, a relatively rich neighbour is allowed to sell *her* kidney for $100,000 to fund home improvements?

There is, however, another, far preferable, way of permitting organ sale, while at the same time eliminating exploitation (or, at least, keeping it to a minimum) – the setting of a minimum fee. This would rule out exploitation, not by excluding the poor from the system altogether, but instead by ensuring that organ purchasers don't take *unfair* advantage of the poor. It's crucial that we include the word 'unfair' here, because taking advantage of other people's misfortune *per se* is neither wrong nor exploitative. What's exploitative is *unfairly* taking advantage of people's misfortunes. Hence, there's nothing necessarily exploitative about setting up in business as an emergency plumber, or a roadside vehicle-repair service, or – for that matter – an emergency-room doctor. Each of these services *could* be exploitative, but only if it overcharged desperate customers and/or provided them with a shoddy service. The same goes for organ purchasers. They only exploit vendors if, taking advantage of their poverty, they offer them an inadequate fee and/or maltreat them in other ways. Thus, it seems hard to escape the conclusion that the setting up of a regulatory regime which enforced a fairly generous minimum fee not only would neutralise the exploitation argument, but may result in a considerable level of benefit for some of the poorest people in the world. As Cameron and Hoffenberg put it,

> It is the financial circumstances that make it necessary for someone to consider offering body parts for sale that defines exploitation of the individual. Prohibiting this often removes the best or only option the 'donor' might have of earning money for a really important cause.[73]

7.7 Summary and conclusions

At the start of this chapter, it was (I hope) made clear that all or most of the organ trade, as it is practised today, is morally unjustifiable. Its unpalatable features include the complete absence of regulation and supervision, the coercion and underpayment of vendors, and – in the most appalling cases – the theft of organs and murder of 'donors'. Nothing that I state here should be construed as an attempt to excuse or justify the actions of those presently involved in organ trafficking. The awfulness of present practice, however, doesn't get us very far when we attempt to answer questions such as: is organ sale *per se* morally wrong and should it be criminalised? This is mainly because what makes present practice so objectionable isn't payment *per se* but additional factors – for example, assault, coercion, murder, theft, torture, and underpayment – factors which could, in principle, be removed from an organ trading system. Furthermore, when it comes to the legal prohibition issue, it has been plausibly argued that banning organ sale is partially responsible for the awfulness of present practice. Cameron and Hoffenberg, for example, claim that it's the 'marginalization of paid organ donation that leads to its performance in less than ideal circumstances'.[74] Hence, far from being a reason to continue the ban on sale, the dreadfulness of present practice may be a reason to *dis*continue prohibition, so that the organ trade can be brought 'overground' and properly regulated.

Given this, the main body of Chapter 7 was concerned not with an analysis of present practice, but rather with ethical arguments that attempt to show that the act of paying a person for a part of her body is somehow objectionable in itself. Five anti-sale arguments were considered, focussing respectively on harm and risk to the vendor, the role of free donation in promoting altruism and social solidarity, valid consent, coercion, and exploitation.

In section 7.2, the harm and risk argument was rejected (a) because donating a kidney isn't (or needn't be) terribly harmful, and (b) because it certainly isn't any *more* harmful than other widely accepted forms of 'risky labour'. In section 7.3, I conceded that altruism arguments may have some force if there is already a successful and predominantly free system of donation in place, such as the UK's free blood donation service – or if there is a realistic prospect of such a system being brought into being. However, altruism arguments won't work against practices like kidney sale, because free donation between non-relatives is very rare indeed and is unlikely to become much more common in the foreseeable future. Where we have a choice between an altruistic system and a commercial system, then the altruistic system will normally be preferable. But where an altruistic system is not a practical possibility and the real choice is between a commercial system and (virtually) no system at all, it makes little sense to opt for not having a system at all just because an altruistic system, if possible, would have been better than a commercial one.[75] Section 7.4 assessed the view that financial inducements invalidate organ donors' consents: the claim that financial inducements make the offers that they support irresistible to (certain kinds of) offeree and/or that inducements incite people to act on non-autonomously held desires. Such views were found to be either implausible, or plausible but insufficient to ground a consent argument against organ sale. Section 7.5 discussed the coercion argument, the idea that organ sellers would be the victims of coercion. It was conceded that many actual organ vendors are coerced. However, it was concluded that there's no reason to suppose that a properly regulated market in human organs would involve any more coercion than a properly regulated system of free donation – or that it would be any more coercive than capitalism in general. Finally, section 7.6 examined exploitation arguments against organ sale. As with coercion, it was conceded that many *actual* organ vendors are exploited. It would, however, be possible to make a suitably regulated market in human organs non-exploitative, or *comparatively* non-exploitative. In particular, the imposition of a generous minimum fee could help to alleviate poverty and save lives, while at the same time all but eliminating exploitative kidney purchases.

The overall conclusion in this chapter, then, is that the moral case against the establishment of a properly regulated commercial market in human organs is weak. As I stated at the outset, this has direct implications for criminal law in this area. Permitting organ sale would deliver very substantial practical benefits (the saving of lives). Hence, in the absence of a defensible moral argument for prohibition, the case for decriminalisation looks compelling.

8

BABIES FOR SALE?

[G]estational surrogacy is a form of prostitution and slavery.[1]

Nobody wants to see babies treated as commodities or vulnerable people exploited.[2]

This chapter is about surrogacy, or surrogate motherhood. As the opening quotations suggest, this practice, especially the commercial variety, is something that many regard as extremely morally objectionable. Commercial surrogacy has been attacked on an array of different grounds, but almost all of the objections concern themselves primarily with one or more of the following: *harm* to surrogates or children; the *commodification* of surrogates, children, or (more generally) reproduction; or the *exploitation* of women, especially those who are poor or vulnerable in some other way.

In some ways, then, the commercial surrogacy debate resembles the kidney sale debate. For example, in both there are concerns about exploitation and about people's consents being invalid because they are 'forced by poverty'. So from time to time during this chapter, I'll be referring the reader back to arguments and distinctions deployed in the earlier discussion of organ sale (not least in order to avoid unnecessary repetition). There are, however, some interesting and important differences between the two debates.

One is that the altruism objection, which (as we saw) figures prominently in the case against kidney sale, is used much less against commercial surrogacy. This is perhaps surprising given that some surrogates seem to have precisely the kind of altruistic motives that are lauded in discussions of organ donation. The UK organisation COTS, for example, claims that

> in general women are motivated to be surrogates because they feel a desire to help others. Many potential surrogates place great value on their own children and family life, and recognise the

pain and suffering felt by women who face a lifetime of childlessness. Some have seen members of their own family or friends
battle against infertility. Most surrogates derive a great deal of
satisfaction from knowing that they have changed peoples' [sic]
lives for the good, making what would otherwise be an
impossible dream come true.[3]

Why, then, doesn't the altruism objection have a higher profile in the
surrogacy debate? One reason is simply that other concerns ('baby selling', commodification, exploitation, and similar) seem more pressing.
Another reason, I suspect, is that commercial surrogacy's opponents
don't regard unpaid surrogacy as unproblematically good – whereas
organ sale's opponents, for the most part, see free organ donation as not
merely permissible, but as a good which law and policy should actively
encourage. Indeed, I'd go further and conjecture that a lot of commercial
surrogacy's opponents are against surrogacy in general – their view being
just that paid surrogacy is *even worse* than altruistic surrogacy. I wouldn't,
however, want to overstate this difference between organ sale and surrogacy. For while the idea of altruism has a *relatively* minor role in the
surrogacy debate, it is invoked by some people. For example, the UK's
Brazier Report (discussed below) quite explicitly compares altruistic
surrogacy with blood and organ donation:

> 4.36 – We believe that the core value here, on which many social
> arrangements in the United Kingdom are based, including blood
> and live organ donation, is the 'gift relationship'.
>
> 5.13 – In the UK, bodily parts may be donated only as a gift for
> which no payments are allowed. We believe that surrogacy
> should be informed by the same values.[4]

This leads us at once to the second difference between organ sale and
paid surrogacy, which is that while few people (and hardly any secular
bioethicists) think that there's anything wrong with free kidney donation,
many people (ranging from conservative moralists to radical feminists)
think that there's something troubling about surrogacy *in general* – i.e. not
just the commercial sort. Since this book is about the *commercial* exploitation of the human body, this general anti-surrogacy view isn't really
my concern. However, as we'll see later, it is sometimes hard to keep
anti-surrogacy arguments and anti-commercialisation arguments apart.

A third difference between organ sale and paid surrogacy is that the
latter raises what might be termed 'gender issues', whereas the former
doesn't (or, at least, doesn't obviously or necessarily). In essence, this
boils down to the fact that whereas many organ vendors are men, surrogates are all women. Hence, if (for example) surrogates are commodified

and/or exploited, this may be related in important ways to more general concerns about women being commodified and/or exploited. Again, prostitution is a good comparator, insofar as most sex-workers are female and most consumers of sexual services are male; thus, moral concerns about prostitution can be plugged into more general concerns about the exploitation and oppression of women. Moreover, it is often suggested, rightly or wrongly, that surrogacy is similar to prostitution in important ways. For example, Andrea Dworkin writes:

> Motherhood is becoming a new branch of female prostitution with the help of scientists who want access to the womb for experimentation and power ... Women can sell reproductive capacities the same way old-time prostitutes sold sexual ones but without the stigma of whoring because there is no penile intrusion. It is the womb, not the vagina, that is being bought.[5]

A fourth difference is that the moral concept of commodification (explicated in Chapter 3) figures more prominently in the debate about surrogacy than it does in the debate about organ sale. As I mentioned in Chapter 7, there certainly are commodification arguments against organ sale, but these tend to take a back seat.[6] In discussions of surrogacy, though, commodification claims loom large. One reason for this is that, as I just suggested, surrogacy raises gender issues in a way that organ sale does not. Hence, people are often keen to link the commodification of surrogates to wider patterns of social behaviour in which women and/or their bodies are commodified – in which women are seen as reproductive or sexual objects.[7] Another reason is that (unlike organ sale) paid surrogacy is often compared to slavery, or described as the buying and selling of complete human beings.

The rest of the chapter proceeds as follows. First, section 8.1 outlines contemporary regulation and practice, focussing principally on the present position in the UK and on proposed reforms. Subsequent sections critically assess a number of arguments against commercial surrogacy: that it is baby selling and commodifies children (section 8.2); that there are serious concerns about the welfare of children created through surrogacy arrangements (section 8.3); that surrogates would be exploited (section 8.4); that surrogates wouldn't validly consent (section 8.5.); and that commercial surrogacy constitutes and/or encourages the commodification of women (section 8.6). Finally, section 8.7 provides a summary of the chapter's main findings.

Surrogacy raises many deep and difficult moral problems. So even though this chapter is comparatively long, I don't claim that the list of arguments covered in it is exhaustive. For example, there is no sustained discussion of paternalistic arguments against surrogacy, or of those feminist arguments that concentrate on the subjugation rather than the commodification and exploitation of women. It does, however, seem to me that the arguments analysed in this chapter are the most interesting and popular ones.

8.1 Contemporary regulation and practice

This section starts with a general introduction and an identification of what the issues and options are. It then provides a more detailed discussion of the legal position in the UK.

First, what exactly is commercial surrogacy? By 'commercial surrogacy' I mean situations in which a woman is paid a fee (not merely compensation) for carrying and giving birth to a foetus/child and for subsequently giving up that child (and all associated parental rights) to the commissioning parent or parents. In some cases, the surrogate mother is the genetic mother because she is also the egg provider. This is termed *partial* surrogacy, or *straight* surrogacy. Partial or straight surrogacy isn't medically complex. On the contrary, surrogates can simply inseminate themselves using a syringe. In other cases, the surrogate provides only gestational services and the gametes are provided by others (often, but not necessarily, the commissioning parents). This is termed *full* or *host IVF* surrogacy.

Surrogacy's legal and regulatory status is less straightforward than that of organ sale. One reason for this is that, for surrogacy, there is a wider range of legislative options. These include (in order of 'restrictiveness'):

1 prohibiting surrogacy altogether;
2 prohibiting commercial surrogacy – by making it illegal to 'procure', and/or to 'supply', and/or to act as an intermediary (for money);
3 not criminalising commercial surrogacy, but making surrogacy contracts unenforceable;
4 allowing surrogacy contracts to be enforceable, but only within a specific statutory regulatory framework; and
5 a *laissez-faire* approach under which surrogacy contracts are governed by the general principles of contract law (and other relevant provisions).

A second (related) reason why surrogacy is less straightforward than organ sale is that its legal status varies substantially from place to place. Even within the US, for example, there is considerable variation. Some states have criminalised paid surrogacy. Others formally recognise surrogacy contracts and, with varying degrees of state involvement, allow for their implementation. Others, while not criminalising surrogacy contracts, have laws which render them unenforceable. Finally, many have no specific surrogacy legislation. Within the EU, there is also considerable diversity.

In the UK, surrogacy is governed principally by the Surrogacy Arrangements Act 1985 and the Human Fertilisation and Embryology Act 1990. According to many commentators, the former was something of a knee-jerk reaction to 'moral panic over the "Baby Cotton" affair'.[8] Freeman, for example, calls it 'an ill-considered and largely irrelevant panic measure'[9] and writes

> There are few better modern examples of morally panicked legislation than the 1985 Act (one MP said it 'rightly outlaw[ed] the hell and wickedness that exists in America – where women are exploited and handled in an undignified manner for gain').[10]

The case in question was a controversial and heavily publicised one in which Kim Cotton (dubbed 'Britain's first surrogate') was paid £6,500 to have a baby for an infertile couple in 1985.[11] Kim Cotton later became a leading figure in the UK surrogacy movement and in 1988 founded COTS (Childlessness Overcome Through Surrogacy) – a not-for-profit organisation which aimed to help British people involved in surrogacy arrangements. She announced her resignation from the chair of COTS in 1999, partly as a reaction to the Brazier Report (discussed below), which recommended a 'tightening up' of the law regarding surrogacy. Kim Cotton said at that time:

> I'm resigning as chairperson of COTS and from surrogacy altogether because I feel that we just can't battle on. Surrogacy will continue, in one form or another, and I don't think you can ever underestimate what infertile couples will do to overcome their childlessness. Instead of open and honest payment for surrogates, everything above board, it's going to actually drive it underground.[12]

The UK legislation was also very much a response to the work of the Committee of Inquiry into Human Fertilisation and Embryology which, in 1984, produced the Warnock Report (which Freeman describes as 'increasingly recognised as incoherent and philosophically muddled').[13] Warnock's recommendations were generally hostile to surrogacy, and parliament didn't go quite as far as the authors of Warnock would have liked in enacting anti-surrogacy legislation.[14] I won't spend a great deal of time here explaining or critiquing Warnock, since this has been done extensively and well elsewhere.[15] However, the arguments contained in the report will be mentioned from time to time.

To turn now to the content of the UK legislation, the Surrogacy Arrangements Act stops short of criminalising paid surrogacy *per se*. However, it does contain provisions designed to prevent the development of commercial agencies. Section 2(1) contains the main anti-agency measures:

> 2. – (1) No person shall on a commercial basis do any of the following acts in the United Kingdom, that is –
>
> (a) initiate or take part in any negotiations with a view to the making of a surrogacy arrangement,
> (b) offer or agree to negotiate the making of a surrogacy arrangement, or
> (c) compile any information with a view to its use in making, or negotiating the making of, surrogacy arrangements;
>
> and no person shall in the United Kingdom knowingly cause another to do any of those acts on a commercial basis.

These provisions are bolstered by the anti-advertising provisions in section 3, which criminalises advertising in relation to surrogacy arrangements.

Why, then, doesn't this amount to the total criminalisation of paid surrogacy? The reason is that the next subsection – 2(2) – specifically exempts (prospective) surrogates and (prospective) commissioning parents from the restrictions contained in 2(1) (though not from the anti-advertising measures contained in section 3):

> 2. – (2) A person who contravenes subsection (1) [quoted above] is guilty of an offence; but it is not a contravention of that subsection –
>
> (a) for a woman, with a view to becoming a surrogate mother herself, to do any act mentioned in that subsection or to cause such an act to be done, or
> (b) for any person, with a view to a surrogate mother carrying a child for him, to do such an act or to cause such an act to done.

The Surrogacy Arrangements Act, then, is more concerned with preventing surrogacy agencies from profiting from surrogacy arrangements than with stopping surrogates from selling their own reproductive services; although, of course, the ban on agencies and advertising makes it much more difficult for women to become paid surrogates and, for this reason, many would-be surrogates turn to the US.[16]

Further restrictions on commercial surrogacy were introduced later as part of the more wide-ranging Human Fertilisation and Embryology Act 1990. Section 36(1) of the 1990 Act amended the Surrogacy Arrangements Act by inserting an unenforceability measure, section 1A:

No surrogacy arrangement is enforceable by or against any of the persons making it.

Also of particular relevance is section 30 of the 1990 Act, which covers parental orders in favour of gamete donors:

30. – (1) The court may make an order providing for a child to be treated in law as the child of the parties to a marriage (referred to in this section as 'the husband' and 'the wife') if –

(a) the child has been carried by a woman other than the wife as the result of the placing in her of an embryo or sperm and eggs or her artificial insemination,
(b) the gametes of the husband or the wife, or both, were used to bring about the creation of the embryo, and
(c) the conditions in subsections (2) to (7) below are satisfied.

This measure was helpful in relation to many non-commercial surrogacy arrangements, because it enabled the courts to grant an order (known as a 'section 30 order' or 'parental order') conferring legal parenthood on commissioning parents without their having to go through a very lengthy adoption procedure. The conditions contained in subsections (2)–(7), though, further bolstered the law's anti-commerce stance by stopping paid surrogates from using section 30 orders:

(5) The court must be satisfied that . . . the woman who carried the child [has] freely, and with full understanding of what is involved, agreed unconditionally to the making of the order

and:

(7) The court must be satisfied that no money or other benefit (other than expenses reasonably incurred) has been given or received by the husband or the wife for or in consideration of–

(a) the making of the order,
(b) any agreement required by subsection (5) above,
(c) the handing over of the child to the husband and the wife, or
(d) the making of any arrangement with a view to the making of the order, unless authorised by the court.

So while not criminalising paid surrogates or commissioning parents, conditions (5) and (7) (above) strongly discourage commercial surrogacy (especially when allied with the amendment to the 1985 Act).

More recently, a committee chaired by Professor Margaret Brazier, an academic lawyer based at the University of Manchester, has reviewed UK surrogacy legislation. In October 1998, this committee produced *Surrogacy: A Review for Health Ministers of Current Arrangements for Payments and Regulation* (henceforth Brazier). In some respects, the moral climate in which Brazier was conducted was reminiscent of 1985 in that there was a certain amount of moral panic in the air. Public alarm centred around a number of high-profile surrogacy cases, cases which gave the impression (a) that commercial surrogacy was widespread, (b) that the 'expenses reasonably incurred' parts of the legislation were being abused, and (c) that a high proportion of surrogacy arrangements were traumatic and problematic. Brazier cites various stories that appeared in the news media around that time.[17] One concerned the director of an American commercial surrogacy agency who visited Britain in order to recruit commissioning couples; these couples would be charged approximately £30,000 each. In another report, a surrogacy arrangement led to the birth of triplets, who were handed over to the commissioning couple. A third was about an American case in which a couple arranged for a surrogate to gestate their dead daughter's fertilised eggs so that they could become grandparents. And, fourth, there were UK cases in which mothers gestated foetuses for their daughters, and in which daughters gestated foetuses for their mothers.[18]

The Brazier team was given three main tasks by Health Ministers. First, 'to consider whether payments, including expenses, should continue to be made to surrogate mothers'. Second, to investigate the feasibility and desirability of setting up a dedicated 'recognised body' to regulate surrogacy. And third, to propose changes (if deemed necessary) to the Surrogacy Arrangements Act 1985 and/or the Human Fertilisation and Embryology Act 1990. Because my main concern is commercialisation, I'll concentrate just on the first of these, the payments issue (although, clearly, the team's views on payment feed into what it had to say about legislative reform).

Brazier is critical of the state of UK law in the late 1990s, describing the situation as a 'policy vacuum within which surrogacy has developed in a haphazard fashion'.[19] On the question of payment, though, the report is somewhat conservative, endorsing the kind of anti-commerce line found in Warnock and enshrined in the 1985 and 1990 Acts and, in essence, recommending no more than a 'tightening up' of existing regulations. Though to be fair to the committee, their terms of reference

specifically excluded consideration of:

(i) commercialisation i.e. that third parties should be able to profit from surrogacy arrangements, and

(ii) enforceability of contracts i.e. whether the surrogate mother should be bound by a contractual arrangement to give up her child, or whether the commissioning couple should be similarly bound to make the agreed payment.[20]

So, while the committee clearly did in fact have anti-commerce views, it wasn't permitted to take a radically pro-commerce line, even if it had wanted to.

To turn now to its conclusions, the relevant part of the summary of recommendations reads:

3 – The basis on which expenses will be met should be established before any attempt is made to create a surrogate pregnancy, with a requirement for documentary evidence of expenses incurred in association with the surrogacy arrangement to be produced by the surrogate mother.

4 – Legislation should define expenses in broad terms of principle and empower Ministers to issue directions on what constitutes reasonable expenses and the methods by which expenses shall be proven.

In the body of the report, the committee recommends restricting allowable expenses to a specified range of items (maternity clothing, counselling fees, healthy food, legal fees, domestic help, life and disability insurance, travel to and from hospital/clinic, medical expenses, telephone and postal expenses, ovulation and pregnancy tests, overnight accommodation, insemination and IVF costs, child care to attend hospital/clinic, medicines and vitamins).[21] It also recommends disallowing payments for 'potential' loss of earnings and allowing instead only reimbursement for 'actual' loss of earnings (supported by 'documentary proof', and with an expectation that such losses will be 'minimal').

Brazier identifies three arguments against payment:

(1) Payments create a danger that women will give a less than free and fully informed consent to act as a surrogate. (2) Payments risk the commodification of the child to be born. (3) Payments contravene the social norms of our society that, just as bodily parts cannot be sold, nor can such intimate services.[22]

The report also speaks favourably of the exploitation argument against commercial surrogacy, although this is usually linked to the 'free and fully informed consent' issue covered in (1). We'll be taking a critical look at arguments (1) and (2) shortly. Argument (3), however, doesn't merit any attention, since it's not so much an ethical argument as an appeal to public opinion (and to 'norms' which, even if widely accepted, may not be justifiable).

8.2 Is commercial surrogacy baby selling?

> [A] surrogacy agreement is degrading to the child who is to be the outcome of it, since, for all practical purposes, the child will have been bought for money.[23]

> I see no problem with someone collecting – the general going rate appears to be $10,000, getting paid for your pain and suffering, shall we say. I haven't carried a child myself, but from what I've seen, it's a tough program . . . there's nothing wrong with getting paid for nine months of what I understand to be a lot of misery and a lot of bad days . . . they are not selling a baby, they are selling, again, the pain and suffering, the discomfort, that which goes with carrying a child to term.[24]

This chapter is provocatively entitled 'Babies for sale?'. For reasons which we'll look at shortly, though, it's not clear that paid surrogacy really is the selling of a baby. Many people, however, do identify commercial surrogacy with baby selling and, understandably, view this identification as a strong reason to prohibit it.[25] Let's take for granted that these objectors are right to think that baby selling is immoral and ought to be prohibited. With this assumption in place, everything then depends on the question: are paid surrogates baby sellers? Or, to put it another way, *what* exactly do paid surrogates sell: babies, gestational services, or something else?[26]

Like Warnock (quoted at the start of this section), Brazier takes the baby selling argument seriously, as the following passages indicate:

> 4.34 – It was argued by a number of the respondents to our questionnaire that surrogacy need not be equated with 'baby-selling', because any fee paid to the surrogate can be regarded as payment for the pregnancy, i.e. payment for her services, not the baby. We find it difficult to see how this distinction can be maintained, especially because any fully commercial transaction of this kind should be subject to the normal laws of contract. It is unimaginable that a commissioning couple should enter into a contract that required simply that the surrogate become pregnant and give birth. The contract would have to contain a requirement that in return for the fee the child was handed over to those contracting the pregnancy, with penalties for failure to fulfil this aspect of the agreement.

4.35 – It is possible to imagine a new legislative framework, which permitted payment of a fee to the surrogate, whilst maintaining her right to retain the child, but any such legislation would rationally have to contain provision for the contracting couple to obtain redress in the event that the child was not handed over. These legal considerations lead us to the conclusion that any financial arrangement that involves remuneration rather than simply expenses has to be regarded as a form of child purchase.

5.11 – Although a theoretical distinction can be made between payment for the purchase of a child and payment for a potentially risky, time-consuming and uncomfortable service, in practice it is difficult to separate the two, and it remains the case that payment other than for genuine expenses constitutes a financial benefit for the surrogate mother.

The wording of Brazier is, on the whole, slightly more cautious than that of Warnock. Nonetheless, the underlying idea remains the same: commercial surrogacy is 'a form of child purchase', since the distinction between baby selling and gestational services 'cannot be maintained' and 'in practice it is difficult to separate the two'. Quite why the distinction 'cannot be maintained' isn't clear. However, this needn't bother us, since Brazier contains an independent argument for the view that surrogacy is baby selling. This argument appeals to the fact that the surrogacy contract must 'contain a requirement that in return for the fee the child [is] handed over to those contracting the pregnancy'. So even if, it is argued, many parts of the surrogacy contract can be viewed as the sale of gestational services, surrogacy contracts must nonetheless contain 'hand over the baby' clauses. And these clauses amount to baby selling for the simple reason that, in order to be paid, the surrogate must give her baby to the commissioning couple. In others words, a baby is surrendered for money. As Kornegay suggests, this line of argument is both 'typical' and 'seductive'.[27] Moreover, it can be made even more attractive if we remind ourselves that normally

> The surrogate receives the bulk of the payment only if and when she hands a live baby over to the couple. She receives comparatively little money in the case of a miscarriage or stillbirth. Consequently, she is *primarily or exclusively* selling a baby, not child-rearing services.[28]

The 'hand over the baby' clause, then, is not only an essential part of the surrogacy contract, but the most important and most lucrative part. So baby selling isn't just a necessary part of the surrogacy arrangement: it is its major part.

These attractions notwithstanding, the baby selling argument against commercial surrogacy is flawed in a number of ways. Let's start by thinking more carefully about the 'hand over the baby' clause. The claim in Brazier was, roughly, that paid surrogacy is baby selling because if the surrogate doesn't hand over the baby then she won't be paid. This argument seems to rest on the following general principle: *if the contract between A and B includes the condition that B won't pay A unless A hands over x to B, then A is selling x to B*. This principle, however, is false. There are numerous counter-examples. One kind of case concerns repairs carried out on machines. I take my car to the garage. They repair it. I refuse to pay unless they hand back my vehicle. Are they selling me my car? No! Another example is the services of (private-sector) child-minders, midwives, and schoolteachers. For each of these occupational groups, parents would be perfectly within their rights to withhold payment if their children weren't handed over after the service had been delivered. But are they buying (back) their children? Clearly not!

At this point, defenders of the baby selling argument are likely to raise the following objection. The cases that I've come up with (for example, car repairs and schoolteaching) are ones in which B *already owns* the object in question. B then grants A *temporary custody* of it so that a service can be delivered, with the expectation that A will *return* it (as opposed to surrendering it for the first time) at an agreed time. But (the objection goes) surrogacy is not like this, because the surrogate is asked to give up something which is hers, and which is 'new'. The problem with this move, though, is that it *begs the question*, i.e. it assumes the very thing that's at issue. This is because what's assumed is that the surrogate owns the baby. Now, if we make that assumption, then the conclusion that giving it up would amount to selling is hard to resist. But we can't (without begging the question) make that assumption. For precisely what defenders of the gestational services model of surrogacy believe is that the commissioning parents (morally if not legally) *already* own the baby (at least insofar as anybody owns it at all) since the surrogate was just a 'facilitator who provided a service'.[29] On this view, the surrogate's role (especially in host IVF surrogacy, where the commissioning parents are also the genetic parents) is structurally just like that of the child-minder or schoolteacher. She is given an embryo to look after and grow and is paid for looking after it and growing it. The surrogate will, of course, be penalised if she doesn't hand over the baby at an agreed time. But in this respect, she's no different from the schoolteacher who might be penalised for not handing over the schoolchild at the end of the school day. This fact, though, doesn't make the surrogate a baby seller. The surrogate is no more a baby seller than the schoolteacher is a child seller

Kornegay raises another similar objection to the baby selling argument. She draws our attention to the fact that some service delivery contracts have success clauses, while others don't. For example, a surgeon may expect money for (non-negligently) performing an operation, *regardless of whether or not it is a success*, and universities expect fees for teaching their students, *even if the students fail*. These are contracts without success clauses. What's paid for is a service, *with or without the desired outcome*. However, not all contracts are like this:

> It does not follow from the fact that an assassin may perform the same bodily movements in two cases – one in which the victim dies and s/he is paid and the other in which the victim is saved by a passing ambulance and s/he is unpaid – that the assassin is not being paid for services in the former case, but for a corpse. The contract is not for performing bodily movements merely, but *for performing bodily movements which result in the victim's death.*[30]

Some contracts, then, are for *services that deliver the desired outcome*. Contracts with domestic service providers are sometimes like this. If my plumber says that she will install an electric shower for $250, I expect to pay her only when the shower is in place and functioning correctly. 'No win, no fee' arrangements with lawyers are another example; here, I am paying for a service, but I only pay for the service if it brings success. The distinction between the two types of contract – those with success clauses and those without – is chiefly about the distribution of risk between the parties. When there's a success clause, the service provider bears the risk. She won't be paid if something goes wrong and the desired outcome isn't achieved. But when there's no success clause, the service purchaser bears the risk. She will still have to pay, even if there is no successful outcome (as long as the provider has acted within the terms of the contract). To turn now to surrogacy contracts, these (according to Kornegay) can be thought of as the buying of a service which delivers the desired outcome, as contracts with success clauses:

> The reproductive services in question are not *mere* gestation and childbirth . . . Rather, they are *gestation and childbirth that result in . . . having a baby to rear.*[31]

Kornegay's argument seems compelling. The fact that surrogacy arrangements require the surrogate to hand over a live baby does *not* mean that surrogacy is baby selling. This is because we can think of surrogacy contracts instead as service contracts with success clauses.

Let's look, finally, at a different set of objections to the baby selling argument. Each of these tries to show that surrogacy isn't baby selling, not by appealing to the product/service distinction that we've just been discussing, but by pointing to some other relevant feature of the transaction. The main ones are:

1 the child isn't owned by anyone, and so can't literally be sold by or to anyone;[32]
2 the child isn't sold on the open market to the highest bidder but is merely transferred to its genetic parent(s);
3 the commissioning parents' *prima facie* ownership claim (grounded in genetics and/or intentions) is typically at least as strong as the surrogate's (grounded in gestation – or, for partial surrogacy, in gestation and genetics).

Many critics of commercial surrogacy – such as Elizabeth Anderson, quoted below – explicitly deny (1):

> Commercial surrogacy ... requires us to understand parental rights no longer as trusts but as things more like property rights – that is, rights of use and disposal over the things owned.[33]

Anderson thinks that commercial surrogacy involves treating parental rights as if they were fully transferable property rights. However, this is implausible, as McLachlan and Swales explain:

> Parental rights ... are not property rights. Babies are not property and should not (and cannot) be treated in all respects like property. C.S.M. [commercial surrogacy] does not imply that they are property nor that they will necessarily be treated as if they were. Parents are not legally entitled to treat and dispose of their children in the ways ... in which they are entitled to treat and dispose of those things which they legally own ... parents do not own their children, however they acquire them.[34]

So even if we grant that the surrogate sells something in addition to her gestational services, what she sells is (at most) a limited bundle of parental rights, not the baby itself. This is chiefly because children aren't owned by their parents in any very substantial sense of 'own'. Parental rights are limited in numerous ways. For example, parents aren't allowed to abuse their children physically, are required to educate their children, and (importantly) aren't allowed simply to sell their parental rights to the highest bidder, since adoption procedures are heavily regulated. Given this, it would be misleading to claim that parents own their children (or that anyone owns children) and similarly misleading to claim that surrogates sell 'their' babies.

The second difference between surrogacy and baby selling, (2), is that the child isn't sold on the open market to the highest bidder but is instead transferred (for money) to its genetic parent(s). This fact on its own isn't enough to show that the surrogate doesn't sell the baby to its genetic parents. But it does suggest an important difference between, on the one hand, surrogacy arrangements and, on the other, cases in which a woman bears a child and then simply auctions it to the highest bidder. In the latter case, we are looking at a more or less unfettered commercial market in babies. The highest bidder gets the baby. But in surrogacy arrangements, the degree to which the baby is treated as a commodity is much less – not least because of the genetic relationship between the commissioning parents and the baby. So, with this in mind, calling surrogacy baby selling is misleading, because it suggests (wrongly) that surrogacy is exactly like the kind of unfettered market in babies just described.

Another reason for resisting the baby selling model, (3), is the fact that (particularly in full surrogacy) the commissioning parents arguably have an ownership claim (more plausibly, a parental rights claim) which is at least as strong as the surrogate's. The surrogate, admittedly, has gestation on her side. She has carried the foetus for nine months or so, has suffered perhaps during that period, and may even have 'bonded' with the foetus/baby. But against this, we must concede that the commissioning father's parental rights claim is as strong as that of *any* (merely) biological father, since he is the genetic father. And, in full surrogacy, his paternal rights claim is bolstered by a maternal rights claim from the 'commissioning mother', who is as genetically connected to the baby as he is. Furthermore, in all (full) surrogacy cases, the commissioners can argue that the surrogate has been simply looking after and growing what all along belonged to them. All of these claims are contentious and, as Harris notes, the 'gestation versus genetics' dispute is intractable:

> The claims 'I'm your mother, you grew from my egg and carry my genetic make-up within you' and 'I'm your mother because I carried you in my womb, nurtured and gave birth to you' seem equally strong ... and arguments that one is better or more authentic than the other seem well calculated to be both sterile and insoluble.[35]

But at least we can conclude that it is *very far from obvious* that the surrogate's handing over the baby for money is baby selling. This in itself is enough to render the baby selling argument weak, since (in order to justify legal prohibition) its proponents must *demonstrate* that commercial surrogacy *really is* baby selling. Neither merely *asserting* that it is baby selling nor demonstrating that it is *possibly* baby selling is sufficient.

Conclusion

Many of commercial surrogacy's opponents claim that it is not (merely) the provision of a gestational service, but baby selling. The main argument offered is that surrogacy is baby selling because the contract must 'contain a requirement that in return for the fee the child [is] handed over to those contracting the pregnancy'. This argument was found wanting on a number of counts. First, it depends for its validity on a general principle which is demonstrably false: that *if the contract between A and B includes the condition that B won't pay A unless A hands over x to B, then A is selling x to B*. Second, the argument overlooks the fact that some service delivery contracts have success clauses, while others don't. Hence, surrogacy arrangements could be 'pure' service delivery contracts (of the former kind) *even if* they required the production and delivery of a healthy baby to the commissioning couple. Finally, we looked at a number of additional grounds for *not* thinking of surrogacy as baby selling. These include the argument that babies aren't (legally) owned by anyone and hence can't be bought or sold; the fact that surrogacy arrangements don't involve simply giving the child to the highest bidder and are therefore importantly different from a 'free' market in which babies are bought and sold like commodities; and the argument that surrogacy isn't baby selling because the commissioning parents already own the baby. I conclude therefore that the arguments for regarding paid surrogacy as baby selling are weak and, moreover, that there are some independent reasons for not viewing it as baby selling.

8.3 The welfare of the child

In this chapter, two 'child-centred' objections to commercial surrogacy are considered. The first, which we've just discussed, is that commercial surrogacy is baby selling and wrongfully commodifies children. The second, examined in this section, concerns the welfare of children produced by surrogacy arrangements. Again, Brazier is a good place to start, since the report takes seriously child welfare arguments against paid surrogacy and for state regulation:

> 4.16 – there is clear potential of risk to the welfare of [surrogates'] children. Research to identify and quantify that risk is needed urgently. The paramount importance of the welfare of the child is such that we believe that in making judgments about the regulation of surrogacy, the state must act on the precautionary principle. Society has a duty to minimise any such potential risk.
>
> 4.27 – A second reason for restricting . . . surrogacy is the moral imperative to make the welfare of the child our prime concern.

Concern for children's welfare is indisputably laudable. That alone, though, doesn't take us very far, and we're still faced with two tough questions. First (the empirical question), is there any reason to be especially worried about the well-being of children brought into the world through commercial surrogacy arrangements? Is there reason to believe that the lives of children born of commercial surrogacy arrangements will be less happy than those of 'normal' children? Second (the philosophical question), if it turned out that the lives of children born of commercial surrogacy arrangements really were less happy than those of 'normal' children, would this be a reason to restrict commercial surrogacy?[36]

Taking the empirical question first, I suspect that the real answer is a rather disappointing 'nobody knows'.[37] Certainly, the authors of Brazier are keen to bemoan the lack of evidence:

> we found substantial difficulty in obtaining hard evidence about the incidence, nature and outcomes of surrogacy arrangements. We believe that a high priority must be accorded to measures which will help to ensure that such information, including information about the welfare of children born as a result of surrogacy arrangements, is more readily available in the future.[38]

This lack of 'hard' evidence notwithstanding, it's worth briefly rehearsing the arguments for and against the claim that children brought into the world by commercial surrogacy arrangements might somehow be damaged (or, at least, be less well off than other children). The main argument *for* this view is that children born of surrogates may be psychologically harmed. This might happen when they find out that they've been 'sold' by their gestational mothers – a concern which is (even) stronger in the case of partial surrogacy because of the additional genetic link between the child and the surrogate. Elizabeth Anderson goes as far as to ask:

> Would it be any wonder if a child born of a surrogacy arrangement feared resale?[39]

While Munroe claims:

> The kind of problems that the surrogate child may face in forming a coherent sense of self-conception are striking and in need of more serious analysis.[40]

Psychological damage, Brazier suggests, may also be caused if the surrogate refuses to give up the baby. For then the child could be upset about being kept from one or both of its genetic parents:

3.38 – The welfare of the child, who may in infancy be the subject of protracted legal proceedings, and later come to know of the disputed custody and separation from his or her genetic parent(s), must be a matter of concern.

Against this, advocates of the 'pro'-surrogacy position often point out that surrogates' children are unlikely to have worse lives than children who are adopted. Richard Posner, for example, says that the children of surrogate mothers are likely (at worst) to see themselves as (like) adopted children and claims that

> the best evidence seems to be that, on average, adopted children are no more unhappy or unstable than natural children.[41]

Views vary on this, however, and Brazier claims that

> 4.9 – it is important to note that adopted children do tend to show a greater incidence of emotional and behavioural problems in comparison with their non-adopted counterparts.

There are some 'common-sense' arguments for thinking that surrogates' children would fare at least as well as adoptees. The main one is just that surrogacy is structurally very much like adoption insofar as it involves a child's gestational mother giving it to other people who will become its social parents. Indeed, there's some reason to believe that surrogacy is *less* bad than adoption in certain respects. Most obviously, in full surrogacy, the child is (re)united with one or both of its genetic parents – a benefit (if it is a benefit) not afforded to adoptees. Moreover, surrogacy arrangements clearly involve the *intentional* creation of a child, something which is not true of many adoptees, or of many other children who are 'accidents' (for example, those brought into existence by contraceptive failure or neglect). Children born of surrogacy therefore have reason to feel above averagely 'wanted', at least by the commissioning parents. So the answer to our empirical question – *do children born of commercial surrogacy arrangements have below averagely happy lives?* – is that we don't really know for sure. But, that said, there are some reasons for supposing that surrogates' children will fare no worse than adopted children (most of whom undoubtedly have lives worth living).

Let's turn now to the philosophical question: if it were established that most children born of commercial surrogacy arrangements are below averagely happy, would this justify banning or discouraging the practice?[42] We need to start by making a general distinction between two kinds of policy. First, there are 'make people happier' policies; these aim to make actual (present or future) people happier than they otherwise would be. Second, there are 'prevent unhappy people' policies, which aim to prevent unhappy people from coming into existence. 'Make people happier' policies are ubiquitous (though how many of them work is an open question). 'Prevent unhappy people' policies, on the other hand, are much rarer and often highly controversial because they are perceived to be 'eugenic'. An example of a 'prevent unhappy people' policy would be permitting and/or encouraging the killing of foetuses with severe disabilities.[43]

Within this category ('prevent unhappy people' policies) a further distinction can be drawn. First, there are policies that aim to prevent the creation of A so that B (who will be more happy than A would have been) can be created instead (B, in a manner of speaking, takes A's place). Singer and Kuhse provide what seems to be a good example of this way of thinking:

> If the test shows that the foetus does have Down's syndrome, the woman is able to have an abortion. The same happens with women who are shown to be carriers of the gene for haemophilia: the foetus can be checked to see if it has the disease. If it does, the woman can have an abortion, and then try again, so that she can have a normal baby. Why do we regard this as a reasonable thing to do, even when the handicap is one like haemophilia, which is quite compatible with a worthwhile life? . . . [Because] *we are offsetting the loss of one possible life against the creation of another life with better prospects.*[44]

Second, there are policies that simply aim to prevent the creation of A – the thought being that, if A were to be born, she'd have a not merely low, but *negative* quality of life, one such that she'd be 'better off dead' and/or 'better off not having been born'. As Glover puts it,

> some kinds of life are perhaps worse than not being alive at all . . . if it makes sense for people to see death as in their interests, there seems a parallel possibility of parents or doctors thinking that not being born may be in the interests of a potential child.[45]

Many of the regulations governing surrogacy are of the 'make people happier' kind. The idea (roughly) is – given that surrogates will give birth to (say) 100 babies per year, we should aim to make these 100 children as happy as we can. Other (actual or possible) surrogacy legislation, though, isn't about making surrogates' children happier but is, rather, about reducing the number of children born to surrogates – either directly, through prohibition, or indirectly, through measures which are calculated to discourage. Such legislation (which would include most of the anti-commercialisation provisions outlined earlier in this chapter) clearly falls into the 'prevent unhappy people' category. And this appears to be what the authors of Brazier have in mind when they talk of 'restricting' surrogacy because of 'the moral imperative to make the welfare of the child our prime concern'. For *restricting* surrogacy can only mean one thing here: stopping (some) women from acting as surrogates and thereby stopping certain potential people from coming into existence.

We should now ask: can child-welfare considerations justify such restrictions? What's proposed is a 'prevent unhappy people' policy. As we've seen, this could be defended in one (or both) of two ways. The first justification is that it leads to the 'replacement' of less happy future people with more happy ones. The second is that it prevents misery and suffering by stopping the births of people with 'negative quality lives' – people who (if alive) would (for their own sakes) be 'better off dead'.

Let's take the second (putative) justification first. This is extremely unlikely to work, even if surrogates' children face very severe psychological problems (for example, because they see themselves as having been 'sold'), since

> To give the 'highest priority to the welfare of the child to be born' is always to let that child come into existence, unless existence overall will be a burden rather than a benefit. Wherever that child's life, despite any predictable sub-optimality's [*sic*], will be thoroughly worth living, then it cannot be that child's interests which justify any decisions or regulations which would deny it opportunities for existence.[46]

In the absence of other unconnected problems (for example, severe painful disability) the chances of surrogates' children having *negative*-quality lives are remote. Are we *really* expected to believe that these children will live lives that are 'worse than not being alive at all', which is what *negative* quality of life means?[47] I suspect not and, if we are, then this is simply a preposterous expectation. Interestingly, Alastair Campbell (one of the Brazier team) accepts this point, which suggests that the report's authors had some other justification in mind:

> It need not be denied that most people, whatever the problems they face, are happier to be alive than never to have experienced the richness of existence. Thus *the failure to regulate need not mean that those who are born in an unregulated environment would be better dead.*[48]

Also relevant here are thoughts about how our attitudes to surrogates' children might relate to our attitudes to disabled children. Laura Purdy writes:

> those who oppose surrogacy . . . [often] also oppose attempts to reduce the number of handicapped babies born. In the latter context, it is argued that despite their problems handicapped persons are often glad to be alive. Hence it would be paternalistic to attempt to prevent their birth. Why do we not hear the same argument here?[49]

Purdy's objection isn't quite decisive, because paid surrogacy's opponents could, if they wanted to, render their positions consistent by simply dropping their opposition to prenatal screening and selective termination. She nonetheless usefully reminds us that in the debate about prenatal screening, selective termination, 'eugenics', and similar, the thought that even people with severe and painful disabilities are 'glad to be alive' is taken seriously. If we allow (as we probably should) that these people, faced with extraordinarily unfavourable circumstances, have lives worth living, then surely we must also allow that most children born of surrogacy arrangements will have lives worth living too. Similarly, if we grant that it would be wrongfully 'eugenic' to legislate so as to prevent people with severe and painful congenital disabilities from coming into existence, then surely we must say the same about children born through surrogacy arrangements.

This means that proponents of restrictive regulation are forced to fall back on the first (putative) justification: commercial surrogacy should be discouraged because official dissuasion will lead to the children who would otherwise have been born through such arrangements being 'replaced' by a roughly equal number of other 'happier' children (children who would not have existed at all if commercial surrogacy had been allowed). This attempt to defend restrictions on surrogacy, though, is flawed in two ways. First, the empirical assumptions made are implausible: in particular, it is not clear that 'replacement' would in fact occur. Second, there are general theoretical reasons for not allowing *any* arguments of this sort ('replacement arguments') to influence surrogacy policy, *even if* their empirical premises are true.

To take the first point first, most commissioning couples turn to surrogacy only because of serious infertility problems and, in most cases, if they don't have a child using surrogacy then they won't have a child at all: i.e. there will be no 'replacement'. For example, in the UK, roughly 50 per cent of commissioning mothers don't have uteruses, and many others have clinical indications such as repeated IVF failure (almost 30 per cent) or repeated miscarriage (almost 10 per cent).[50] For these women, given the present state of reproductive technology, surrogacy is the only option.

In response to this, it might be argued that anti-commercialisation regulation will simply drive these women away from commercial arrangements and towards non-commercial ones. However, given the powerful incentive of money, it seems likely that anti-commercialisation regulations will result in there being fewer surrogates available than there otherwise would be. Hence, fewer children will be born, unless there are already more than enough altruistic surrogates. But if this is so then regulation seems unnecessary because, other things being equal, commissioning couples will always prefer a free service to one which costs thousands of pounds.

It appears, then, that, on empirical grounds, the 'replacement' argument for the anti-commercialisation policy fails. Before we move onto the argument's more general or theoretical problems, though, it's worth mentioning that this style of argument *may* work specifically against what's sometimes termed *convenience surrogacy*: i.e. cases in which the commissioning couple use a surrogate not because of infertility, but just because the woman prefers not to carry her own foetus (for example, because of career considerations). Convenience surrogacy is commonly thought to be the morally worst kind, with Warnock going as far as to call it 'totally ethically unacceptable'.[51] The precise reasons for this widespread condemnation are far from clear, but the 'replacement' argument may provide one rationale. For it could plausibly be argued that, in many cases of convenience surrogacy, if the commissioning mother didn't employ a surrogate, she'd gestate the foetus herself. (This won't be true in *all* cases, because some women may so loathe the idea of pregnancy that they'd only be willing to have a child if a surrogate carried it.) If this is combined with the thought that the child would be happier if carried by its genetic mother rather than by a surrogate, then we have a *prima facie* 'replacement' justification for discouraging convenience surrogacy.

Let's look now at the general theoretical reasons for not allowing 'replacement arguments' to influence surrogacy policy (even when their empirical premises are true). The main one of these is that if arguments of this type are acceptable, then there seems no reason to restrict their application to particular practices like surrogacy. There are lots of reproductive interventions that may lead to the 'replacement' of one group of potential persons with another 'happier' group. Accepted (though controversial) examples include the use of prenatal screening (accompanied by selective termination) and the use of pre-implantation genetic diagnosis (accompanied by selective implantation) so that disabled potential persons can be 'replaced' by non-disabled ones. Arguably, these practices can be justified by using a 'replacement argument'.[52] But, once we start thinking in this way, it is hard to limit the scope of such arguments. This is because, as Glover suggests,

If someone with a handicap is conceived instead of a normal person, things turn out less well than they might have done. It would have been better if the normal person had been conceived. But things of this sort can be said about almost any of us. If my own conception was an alternative to the conception of someone just like me except more intelligent, or more athletic or more musical, it would have been better if that person had been conceived.[53]

This has troubling implications for commercial surrogacy. The main one is that *if* a 'replacement argument' is deemed sufficient to justify the prohibition of commercial surrogacy then (other things being equal) parallel arguments should, for reasons of consistency, be deemed sufficient to justify (amongst other things) making compulsory the use of prenatal screening or pre-implantation genetic diagnosis so as to reduce the amount of disability in the world, and making women impregnate themselves with enhanced donor sperm rather than the 'inferior' sperm of their partners. All of these interventions (including the prohibition of commercial surrogacy) are similarly structured in that they restrict people's procreative autonomy on the grounds that it would be better if a 'happier' group of future persons came into existence than a 'less happy' group. (It may admittedly be argued that they differ in the *extent* to which they curb procreative autonomy.) None of this counts decisively against the restrictive regulation of commercial surrogacy, since one might argue either (a) that all of these restrictions of procreative autonomy are justified, or (b) that there are differences between the practices which I haven't had space to consider here (which may well be true). However, we have at least raised a problem for 'replacement arguments' and, hence, for those who want to use them to justify the restrictive regulation of surrogacy.

It will be evident by now that the child-welfare arguments for restricting surrogacy are weak, both empirically and philosophically. As Brazier admits, there's very little hard evidence about the welfare of surrogates' children. And, in any case, the preceding few pages have shown that – even if there were such evidence – it wouldn't be sufficient to justify restrictive legislation, unless (astonishingly) it could be shown that many surrogates' children don't even have lives worth living. That is, in brief, the conclusion of this section. I would, however, like to add a postscript concerning a further passage from Brazier, in which its authors dismiss arguments like the ones I've been propounding here. The report states:

4.29 – we do not have to show certainty of major harm to potential children before we are justified [through] . . . legislative restriction, in avoiding conceptions on grounds of risk to the welfare of the child. It is sufficient to show that, if such lives are brought into being, they could be significantly compromised physically or emotionally. By not bringing them into being we do no harm to a child, since none exists. This is not to say that people should aim for perfection in their progeny, or that the state should institute draconian measures to narrow people's procreative choices.

There are a number of interesting claims here. Perhaps the most important is that all that needs to be shown in order to justify prohibiting a particular class of pregnancies is that the children created could be 'significantly compromised physically or emotionally'. It's not clear what exactly 'significantly compromised' means. However, I presume that it doesn't mean anything as narrow as having a negative quality of life (a 'life not worth living') and that children with positive but nonetheless substantially below average quality lives would count as 'significantly compromised'. (And, as we've seen, if it does mean having a 'life not worth living', then it's unlikely to apply to most surrogates' children.) Thus, it seems that the report's authors believe that the fact that a certain class of (potential) children, if born, will have substantially below average quality lives is a sufficient reason to prohibit (or otherwise officially discourage) the relevant pregnancies. This principle is astonishingly illiberal; we might even go as far as to say eugenic, if we think about how it would apply to congenital disabilities, or to the children of the poor, or to the children of alcoholics or other addicts, to name just a few examples. Moreover, the principle becomes even more illiberal and wide-ranging once we factor in its evidential element, which says that the mere fact that a child COULD be 'significantly compromised' is enough to justify preventing its existence. So, while I think that Brazier's authors are probably right to think that this principle is an indispensable premise in their child-welfare argument, they are wrong to subscribe to the principle (and hence to the argument) because of its outrageous implications elsewhere. If such a principle were implemented, we'd be living in something of a procreative police state – one in which not just those who would, if born, have thoroughly miserable lives, but also those who would have 'mediocre' or 'slightly bad' lives were stopped from coming into existence.

It's rather hard to fathom what's going on in the authors' minds here and to tell what reason they might have for endorsing such an oppressive principle (except perhaps that it can be used to shore up their intuitive hostility to surrogacy – especially the commercial variety). The only (putative) reason offered in Brazier is the following:

4.28 – Unless we have a belief in the pre-existence of the soul, there is no person who suffers from not being alive. A decision not to proceed with a conception because of particular circumstances – or the prevention of achieving conception because of restrictive legislation or lack of adequate resources for infertility treatment – certainly causes unhappiness and a sense of loss to the would-be *parents*. But there is no child who suffers this loss or to whom we or the parents have moral obligations.

Alastair Campbell makes a similar point:

> there is no such thing as the harm of non-existence . . . no one is denied anything if there is no person who exists – there is no abandoned pre-existing soul. It follows that regulation which might prevent some surrogacy arrangements and . . . resulted in no birth from the gametes of one or both of these parents, has caused no harm to any child. (It has of course caused harm to the parents, but this is not denied.) Thus no child is harmed by such regulation.[54]

What do these statements mean? Lurking behind them is, I suspect, an argument something like the following. Legislators are sometimes faced with a choice. Either they can enact restrictive laws and thereby prevent certain pregnancies from occurring, or they can opt for a more permissive system and allow those pregnancies to take place. If they go for the first option, no child is harmed because 'there is no person who suffers from not being alive' – although such policies may, it's conceded, harm prospective parents. But if they go for the second option (it's claimed) there may be children who suffer – for example, because they are psychologically scarred when they find out that they were 'sold'. Therefore, if the interests of the child are paramount, legislators should go for the restrictive option, because this minimises (by reducing to zero) the chances of any child being harmed.

This argument is deeply flawed in two closely related ways. First, there is a suggestion that we can use the fact that when we prevent a birth 'there is no person who suffers from not being alive' to justify restrictive birth-preventing legislation. But clearly this can't be right. If this style of reasoning were adopted it would lead to (what I earlier termed) a procreative police state. For such a principle could be used to justify preventing *any* birth, because (as Campbell himself points out) 'there is no such thing as the harm of non-existence'. In other words, if harmlessness (to prospective children) is what justifies the legislation, and given that preventing births is always harmless (to prospective children), preventing any birth whatsoever would be justified.

Second, there is a *precautionary principle* at work in the argument: if the interests of the child are paramount, legislators should go for the restrictive option, because this minimises (by reducing to zero) the chances of any child being harmed. This goes hand in hand with what we might term an *asymmetry principle*: one which says that you *can't* harm someone by preventing her from coming into existence, but that you *can* harm someone by bringing her into existence (or by allowing her to be brought into existence). However, if we combine these two principles with the view that minimising harm to future children is paramount (which appears to be the Brazier view), we have an argument for the discontinuation of the species. We should favour non-conception to conception *in every case* because this will minimise (by eliminating) harm. This position (not one which we should accept) is rather like a crude version of negative utilitarianism, which says that 'minimise pain' is the only basic moral principle. Laudable though minimising pain is, negative utilitarianism is flawed because the best way of minimising pain is (painlessly) to put an end to all conscious life.

8.4 Exploitation

Like organ sale, paid surrogacy is repeatedly criticised for being exploitative:

> Even in compelling medical circumstances the danger of exploitation of one human being by another appears to the majority of us to far outweigh the potential benefits, in almost every case. That people should treat others as a means to their own ends, however desirable the consequences, must always be liable to moral objection. Such treatment of one person by another becomes positively exploitative when financial interests are involved. It is therefore with the commercial exploitation of surrogacy that we have been primarily . . . concerned.[55]

Warnock's authors (quoted above) make a number of errors here. First, treating people as means isn't, in and of itself, exploitative or objectionable. Second, the introduction of payment doesn't obviously or necessarily make an activity any more exploitative than it would be if it were done for free. Indeed, sometimes payment reduces the level of exploitation. Third, one might question the wisdom of using the expression 'commercial exploitation' in this context, as this tends to obscure the distinction between the moral senses of exploitation and its non-moral sense.

Brazier does much better than Warnock on the issue of exploitation, and its authors are to be commended for noting the following points:

> 4.23 – Payment for their services does not make people into mere means: on the contrary lack of payment (as in slavery or breadline wages) may be much more exploitative.

4.24 – Even where there is risk in an occupation (e.g. working as a soldier, or in the police or fire service) payment does not of itself necessarily constitute exploitation. There is unlikely to be exploitation providing that people choosing to undertake such jobs do so with full knowledge and understanding of such risks, and that the payments made to them are not of a nature or at a level to induce them to take such risks against their better judgement.

Brazier's conclusions aren't, however, far removed from those of Warnock. For it's concluded that that there is a powerful exploitation argument against paid surrogacy:

4.46 – the nature of surrogacy arrangements are such that the adult parties, not only surrogates themselves, but commissioning couples too, are vulnerable in certain circumstances to exploitation.[56]

5.16 – the payment of a surrogate by a commissioning couple to bear a child for them creates a potentially exploitative situation, and we wish to minimise the opportunity for exploitation to occur.

It seems to me that the authors of Brazier are worried principally about valid consent rather than exploitation. Even so, an exploitation argument can be constructed based loosely on what they say. I do so below, not principally in order to critique Brazier, but because this style of argument is of general interest and widely used.

1 Being a surrogate is dangerous and/or harmful.
2 Commissioning couples typically derive considerable benefit from surrogacy arrangements. (They get a child.)
3 Relative to the level of danger and/or harm cited in (1), and the level of benefit cited in (2), surrogates' pay levels would be unfairly low. (Brazier, in fact, doesn't say anything like this – which is why I believe that its authors aren't really worried about exploitation, even if they think that they are.)
4 *Therefore* (from (1), (2), and (3)) commercial surrogacy arrangements would involve an unfair 'disparity of value'. What the surrogates get is unfairly small compared to what they give and what the commissioning couple get.
5 Surrogacy involves unpredictable risks, risks which (according to Brazier) 'become fully evident only after an agreement has been entered into, perhaps even some time after the baby has been handed

160

over to the commissioning parents'. It is 'an activity whose degree of risk the surrogate cannot, in the nature of things, fully understand or predict', and 'a difficult personal choice, with an unknown degree of psychological risk'.

6 *Therefore* (from (5) – i.e. because of lack of information and/or her ability to understand the available information) the quality of the surrogate's consent will typically be poor; such consents will often be invalid.

7 In general, a combination of (a) 'disparity of value' and (b) invalid consent provides good grounds for saying that there is exploitation.

8 *Therefore* (from (4), (6), and (7)) surrogacy arrangements are often exploitative.

9 Many of these points apply equally to altruistic and paid surrogacy. (Indeed, some apply more strongly to altruistic surrogacy, because the 'disparity of value' is greater.) However, commercial surrogacy is *especially* objectionable for the following reason. Payment increases the risk of invalid consents being given because it (sometimes) constitutes (undue) inducement. Brazier (5.16) says 'the absence of payment would reduce the likelihood of undue pressure being placed on the surrogate mother'. Conversely, it is claimed that payment increases the likelihood of (or constitutes) undue pressure.

10 Thus, commercial surrogacy may be condemned *either* on the grounds that commercial surrogacy arrangements are more exploitative than altruistic ones, *or* because commercialisation would cause there to be more surrogacy, which (whether paid or not) is often exploitative.

In the rest of this section we'll take a critical look at the first few parts of this argument. This will be a relatively brief process, partly because exploitation arguments have already had a good airing in the discussion of organ sale, and partly because the most contentious and interesting exploitation issues in this area hinge on the question of whether surrogates validly consent, which is dealt with in the following section.

Harm to surrogates

The risks envisaged in (1) are both the normal physical risks associated with pregnancy and the risk of psychological damage caused by having to give up the resulting baby. Anderson, for example, claims that

> Most surrogate mothers experience grief upon giving up their children – in 10% of cases seriously enough to require therapy.[57]

There are lots of difficult empirical questions here about the extent to which surrogates are harmed by surrogacy. Nonetheless we should grant, at least for the sake of argument, that surrogacy is a risky business, while noting that it may also be both financially and otherwise beneficial to the surrogate, that lots of jobs are hazardous, and that

> many occupations which we call upon people to perform or which we are pleased they perform on our behalf, occupations such as the fire, police, ambulance services, military personnel, [and] health care professions ... violate [the] ... principle [that people should not be asked to undergo risks for money].[58]

Benefit to the commissioning couple

The view that commissioning couples normally benefit substantially is uncontentious. Of course, commissioning couples subject themselves to risks too (what if the baby is severely disabled, or the surrogate doesn't hand it over?), but when things go well, commissioning couples gain a lot (which is why they enter into these arrangements).

Low pay levels

Step 3 is where the trouble starts for this argument. The claim is that, given what commissioning couples gain (a baby) and what surrogates give (in terms of subjecting themselves to danger etc., not to mention giving up the baby), the level of payment would be too low. Such a premise is required, for without a 'disparity of value' (in this case, under-payment) there can be no exploitation. (There may, of course, be instru-mentalisation or objectification without 'disparity of value'; this is covered in section 8.6.) As we saw during the discussion of organ sale in the previous chapter, the problem with claims of this sort is: if under-payment is the problem, then why not just put in place rules that would ensure a fair minimum level? As Wertheimer notes, it's rather surprising that those who argue against commercial surrogacy on the grounds that it is exploitative tend not to propose this:

> unlike other contexts in which it is uncontroversial that exploit-ation can be eliminated or decreased by increasing the compensa-tion to the exploited party, it is rarely argued that surrogacy would be less exploitative if the surrogate were paid more. In fact, unpaid surrogacy is typically regarded as less exploitative than paid surrogacy. Among the critics of surrogacy, higher pay is the dog that doesn't bark.[59]

Step 3, then, is implausible unless we assume that there is some feature of surrogacy that makes fair payment impossible. If we conceive of commercial surrogacy as the provision of a service, then it's hard to see what such a feature might be. If, on the other hand (as some would), we think of it as 'baby selling', then, given the further assumption that babies are literally 'priceless', perhaps the view that underpayment is unavoidable makes some sense. However, as we saw in section 8.2, the view that surrogacy is baby selling is itself implausible.

Disparity of value

Another feature of (3) which is worth noting is its inability to differentiate paid from unpaid surrogacy. What we are looking for is a feature of commercial surrogacy in virtue of which it's more exploitative than unpaid surrogacy. The candidate is underpayment. But if commercial surrogacy is underpaid then surely *a fortiori* so is unpaid surrogacy, which (by definition) involves no financial reward at all for the surrogate. This shows that *if* commercial surrogacy is more exploitative than altruistic surrogacy, that can't be just because commercial surrogacy involves a greater 'disparity of value' (since, on the contrary, the 'disparity of value' is more in the case of altruistic surrogacy). Rather, it must be on account of the effect that payment has on the quality of the consent given by the surrogate. With this in mind, we'll leave exploitation to one side now and turn to look in more detail at the issue of consent.

8.5 Consent

Payments create a danger that women will give a less than free and fully informed consent to act as a surrogate.[60]

Many feminists have said that women are exploited by surrogacy. They point out that in our society's social and economic conditions, some women – such as those on welfare or in dire financial need – will turn to surrogacy out of necessity, rather than true choice.[61]

Consent issues occupy a pivotal role in the surrogacy debate. For as well as constituting freestanding arguments against commercial surrogacy, consent objections feed into exploitation arguments (as we've just seen) and into commodification arguments (as we'll see in section 8.6). Indeed, one might usefully regard exploitation and commodification arguments as simply consent arguments with added components ('disparity of value' in the first case, 'instrumentalisation' in the second). For this reason, section 8.5 looks at surrogacy and consent in considerable detail. The section is divided in two subsections, corresponding to a distinction between two different types of argument:

general consent arguments, which say that the surrogate's consent is problematic in *all* surrogacy arrangements (i.e. both paid and unpaid); and

specific consent arguments, according to which commercial surrogacy arrangements are more problematic (as far as consent is concerned) than altruistic ones.

Either may be used to justify banning and/or condemning commercial surrogacy. On the first view, the (putative) justification is simply that the commercialisation of surrogacy encourages surrogacy; while, on the second, it is that commercial surrogacy is *worse than* altruistic surrogacy (because the consents given are generally of a poorer quality). In what follows, we'll look first at *general* consent arguments.

(A) General consent arguments

Why might one think that surrogates can't give valid consent, or that they're at risk of not doing so? A number of different reasons are offered. The first is the likelihood of emotional damage. Brazier makes the point as follows:

5.15 – Embarking on a surrogate pregnancy carries with it emotional risks in addition to the physical risks of pregnancy, and these risks may not become apparent until a pregnancy occurs. For example, the surrogate mother may regret her decision to enter into such an arrangement when she is expected to relinquish the baby, or later in life, perhaps when she enters into a new relationship or finds that she herself is unable to bear another child.

There's no denying that these are serious issues and that the emotional and physical risks alluded to are perfectly real. Indeed, it may be that surrogacy is so hazardous that a paternalistic case can be made against it: i.e. one which argues that prospective surrogates shouldn't be allowed to subject themselves to these risks even if they validly consent. But claiming not merely that surrogacy is dangerous but that its dangerousness is likely to invalidate the surrogate's consent is another matter, and it is not clear why anyone should think this.

One reason for doing so, suggested by the extracts from Brazier quoted above and below, is that surrogates may come to regret their decisions later in life:

6.2 – We have received some personal accounts of uncertainty and unhappiness among some surrogate mothers who did hand over the baby, and we remain unconvinced that all surrogacy arrangements are entered into with genuinely informed consent by all parties.

This, however, won't work, because it is (of course) possible for people validly to consent to a decision that they may come to regret. For example, some years ago I took out a fixed-rate stockmarket-linked mortgage. Now, I regret that decision because interest rates and stock values have both declined and I would have been much better off with a different product. But since I was fully aware of the risks involved when I made my decision (including the possibility of coming to regret the decision later) my present regret doesn't cast any doubt whatever on the validity of my original consent. Similarly, I've met people who say that they regret their decision to marry a particular person, or their decision to have or not have children, or their decision to take a job, or buy a house. Sometimes the quality of such decisions is tainted by lack of information, but generally it is not, and most of these people validly consented to things that they later came to regret. The same goes for surrogacy. Provided that surrogates are fully informed (including about the fact, if it is a fact, that they are likely to have regrets later on), then the possibility of regret doesn't cast any doubt on the validity of their original consents (although, as I've said, it might underpin a paternalistic argument against surrogacy).

A second informed consent worry is that some of the risks attached to surrogacy are unpredictable. This is suggested both by the line quoted above – 'risks may not become apparent until a pregnancy occurs' – and by an earlier passage:

4.25 – surrogacy does carry some unpredictable risks which become fully evident only after an agreement has been entered into, perhaps even some time after the baby has been handed over to the commissioning parents.

The thought here seems to be that it's impossible (or difficult) for surrogates to give *adequately informed* consent because (a) the risks can't be reliably predicted and so surrogates can't be told in advance what the risks are, *and/or* (b) the risks only come to light after the moment at which consent is required. This line of argument, though, is flawed, for there's reason to think that neither (a) nor (b) is true – or, at least, that they're misleading. To take (a) first, *why* can't the risks be reliably predicted? It may be the case that we presently lack empirical evidence of the right sort and, if so, then further research is to be encouraged. But there is, in principle, no reason why surrogates can't be supplied with information in the following form: '37 per cent experience regret within five years of giving up their babies', '8 per cent suffer significant physical health problems during pregnancy', '18 per cent want to keep the baby for themselves', etc. Of course, what probably can't be reliably predicted is whether *this particular surrogate* will experience regret, physical health problems, or whatever. But in this respect, surrogacy is no different from lots of medical treatments to which people regularly give valid consent, based solely on statistical knowledge of the benefits and risks ('4 per cent of patients experience extreme side-effects' and so forth). So if (as seems to be the case) the complaint in the case of surrogacy is that surrogates can only have statistical knowledge of the risks and can't know in advance whether or not the risk will be realised in their case, this is a pretty weak argument – because cases in which people give valid consent based solely on statistical knowledge of risks and benefits are commonplace.

To generalise, it's tempting to think that underlying this version of the consent argument is a mistaken picture of what risk is, and of what it is to know about a risk. Brazier, for example, says that 'risks may not become apparent until a pregnancy occurs' and that there are 'unpredictable risks which become fully evident only after an agreement has been entered into'. These, however, are slightly odd things to say because they make it sound as if risks are to be identified with adverse events (like becoming ill or experiencing regret). But a risk isn't an adverse event. Rather, an adverse event is *that which there is a risk of*, and to say that there is a certain risk of x is just to say that the probability of x happening, relative to a certain evidence base, is n per cent. So, to turn back to surrogacy, unless the evidence is remarkably poor, it's unlikely that the *risks* won't become apparent until after consent is given, because a risk is just the probability of an adverse event, and we can base such probabilities on statistical data about past cases. The mistake underlying this part of Brazier, then, seems to be that it requires (in order for there to be informed consent) not merely information about the *risks*, but information about the *actual future outcomes*. And, of course, this standard for informed consent is unreasonably demanding. Oakley describes what seems a more sensible alternative view:

> what seems to be required for autonomous decision-making and informed consent is not knowledge or foresight of actual *outcomes*, but rather, an adequate appreciation of the *risks* involved in having made the decision. That is, whether we are talking about marriage, surgery, or investment, informed consent requires that we have some level of understanding of what kinds of consequences might ensue from such risky ventures, rather than foresight of the actual emotional, material, or other states we may be in as a result of undertaking such courses of action . . . [so] not

knowing what her [the surrogate's] future emotional responses to pregnancy and relinquishment will be does not entail that a woman's decision to enter into a surrogacy arrangement is inadequately informed.[62]

Furthermore, even if the evidence is weak or absent, that still doesn't preclude informed consent, since the consent could be based on *knowing that* the evidence is limited *and that* the precise risks are uncertain. A useful comparator here is consent given by biomedical research subjects. These consents are often based on evidence that is relatively flimsy. Nonetheless, research subjects can give adequately informed consent to participate in trials, provided that they are given information both about what the relevant evidence is and (crucially) about its limitations. The same can apply to surrogacy; if it's really true that we don't know what the risks are (which, in any case, is questionable), then telling surrogates that we don't know may well be enough to make their consent sufficiently informed.

Next I'd like to consider briefly a pair of arguments based on the (supposed) fact that childbearing and gestation are intimately connected, in a variety of ways, to intense emotional responses. These arguments lie beneath remarks like this:

> if the woman has never had a child of her own beforehand, how can she possibly be truly informed to give her consent to give up the child she has gestated and delivered?[63]

The first of these arguments is summarised by Oakley as follows:

> emotions have a kind of *sui generis* unpredictability, which, even if we were to talk of risks rather than outcomes, entails that we lack information about them which is crucial to decisions involving important emotional risks.[64]

It's pretty clear, however, that such claims aren't going to work. For even if people's emotional responses do 'have a kind of *sui generis* unpredictability', then (thinking back to the comparison with research subjects) we could still secure sufficiently informed consent by telling prospective surrogates about this fact. (It also seems to me, as it does to Oakley, that the unpredictability of the emotions is frequently overstated, since it's very often possible to forecast accurately what one's feelings will be on the basis either of one's own past or of finding out about the reactions of others.)

The second argument isn't based on the (supposed) unpredictability of people's emotions, but instead on the idea that there are certain things which can only be understood by those who have *experiential* knowledge of them: i.e. by people who have firsthand knowledge based directly on experience. Things which fall into this category might include (to name but a few) beauty, love, music, pain, sex, sounds, and tastes. When this is applied to surrogacy, the idea is (a) that it involves experiences and feelings that can only truly be understood by someone with experiential knowledge (for example, of what it's like to give birth and/or give up a baby) and (b) that (therefore) in order to supply adequately *informed* consent, experiential knowledge is required. But since (so the argument goes) surrogates don't (normally) have the right sort of experiential knowledge, the quality of their consent is (normally) compromised, because it is insufficiently informed.[65]

There may well be some truth in this argument or, at least, in its premises. For example, it's reasonable to suppose that a woman can't *fully* understand what it's like to be a surrogate unless she's actually been a surrogate – and that women who already have children of their own are (other things being equal) best placed, because of their experience, to predict what carrying, bearing, and giving up a child will be like. But what exactly follows from this? One possibility (which perhaps we should accept, at least for the sake of argument) is allowing only women who already have children of their own to be (paid or unpaid) surrogates. This is not because other women aren't capable of validly consenting, but just because women who are already mothers are in a *better* position to predict their own emotional responses. This makes them less likely to suffer harm and more likely to give good-quality consent. It might, however, be objected that even women with children lack experiential knowledge of carrying a child and then having to give it up (perhaps for money). And so their consent to a surrogacy arrangement would be insufficiently informed.

This way of thinking, however, is flawed. It's tempting to think that the error is in postulating a standard of information which is so high that it automatically rules out informed consent from anyone who hasn't already been a surrogate. This isn't, however, *necessarily* a problem, even though it's certainly true that, normally, one doesn't need experiential knowledge of x in order to consent validly to x. For we might concede that there are certain *special* experiences which can only be validly consented to on the basis of experiential knowledge: for example, torture. If so, the question then becomes: is being a surrogate one of these special experiences? Provided that we restrict surrogacy to women who are already mothers, there's some reason to answer *no* to this. For these women have already had direct experience of gestation, childbirth, and (perhaps most importantly) their own relevant emotional states – including love for their children and some resultant sense of how bad they would have felt if they'd had to give them up. Of course, the past isn't an infallible guide to the future, and it's *possible* that their emotional states will be different next time around, but this applies to experiential knowledge in general and seems to count against taking such knowledge too seriously. It seems, then, that even if we concede that there are some exceptional activities which can only be validly consented to on the basis of experiential knowledge, this is unlikely to be true of surrogacy (at least if we restrict the class of prospective surrogates to women with children).

The final general consent argument that we're going to consider is closely connected to the idea that surrogates are exploited. The main claim here is not that surrogates lack information, but that they (often) lack the *capacity* to consent because of their emotional needs and vulnerabilities. Anderson, for example, argues that the surrogate

> is exploited, because her emotional needs and vulnerabilities are ... treated ... as factors which may be manipulated to encourage her to make a grave self-sacrifice to the broker's and adoptive couple's advantage.[66]

Amongst her reasons for thinking this are that

> most surrogate mothers are motivated by emotional needs and vulnerabilities which lead them to view their labor as a form of gift and not a purely commercial exchange. Only 1% of applicants to surrogate agencies would become surrogate mothers for money alone; the others have emotional as well as financial reasons for applying.
>
> Many surrogate mothers see pregnancy as a way to feel 'adequate', 'appreciated', or 'special'. In other words, these women feel inadequate, unappreciated, or unadmired when they are not pregnant.[67]

Anderson makes two closely related points here, each of which is supposed to impact negatively on the quality of the surrogate's consent and to put her at risk of being exploited. The first is that surrogates have a 'gift' mentality. The second is that they have feelings of inadequacy which only surrogacy can only alleviate.

Why are these mental characteristics supposed to threaten the quality of the surrogate's consent? One answer is that they make her too keen to be a surrogate, and (hence) too willing to accept a bad deal. If we accept Anderson's empirical premises (which we shall, at least for the sake of argument), then it's reasonable to suppose that many surrogates are excessively eager, and that they are therefore at risk of being exploited. (We should think back here to Wood's suggestion that the typical victims of exploitation – such as starving people – are likely to be *all too willing* to be exploited.)[68] It's not clear, however, that eagerness *per se* damages the quality of a consent. Indeed, one might ask: what could be more consensual than people doing what they're keen to do?

A better answer is one which doesn't simply cite the surrogate's excessive eagerness, but goes beyond that to look at *the reasons why* she's so keen. The idea here is that we can then distinguish between eagerness based on autonomously held preferences and eagerness based on non-autonomous mental states. (See section 7.4 for a more detailed account of this distinction.) Eagerness of the first sort doesn't in any way compromise the quality of the consent. But eagerness of the second kind, because it is non-autonomous, may render the consent invalid.

How does this apply to what Anderson says about surrogates' motives? First, there's the claim that many surrogates regard surrogacy as a 'gift and not a purely commercial exchange'. In order to say much about this, we'd need to know, in any given case, more about *why* the surrogate has this gift mentality. If (for example) the surrogate is a *compulsive* giver, then we may well have legitimate concerns about the quality of her consent. But if she's not compulsive and simply generously inclined, or has a well-thought-out moral belief that it's good to be a surrogate, then the gift mentality doesn't, on its own, seem to threaten her consent, as it's autonomous and rational. Perhaps a useful comparator here is nursing. Some people enter the nursing profession not just for personal satisfaction or for money, but for altruistic reasons – because they want to help people. Such altruism, though, surely doesn't reduce the quality of their consent to become nurses.

Similar considerations apply to Anderson's claim that many surrogates use surrogacy as a way of feeling adequate, appreciated, or special. This fact can't, in and of itself, be enough to preclude valid consent, because people in a variety of different professions use their jobs in this way and, clearly, it would be bizarre to say of all such cases that there was no valid consent (for example, to the contract of employment). It's hard to see why surrogacy should be any different in this respect. The fact that the surrogate is made to feel better than she otherwise would doesn't invalidate her consent. Furthermore, if she derives psychological benefits from the arrangement, one might simply say 'so much the better'. For at least, if the arrangement is exploitative, it is exploitation of a mutually advantageous kind. The same goes for women who 'say that they actually enjoy being pregnant but don't want any further children for themselves'.[69] Of course, their desire to be a 'host' might be taken advantage of, but to say that their consent is invalidated by this desire would be rather like saying that people who enjoy their jobs can't validly consent to their contracts of employment. So, as with altruism, everything depends on *the reasons why* the surrogate is made to feel adequate, appreciated, and special. If, for example, it's because she *is* appreciated, then there's no problem. But if, on the other hand, it's because she has an irrational and non-autonomous sense of her own inferiority that can only be got rid of by performing self-sacrificial acts, then we might start to wonder about the validity of her consent.

Conclusion

Those who put forward general consent arguments against surrogacy helpfully remind us of the risks that surrogates face. These include the possibility of regret and emotional trauma, the unpredictability of the emotions, the lack of reliable empirical evidence about surrogacy, and the important role that experiential knowledge (or its absence) can play in decision making. We are also usefully reminded of the importance of carefully scrutinising the prospective surrogate's motivations to make certain that her desire to enter into the arrangement isn't compulsive (or, more generally, non-autonomous) and that she's not coerced. These are important matters, ones that must be taken into account when policy is framed. They don't, however, support the conclusion that surrogacy arrangements can't be properly consensual (provided that the practice is suitably regulated). There are various different reasons for this, as we've seen. But perhaps the foremost is this: *if* (as is suggested) it's true that women's emotions are unpredictable, and that surrogates often have regrets, and that there's much that we don't know about surrogacy arrangements, and that direct experience changes women's attitudes to pregnancy and childbirth, then *simply by telling prospective surrogates in some detail about these facts* we go a long way towards making sure that their consents are adequately informed. Consequently, it seems to me that the general consent arguments considered here (most of which are to do with surrogates' consents being insufficiently informed) are weak and don't provide a justification for banning commercial surrogacy or even for morally condemning it.

(B) Specific consent arguments

[T]he prospect of payment further complicates decision-making and results in an increased likelihood of women entering into a surrogacy arrangement when they would not otherwise have done so, particularly women experiencing financial difficulties.[70]

Specific consent arguments are ones which, rather than asserting that consent is problematic in *all* surrogacy arrangements, claim that it is problematic specifically in *commercial* ones. We can deal with these arguments relatively quickly, because most of them are exactly like ones that we

looked at during the discussion of organ sale in Chapter 7. This is principally because, whereas general consent arguments focus on the nature of
surrogacy and of surrogates, specific consent ones are concerned with
worries about the impact that payment has on consent – worries which
are pretty much the same whether we're talking about surrogacy, or
organ sale, or prostitution, or participation in biomedical research. In
what follows, I'll do no more than very briefly rehearse arguments
which we've already looked at in much more detail elsewhere (chiefly in
Chapter 7).

The first is the claim (suggested by the above extract from Brazier) that
payment damages consent because it *influences* prospective surrogates,
resulting 'in an increased likelihood of women entering into a surrogacy
arrangement when they would not otherwise have done so'. This, however, won't suffice, because there are numerous cases in which payments
influence people without invalidating their consents. Indeed, the whole
economy is based on people using money to influence each other – often
in entirely innocent ways, and (most importantly for our present
purposes) in ways which in no way rule out free and informed consent.

The second argument relates specifically to the (supposed) fact that
commercial surrogacy does, or would, attract mostly poor women. Brecher, for example, envisages that

> a pool of surrogates could well be created on the model of work-
> ing class prostitution; women would come to be imported from
> poor countries for the purpose of serving as surrogates.[71]

This, it is supposed, would generate consent problems because such
women would in effect have been *forced* into surrogacy by poverty and by
lack of alternatives. Thus, Ber asks:

> It is presumed that a woman who decides to serve as a surrogate
> mother is autonomous, but is she truly free from economic
> pressures in commercial surrogacy?[72]

There are two main interpretations of the claim that women are forced
into surrogacy by poverty. One is simply that they lack choice, that they
don't have any acceptable alternatives; the second is that they are coerced.
I'll deal with each in turn.

There's undoubtedly a sense in which women who have to choose
between paid surrogacy and extreme poverty aren't free to decline paid
surrogacy. Indeed, this is an entirely general point. People who have to
choose between *anything* and extreme poverty are (in that respect) unfree.
I argued in Chapter 7 that unfreedom of this sort is best understood as a
lack of choice relative to one's fundamental goals. The idea is that A is unfree

to decline X insofar as *in order to achieve A's fundamental goals* (which usually include or require staying alive) A *has to* accept X. But I also argued that unfreedom of this sort doesn't preclude valid consent. One reason for this is that, if it did, then it would be impossible to consent to (for example) lifesaving medical treatments. So not having any acceptable alternatives isn't, in and of itself, enough to render poor surrogates' consents invalid – because it's possible to consent validly *even when* one is unfree in this 'lacking options' sense.

To turn to the second interpretation, are there grounds for seeing poor surrogates as the victims of coercion? If so, then this would be a good reason to view their consents as invalid. I argued in previous chapters that although poverty can't itself coerce, because coercing has to be done by an agent, it can nonetheless be used as a *method of* coercion. This leaves open the possibility that poor surrogates are being coerced, with actual or threatened poverty being the method of coercing. But it also leaves us with the tricky question of *who* is doing the coercing.

In order to answer this, we need to know who (if anyone) has a free-standing duty to alleviate prospective surrogates' poverty – who is (what, in Chapter 7, I termed) a rescuer. This is because being a rescuer is a necessary condition for being an omissive coercer. (See sections 4.4 and 6.3 above.) One possibility is that the (prospective) commissioning parents are rescuers. This would mean that they had an independent obligation to alleviate the (prospective) surrogates' poverty, without requiring anything (for example, surrogacy services) in return. However, the claim that the prospective commissioners are rescuers is hard to justify (except perhaps in cases where the couple are obscenely rich and the potential surrogate desperately poor). For, first, many prospective commissioners aren't terribly rich, especially if they've blown their life savings on unsuccessful infertility treatments. And, second, it's hard to see why potential commissioners should be singled out as rescuers. Why not some *other* couple, individual, or group?

A more promising option is for us to turn our attention to groups rather than individuals. One might argue, for example, that relatively rich people have a duty to alleviate poverty. With this assumption in place, it could then be argued that when the rich couples 'offer' poor women money in return for surrogacy services, this isn't really an offer, but rather coercion. This is because the rich people should be giving the money anyway, not demanding surrogacy services in return for it. So what the rich are doing is threatening to withhold resources to which poor women have a right, unless these poor women become surrogates. This argument is fine as far as it goes. However (as we saw during the discussion of organ sale), the trouble is that it proves too much. What I mean is that it works equally well against *all* trade between the rich and the poor. For (in simplistic terms) if the rich have a duty to *give* resources to the poor, then any time that the rich insist on trading (for example, money for services) rather than donating, they will be practising omissive coercion – threatening to withhold money that they should be giving anyway, unless they're provided with goods of one sort or another. And, in this respect at least, there's no reason to single out commercial *surrogacy* for special treatment, since parallel coercion arguments will apply with equal force to (say) cleaning, or to factory or secretarial work. This is a decisive objection. Either the coercion argument doesn't work at all, or it works but proves too much and gives us no reason to single out commercial surrogacy for denunciation or prohibition.

8.6 Commodification

> Whatever benefits [commercial surrogacy] might bring . . . would be outweighed by the harm done to the general interests of women – and . . . to the general interests of all. In brief, these are: the further commoditization of women; the resulting further commoditization of all of us; the further development of consumerist values.[73]

We've already looked at the idea that commercial surrogacy commodifies children. In this section, we're going to examine the claim that it commodifies women. Such commodification arguments can usefully be divided into two categories. First, there are those that see commercial surrogacy as a sort of *sui generis* evil which in some way reduces women to wombs, incubators, or foetal containers. Andrews, for example, reports that

> Surrogate motherhood has been described by its opponents . . . as reproductive prostitution, reproductive slavery, the renting of a womb, incubatory servitude, the factory method of childbearing, and cutting up women into genitalia. The women who are surrogates are labelled paid breeders, biological entrepreneurs, breeder women, reproductive meat, interchangeable parts in the birth machinery, manufacturing plants, human incubators, incubators for men's sperm, a commodity in the reproductive marketplace, and prostitutes.[74]

These claims are to be contrasted with those which say that, while in most respects surrogacy is nothing special and no worse than many other widely accepted practices, it is nonetheless wrong insofar as it encourages or perpetuates a particular moral climate: one in which women are seen as commodities and valued for their bodily attributes rather than their personal ones. One of the clearest and most explicit advocates of this line is Bob Brecher, who writes:

> I am not seeking to argue that surrogacy is *especially* problematic ... Issues such as advertising, pornography, the privatisation of health care and education, the notion of property-owning democracy and many others may well be far more important.[75]

> It is not what surrogacy is, mythically, like *per se* which is the problem, but the consequences, both direct and indirect, of its being institutionalised: and any discussion of these must take into account the dialectical relationship between 'harms' and the moral climate.[76]

The thought here is that women are already commodified and that permitting commercial surrogacy would simply make matters worse by encouraging and perpetuating the 'consumerist' moral climate (either in general or specifically as it relates to women).

In what follows, I'll start with arguments of the first kind – by asking whether or not commercial surrogacy is *especially* commodificatory. I'll then turn to the question of surrogacy's effects on the moral climate.

(A) Is commercial surrogacy especially commodificatory?

The view that there's something in the *nature* of either surrogacy in general or commercial surrogacy in particular that makes it commodificatory is, it seems to me, implausible. In what follows, I'll explain why.

In Chapter 3, I argued that commodification (in the pejorative sense) is a form of objectification. For this reason, I'll focus on the general question of whether surrogacy *objectifies* women. For if it doesn't, then nor does it commodify them. To objectify is to treat as an object something which isn't really (or merely) an object. Thus, surrogacy objectifies women if and only if it involves treating them as mere objects. Why might one think that it does this? The main reason is that surrogates are treated (by commissioning couples, agencies, and others) as wombs, incubators, or foetal containers. This is reasonably plausible, but what's much less plausible (and what's required for a strong anti-surrogacy argument) is the claim that surrogates are *necessarily* viewed as *mere* wombs, incubators, or foetal containers. For it's hard to think of anything in the *nature* of surrogacy that precludes fully recognising the personhood of the surrogate – recognising that she's much more than simply an incubator.

Anderson (an opponent of surrogacy and a proponent of commodification arguments) claims that

> The application of commercial norms to women's labour reduces

the surrogate mothers from persons worthy of respect and consideration to objects of mere use.[77]

But the problem with such arguments is that it's not clear why 'women's labour' can't have commercial norms applied to it while *at the same time* the women providing the labour are treated with consideration and respect. Crucial here will be consent and the welfare of the surrogate. Clearly, it's *possible* for surrogates to be treated as mere objects of use. For example, they could be forced to be surrogates against their wills, chained up for nine months, subjected to sexual abuse, and denied medical treatment after the birth. Such behaviour would undoubtedly amount to treating these women as mere incubators, with no concern for their welfare or respect for their autonomy. But what if the commissioning couple have a personal relationship with the surrogate, take care of her, and ensure that she gives free and informed consent before entering the surrogacy arrangement? Can we credibly say of such cases that the surrogate is treated as an object of mere use? She is certainly *made use of*, as almost all of us are (normally entirely innocently) every day. But there seems no reason to suppose that she's object*ified*, treated as a *mere* object. McLachlan and Swales, responding to a later paper by Anderson, make a similar point:

> Is [Anderson] saying . . . that, as a matter of fact, (some) people do not treat women who are surrogate mothers with the dignity and respect which they are due? This might be true but if it is, *it indicates a problem not about surrogate motherhood but one about these particular people.*[78]

This seems completely right. There's nothing in the *nature* of surrogacy which means that commissioning parents (or others) *necessarily* fail to treat surrogates with consideration and respect. So the objection must be that, as a matter of fact, many commissioning parents fail to treat surrogates sufficiently well. If this is true, then these commissioners deserve censure, and tougher regulation is justified – regulation which ensures that surrogates get fair treatment, higher welfare standards, and an opportunity to give (or withhold) free and informed consent. But it's hard to see how a ban on, or 'blanket' moral condemnation of, surrogacy is warranted.

Responding to this, Anderson says:

> This is like saying: there is nothing inherent in a slave contract that violates the dignity and autonomy of the slave. After all, many slave owners treat their slaves decently and permit them a wide range of freedoms . . . This argument is flawed, because

176

slave contracts give slave owners a *license* to disrespect their slaves, and an *incentive* to do so. Even if slave owners did not act on their incentive, the mere license to abuse the slave is enough to render the slave contract an objectionable form of commodification.[79]

What she says about slavery is right. Even if slave owners didn't exercise their oppressive legal rights, the mere possession of those rights would still be abhorrent. But to imply, as Anderson does, that surrogacy is like slavery begs some important questions. In particular, in what ways (if any) is surrogacy like slavery? And are the legal rights that surrogacy arrangements give to commissioning parents oppressive or otherwise objectionable? In response to questions like these, defenders of a regulated commercial market in surrogacy services will rightly point out that, even if some actual surrogacy contracts treat surrogates as if they were slaves, there's certainly no reason in principle why surrogacy contracts *need* to be like that, or why proper regulation couldn't do away with such contracts, replacing them with fair and non-oppressive (or at least much less oppressive) ones. In her defence, Anderson writes:

> I am not trying to argue that pregnancy contracts reduce women to slaves. Rather, my point is that both pregnancy contracts and slave contracts wrongly treat someone's inalienable rights as if they were freely alienable. Pregnancy contracts treat *the mother's inalienable right to love her child*, and to express that love by asserting a claim to custody in its own best interests, as if it were alienable in a market transaction.[80]

However, such strong claims stand in need of justification, for, as we saw earlier, it's not clear (a) that the child is really *hers* (the surrogate's) or (b) that the surrogate is really *the child's mother* (*a fortiori* that she is the child's *only* mother) or (c) that gestational mothers' rights to love 'their' children (if such rights exist at all) are *inalienable*.

I conclude, then, that there's nothing in the nature of either surrogacy in general, or commercial surrogacy in particular, that makes it necessarily commodificatory. This is chiefly because it's possible for commissioning parents (and other prospective commodifiers) to treat the surrogate with consideration and respect by (for example) taking steps to minimise any harmful effects, paying a fair or generous rate, and ensuring that free and informed consent is obtained prior to the arrangement's being made. Moreover, it's possible more or less to guarantee that commissioners act in this way by having an appropriately regulated commercial market in surrogacy services.

This may seem like a rather swift dismissal of the (first) commodification objection and, in a way, it is. But there's a reason for this. The reason is that we can build on some of the important conclusions established earlier in relation to consent. Of particular significance is the principle defended in Chapter 3 – that if A seeks and obtains from B valid consent to do x to B, and x is not substantially harmful to B, this is sufficient to guarantee that B's status as an end-in-herself is respected by A. This principle, when combined with the conclusion of section 8.5 (which says that, at least in normal circumstances, there's no reason why paid surrogates can't supply valid consent), gives us a powerful way of countering commodification arguments against surrogacy. For (in brief) where valid consent is sought and supplied, there's no objectification and, hence, no commodification.

This just leaves the question of *substantial harm*. For I've conceded that A may fail to respect B's status as an end-in-herself *either* by failing to seek and obtain valid consent, *or* by inflicting substantial harm on B. Someone like Anderson may then argue that, even if valid consent is forthcoming, surrogacy still (often) objectifies women insofar as they are harmed for the benefit of third parties. There's no doubt that *some* surrogates will be harmed no matter what system we have. However, there's no reason why harm can't be kept to a minimum in a properly regulated commercial system. What's more, if regulations ensured that surrogates received fair or generous remuneration, this would (if the level were set high enough) ensure that most surrogates stood to benefit from surrogacy (once financial benefits were factored in). Hence, in advance of the pregnancy, both the commissioning parents and the surrogate would have every reason to believe that she would benefit. Thus, even in those cases where there was harm, the harm would be 'accidental' (not intended or rationally expected), and this is almost certainly not the kind of harm that can underpin an objectification claim.

(B) The moral climate argument

The moral climate argument is about consequences – in particular, about the effects that permitting surrogacy would have on the way in which people treat each other (or, more specifically, treat women). The core idea is that commercial surrogacy encourages wider patterns of commodification. If, however, this is going to be a truly *independent* argument (i.e. one which might be sound even if the commodification argument just considered in (A) isn't), then it must make the following claim: *even if* there's nothing in commercial surrogacy's nature which makes it (intrinsically, necessarily, etc.) commodificatory, and *even if* actual cases of surrogacy rarely (if ever) involve commodification, it's still the case that commercial surrogacy would cause there to be additional commodification in society at large. The moral climate argument needs this thesis because otherwise we could refute it just by citing the conclusion of (A) – that, given suitable regulation, there's no need for commercial surrogacy to involve the commodification (in the pejorative sense) of women.

It seems that this is exactly what Brecher (a clear advocate of the moral climate argument) has in mind:

> if someone walks across a patch of grass with a 'Keep Off' sign, it may not result directly in any damage to the grass, but might encourage, however indirectly, other people to reject injunctions of a similar sort, thereby doing harm. Here . . . something which is 'in itself' harmless may nevertheless constitute a morality-affecting harm.[81]

Presumably, this idea applies to surrogacy in something like the following way:

1 The commercial exploitation of women's (people's) bodies is, generally speaking, a bad thing because it encourages objectification: the treatment of women (people) as *mere* bodies.
2 A carefully regulated commercial market in surrogacy services wouldn't be harmful or wrong 'in itself' (just like walking over the piece of grass in Brecher's analogy).
3 However, such a market would encourage people to disregard or disbelieve a moral principle like 'the commercial exploitation of women's bodies is generally a bad thing'. (This principle is comparable to the 'Keep Off' sign.)
4 The erosion of people's commitment to this principle will have bad consequences. In particular, it will lead to an increase in the amount of commodification (of women/people) that occurs.
5 Therefore, there's reason to view commercial surrogacy as wrong, because it's a morality-affecting harm.

As Brecher puts it,

> To institutionalise surrogacy would be likely . . . to lead to an even greater acceptance of people's making use of each other . . . either in explicitly commercial terms, or in terms of the power and control exercised to a large extent by society over women, a phenomenon I would characterise . . . in terms of treatment as commodity.[82]

In one important respect, it's hard to assess such arguments, since they're based on *empirical* claims about what will happen to the moral climate if we permit surrogacy. Such claims are notoriously difficult to confirm experimentally. We might, I suppose, compare the moral climate in countries with commercial surrogacy to that in countries where it's banned, and discover that the countries in the first group contain more commodificatory actions and attitudes than the others. But this would be inconclusive, since it's almost impossible to tell whether or not commercial surrogacy is a *cause* of additional commodification or merely a *symptom* of it. So we can at least conclude that the moral climate argument is unpersuasive insofar as it relies on an empirical premise that (while 'intuitive' to many) is very hard to establish scientifically.

A more philosophical objection to the argument concerns the status of the moral principle cited in (3) ('the commercial exploitation of women's body parts is generally a bad thing'). First, we should note that 'exploitation' here is used in its non-moral sense. Second, we have to ask what exactly 'generally' means here. Clearly, it doesn't mean *universally*, since it's already been granted that commercial surrogacy isn't wrong 'in itself' (if properly regulated, etc.). So it must mean *usually* or *more often than not*. If this principle is to be believed, then there's an important distinction between the *majority* of commercial exploitation cases (those in which women's bodies are wrongfully used) and the *minority* (those in which they're permissibly, 'innocently', used). But, given this distinction, it's tempting to ask *why* the official acceptance of commercial surrogacy (which is, *ex hypothesi*, not intrinsically wrong) is supposed to lead people to disbelieve the moral principle. For believing that commercial surrogacy is permissible is entirely consistent with believing that the commercial exploitation of women's bodies is *usually* a bad thing. So why not just believe both?

The standard response to this is to say that, as a matter of moral-psychological fact, people are bad at distinguishing between wrongful and permissible instances of body-commercialisation. Therefore, it's argued, in order to minimise wrongdoing, people should err on the side of caution and avoid body-commercialisation altogether (even though *really* it's sometimes permissible). Similarly, it might be argued that if commercial surrogacy were publicly sanctioned by the state, this would (mistakenly) be interpreted as a much more wide-ranging endorsement of body-commercialisation *in general*. People sometimes make this kind of move when talking about the legalisation of cannabis. Even if, they say, cannabis is 'in itself' acceptable (or, at least, is no worse than other widely used substances such as alcohol and tobacco), we shouldn't decriminalise it because people will (mistakenly) take this as an endorsement of *drugs-in-general*. This is (it's alleged) because people are unable to make the relevant distinctions within the category 'drugs'.

Again, it's hard to assess arguments of this sort because there're based on empirical premises which are difficult to prove or disprove. It does, however, seem that there are some reasons to reject the argument, at least as applied to surrogacy. The main one is that the kinds of things that differentiate a properly regulated commercial surrogacy system from objectionable forms of body commodification (for example, degrading and violent pornography) aren't exactly 'moral rocket science' and there seems, on the face of it, to be no reason why ordinary people couldn't spot the moral differences in question. One obvious difference is consent; another is the degree of harm involved. I argued in previous sections that it's possible for surrogacy to be validly consensual and for harm to surrogates to be kept to a minimum through the careful regulation of surrogacy contracts. If this is correct, then I see no reason why people can't – at least if suitably informed – understand the difference between surrogacy and (wrongful) body commodification.

Conclusion

In this section, we've looked at two different types of commodification argument. According to the first, commercial surrogacy is a sort of *sui generis* evil which objectifies women by treating them as mere foetal containers. According to the second, although commercial surrogacy isn't fundamentally different from other widely accepted practices, it is nonetheless wrong because it encourages wider patterns of commodification. Both arguments have been found wanting. Arguments of the first sort are weak, because there's nothing in the *nature* of surrogacy which precludes fully respecting the personhood of the surrogate – recognising that she's much more than *merely* an 'incubator' and treating her as such. Arguments of the second sort are consequence-based and empirical in nature and so it's difficult or impossible to refute them conclusively by philosophical critique alone. Such arguments are nonetheless weak insofar as they rely on speculative sociological premises about the effects of permitting surrogacy. Moreover, there are (as I've just argued) reasons to be sceptical about some of these premises.

8.7 Summary and conclusions

Commercial surrogacy is widely regarded as abhorrent. This chapter has provided a critical assessment of the main ethical arguments underpinning this position. Some of these show that careful regulation is necessary, but none of them is sufficient to show that commercial surrogacy should be prohibited or otherwise officially discouraged. As we've seen, appealing to the welfare of the child can't underpin a sound moral argument against paid surrogacy. And commercial surrogacy *isn't* baby selling, *needn't* commodify or exploit women, and *can* be validly consensual.

9

PATENTING LIFE

This chapter attempts to answer two related questions. First, what special ethical issues (if any) are raised by gene patenting? Second, how strong are the moral arguments against this practice? My focus here is on the *human* body. However, a sharp distinction between intellectual property in the human body and that concerning other species is, at least at the level of practical genetics, hard to maintain. For, as Resnik puts it,

> many genes that occur in human populations also occur in pri-
> mate, mammalian, and other animal populations . . . biological
> context determines the humanness of genes: a gene is human if
> and only if it contributes to the structures or functions of human
> beings. Thus, genes that code for hair proteins are human genes
> even though many of these genes also occur in chimpanzee
> populations.[1]

So, while I shall talk about human bodies and human genes, such talk should be interpreted in the light of Resnik's point.

Intellectual property issues are harder to explain and understand than those discussed in the previous two chapters. Admittedly, some of the arguments for and against organ sale and commercial surrogacy are complex, or deploy difficult concepts. But at least it's fairly easy to say what selling a kidney *is*, or what surrogate mothers *do*, and then to divide the arguments and their proponents into broadly 'anti-' and 'pro-' camps. When we turn to *intellectual* property in the human body, though, just making sense of what's actually going on 'on the ground' and of the diverse options that face us is itself a formidable task. This is chiefly because, as Bunting puts it, 'gene patenting combines two immensely complex subjects – genetic science and intellectual property law'.[2] As we'll see during the course of this chapter, then, expressions like 'patent-ing life' and 'gene patenting' are really too simplistic – although I'll be using them from time to time because they provide useful shorthand for a wide range of practices, including the patenting of genetically modified organisms, as well as the patenting of techniques for isolating or testing, methods of replicating, and ways of using naturally occurring genetic material.

Most of Chapter 9 is concerned exclusively with the patenting of (human) DNA. The chapter does, however, start with two more wide-ranging sections. The first (9.1) explains in general terms what intellectual property is and provides a taxonomy of issues and positions. The second (9.2) discusses what's been called 'biopiracy'. The more narrowly focussed discussion of patenting starts (in 9.3) with an account of con-temporary law and practice, something which – as I've already suggested – is far from straightforward. Section 9.4 examines utilitarian arguments for and against gene patenting, while 9.5 looks at the view that gene patenting (or certain forms of gene patenting) is somehow intrinsically wrong.

9.1 What are the issues?

Intellectual property is *intangible* property with wholly or mainly *intellectual content*. I won't attempt to spell out in any detail here what differentiates intellectual from other forms of intangible property, since not much hangs on this for our present purposes. It will suffice to say that the word 'intellectual' is normally understood quite broadly in this context to cover anything informational. The idea of intangibility, however, deserves a little more attention. Moore characterises intangible property as

> non-physical property where [the] owner's rights surround con-trol of physical manifestations or tokens of some abstract idea or type.[3]

Musical composition provides a simple example. Take a case in which I write and record an original song called 'My song'. In such a case, I own not only the physical storage medium (for example, the magnetic disc or tape) on which 'My song' is recorded, but also the intangible entity, 'My song', which is an 'abstract idea or type'. What ownership of this intangible amounts to is that others must not create physical manifestations of the song (such as CDs or live performances) without my consent and/or the payment of a fee. So, as Moore puts it, my rights in respect of the intangible 'surround control of physical manifestations'.

One important fact which follows from the non-physicality of intangible property is that it 'can be shared without diminishing the owner's ability to use it'.[4] Some economists and philosophers have called such goods 'non-rivalrous' or 'joint', meaning that their consumption by one person does not in itself make it more difficult for others to consume them. Exclusion is therefore not a *necessary* consequence of their consumption.[5]

The idea is that if, for example, Anne invents a new logical method and makes it available to her colleagues, Andrew and Angus, this won't in any way prevent her from using it, or diminish its usefulness for her. But if she owns a tangible thing, such as a lawnmower, and makes *that* available to Andrew and Angus, their use of it may well compete with hers and diminish its usefulness to her. Another way of putting this is to say that intangible property, unlike tangible property, is 'non-zero-sum':

> when I eat an apple there is one less apple for everyone else – my plus one and everyone else's sums to zero. With intangible property it is not as if my acquisition leaves one less for everyone else.[6]

The fact that intellectual property is 'joint' or 'non-rivalrous' is important, not least because ideas about the just distribution of *scarce* goods, which have a major role in our thinking about tangibles, don't seem to apply directly to intellectual property.

We can turn now to look at the ethical issues which fall under the heading 'Intellectual property rights in the human body'. Such issues arise at a number of levels and certainly don't *necessarily* have anything to do with genetics. For example, there's no reason in principle why someone couldn't own the 'design' of a particular arm or leg or, for that matter, an overall body shape or 'look'. For the rest of this chapter, though, I'm going to concentrate on the ownership of genetic information. This, in particular the practice of DNA patenting, is the intellectual property issue which has most interested bioethicists. It has also provoked widespread public protest from religious groups and environmental pressure groups, such as Greenpeace,[7] as well as from individuals.[8] Donna Maclean, a 'poet and casino waitress' from Bristol, is a fascinating example of the latter.[9] Ms Maclean applied to patent *herself* in order 'to register her anger at the mass patenting of genes':

> 'There's a kind of unpleasant, greedy atmosphere around the mapping of the human genome', Ms Maclean told *The Guardian* newspaper ... Ms Maclean claims it has taken her 30 years of hard labour to discover and invent herself, and she now wishes to protect her invention from unauthorised exploitation, genetic or otherwise. 'I have led a private existence and I have not made the invention of myself public. I am not obvious' she added.[10]

So what exactly is this public concern about? What are people objecting to and, more importantly from the perspective of moral philosophy, what *coherent* views about the ethics of patenting human genes are available and what are the *arguments* for and against these views? There are various different ways of carving up the territory here. Perhaps the best way of starting is as shown in Table 9.1.

In the extreme left-hand column, a distinction is drawn between natural and modified gene sequences or organism-types. Something is modified, in the sense intended, if and only if

1 human intervention is a major cause of its existence;
   and
2 (a) it is brought into existence intentionally *or* (b) its coming to exist is a reasonably foreseeable effect of an intentional action.

Something is natural if and only if it is not modified; in other words, the categories 'modified' and 'natural' are, for our present purposes, mutually exclusive and exhaustive.

The first four views (from left to right) contained in Table 9.1 can be fully characterised in terms of their endorsement or denial of the following two propositions:

1 Ownership (or patenting) of natural gene sequences and organism-types is wrong (and/or should be banned).
2 Ownership (or patenting) of modified gene sequences and organism-types is wrong (and/or should be banned).

The *restrictive view* (Table 9.1, second column from the right) is the conjunction of (1) and (2). According to this view, ownership of gene sequences and organism-types is wrong, irrespective of whether they are natural or modified. The opposite of this position is the *permissive view* (column 2), which denies both (1) and (2).

Table 9.1 Views about bio-patenting

	The permissive view	*The 'no phenomena of nature' view*	*The 'no modified life forms' view*	*The restrictive view*	*Moderate and/or pragmatic views*
Natural gene sequences and organism-types[11]	OK	Wrong	OK	Wrong	Depends
Modified gene sequences and organism-types	OK	OK	Wrong	Wrong	Depends

In between are two intermediate positions. In column 3, there is the *'no phenomena of nature' view*. According to this, while patenting modified organisms is acceptable, patenting naturally occurring ones is not. Most proponents of this position are impressed by one or both of the following arguments. First, there is the idea that phenomena of nature cannot (by definition) be *invented*, as opposed to merely *discovered*. Hence, they cannot rightfully be patented, since patenting is meant only for inventions. Second, there is the idea that natural phenomena should not be patented because they are, in an important sense, collective property. As the US Supreme Court put it in 1948, they are

> part of the storehouse of knowledge of all men . . . manifestations of laws of nature, free to all men and reserved exclusively to none.[12]

The other intermediate position is the *'no modified life forms' view*, which opposes only the patenting of *modified* life forms. What motivates this position normally has little to do with concerns about ownership *per se* and much more to do with a belief in the wrongness of modification, especially genetic modification. The argument, then, would be that we ought not to allow the patenting of modified life forms, because creating such things is immoral, and because permitting the patenting of them encourages this immorality, or amounts to wrongful state endorsement of it. This style of reasoning is widespread, and not just amongst bioethicists.[13] Nonetheless, hardly anyone holds the 'no modified life forms' view. This is not because there is little opposition to genetic modification and associated patenting but, on the contrary, because most people who are opposed to genetic modification are opposed to the patenting of phenomena of nature as well, making them adherents of what I called earlier the restrictive view. Partly for this reason and partly because, as I suggested earlier, the 'no modified life forms' view has more to do with concerns about modification than about *comm*odification, it will not be examined in detail during this chapter.

Finally, in the extreme right-hand column, there are *moderate* or *pragmatic* views. Adherents of these don't take a *principled* stand against (or for) the patenting of modified or natural biological entities. Rather, they assess particular patenting practices and policies on pragmatic grounds. Someone who held such a view might, for example, believe that regulations (ones which may cut across or ignore the modified–natural distinction) are required in order to stop patenting from damaging important goods, such as scientific progress, medical therapy, or respect for human rights.[14] Adherents of these views are often, but needn't be, utilitarians.

So, to sum up, there appear to be five main types of view about which biological types, if any, it is ethical to patent. The restrictive view says that there are no such types. The permissive view says that, at least in principle, any type may be patented. The 'no phenomena of nature' view says that only modified biological types may be patented. The 'no modified life forms' view says that only naturally occurring biological types may be patented. Finally, moderate or pragmatic views disregard the modified/natural distinction and assess particular patenting practices and policies on their merits.

In the remaining parts of this chapter, arguments for the first three of these positions will be examined in more detail. Moderate or pragmatic views will also be revisited in section 9.4, which considers utilitarian arguments for and against gene patenting.

Before we finish this taxonomy of views, a couple of possible difficulties with the modified–natural distinction should be noted. The first is that whether something gets counted as modified or natural depends partly on what 'level' is considered: 'micro-' or 'whole organism'. For example, an engineered animal consisting entirely of elements found in nature (for example, natural gene sequences) might be created. Considered only at the 'micro-' level, such an animal is natural, since each individual component is natural. But at the 'whole organism' level it is modified, since the inventors have caused a new type of organism to exist by recombining these natural elements. Conversely, one could in principle replicate a naturally occurring organism using artificial elements. Such a creature might be natural at the 'organism level' but modified at the 'micro-' level. None of this necessarily presents a problem for the modified–natural distinction, or for ethical views which deploy it. What it does demonstrate, though, is that we must be careful to specify the level at which the thing in question is claimed to be modified or natural. Otherwise, ambiguity and confusion may ensue.

The second complication is that there are difficult borderline cases. One of these is the long-established practice of selective breeding for such creatures as cattle, dogs, and horses. Are, for instance, pedigree dogs modified organisms? I take it that there is no doubt about the intentions of selective breeders; they are clearly engaged in attempts to produce creatures which are, in some sense, new types, with especially desirable characteristics. Hence, on the distinction outlined above, whether (for example) selectively bred dogs count as modified will depend on whether human intervention is 'a major cause' of their existence. It would be unwise to generalise about this, partly because the extent of human involvement will vary from case to case, and partly because the idea of 'major cause' (not something that can be unpacked further here) is necessarily rather vague. I mention this, then, simply to draw attention to the fact that distinguishing between modified and other organisms may be more difficult than it at first appears.[15]

9.2 Biopiracy

> Our land, our culture, our subsoil, our ideology and our traditions have all been exploited and this could be another form of exploitation. Only this time they are using *us* as raw materials.[16]

As well as the views just outlined, there is a rather different group of ethical concerns which we might usefully call the *anti-biopiracy view*.[17] This is not about the wrongness of commercialisation *per se*, although it is often conjoined or confused with more general concerns about commercialisation. Rather, it is about the mistreatment which can occur when, through patenting and other kinds of commercial exploitation, individual scientists or biotechnology companies 'steal' genetic information from the bodies or environments of 'indigenous peoples' or from the bodies of Western individuals who are patients or research subjects.

The web pages of Greenpeace provide a clear statement of the worry about 'indigenous peoples'. Consider, for example, the following extract from a page called simply 'Biopiracy':[18]

> Genetic diversity is at its richest in the countries of the Third World. The rainforests of the South are home to over half the world's plant and animal species. In what the industry calls 'bioprospecting', scouts are sent to these areas to seek out valuable organisms or plants, often drawing upon the wisdom of indigenous peoples. They then take samples back to laboratories where they isolate active ingredients or genetic sequences and patent them as their own invention . . . in many cases, communities end up having to pay multinational corporations for the right to use something that was previously part of their legacy.[19]

Similarly, the Blue Mountain Declaration contains a strong statement about the rights of 'indigenous peoples' and the dangers that they face:

> Indigenous peoples, their knowledge and resources are the primary target for the commodification of genetic resources. We call upon all individuals and organizations to recognize these peoples' sovereign rights to self-determination and territorial rights, and to support their efforts to protect themselves, their lands and genetic resources from commodification and manipulation.[20]

Numerous examples of alleged biopiracy have been reported. One often-cited and controversial example is the Human Genome Diversity Project (HGDP), referred to by some as the 'vampire project'.[21] This aims to

188

provide useful information about the causes of diseases and also about social and historical questions, such as patterns of migration, human origins, and sources of ethnic diversity. The purported goal of the research is nothing less than finding out who we are and how we came to be.[22]

HGDP was originally supposed to involve the taking of DNA samples from more than 700 human populations, including many 'indigenous peoples'. According to Greenpeace, these include the San peoples of the Kalahari, Australian aborigines, the Penan of Sarawak, Latin American Indians, and the Saami of northern Scandinavia.[23] Some of these groups were viewed and described by researchers as 'dying tribes', 'disappearing peoples', 'vanishing opportunities', and 'endangered species'. Thus, part of the motivation for the project was to stop genetic resources from being 'lost forever'.[24] The idea was that, eventually, the DNA samples would be fed into 'tissue museums' which would be accessible to researchers, including those belonging to biotechnology companies. Opponents, however, feared that this could lead to much more systematic and widespread commercial exploitation of the genetic heritage of 'indigenous peoples'. Speaking of this, Debra Harry, a Northern Paiute activist, says:

> Our lives and lands have been under continual assault for the past 500 years . . . we've endured generations of outright war and genocidal policies. Now they've come to take our blood and tissues.[25]

Andrews and Nelkin report that the extraction of blood and tissue for research purposes spawned a great deal of 'angry opposition . . . reflecting deep historical resentments and cultural conflicts' and that, for this reason, HGDP 'foundered and greatly scaled back its goals'.[26]

Another example of alleged biopiracy is the case of the Samoan traditional healers. For hundreds of years, these healers have been using the small tree *Homalanthus Nutans* for medicinal purposes. Its stem wood is used to treat yellow fever, its root to treat diarrhoea, and its leaves to treat back pain.[27] According to a report in the *Guardian* (21 December 2000) samples of this plant have been collected and taken back to the US by the National Cancer Institute, as it contains prostratin, a possible drug for the treatment of HIV. It is claimed that this drug is now being developed and has 'the potential to earn millions'.[28] Keith Perry writes:[29]

> It might have been a good example of traditional medicine and modern science working hand in hand, with the financial rewards being channelled back to the developing countries which

originally shared the medical knowledge of their ancestors. But sadly for the Samoan villagers, there is no record of the American scientists having sought any prior agreement with the Samoan government, local communities or healers for the collection and use of the plant and the associated knowledge. They are unlikely to receive a penny.[30]

As I suggested earlier, these concerns have no *necessary* connection with opposition to the ownership of genetic information. This is because one way of framing them is to say that, through bioprospecting, Western companies are stealing *what should really belong to* 'indigenous peoples'. Furthermore, one obvious remedy is to assign to indigenous peoples property rights in profitable products developed as a result of samples taken from their environment, or from their traditional medicines. So the ethical worry here is not about ownership *per se*, but rather about *who* comes to own the genetic information and *how* they come to own it: about whether the present ownership arrangements are exploitative, unjust, or harmful to indigenous peoples.

Very similar issues are raised by individuals whose genetic material has been 'stolen'.[31] One of the most famous cases of this type is *Moore v. Regents of the University of California*.[32] Moore was treated at UCLA's medical centre in the late 1970s for a rare disease called hairy-cell leukaemia. Moore's doctor, David Golde, recommended the removal of his spleen, which was duly done. During the next seven years, Moore returned to the UCLA Medical Centre on a number of occasions. He was asked to give samples of blood, bone marrow, skin, and semen and told that these were necessary to monitor and maintain his good health.

Dr Golde discovered at an early stage that Moore's body was over-producing lymphokines. These have an important role in human immune systems. With this in mind, Golde arranged, before its removal and without Moore knowing, to have parts of the spleen held back for research purposes. He also (again, without Moore's knowledge) used samples provided at follow-up visits for his research. The outcome of the research was that Golde managed to

> create a culture of cells producing lymphokines. This cell line differed from Moore's ordinary cells only in that, through a well-known but sometimes difficult process, the cells in the cell line were enabled to reproduce themselves indefinitely.[33]

This cell line and its derivatives had huge commercial potential, valued at around $3 billion. It was patented and both Golde and the University of California made sizeable amounts of money from it, again without informing Moore. Later Moore found out for himself what had been going on and initiated legal action. The ensuing legal battle was complex but, in brief, Moore lost his main claim (for compensation for conversion), the California Supreme Court finding that he had no proprietary interest in his removed cells.

Moore is less obviously a case of intellectual property theft than some of the indigenous peoples' cases, in particular, those which involve traditional medicines. For whereas, in the traditional medicine cases, a person's, or a community's, *invention* (or, at least, discovery) is patented non-consensually by a third party, such as a biotech company, in *Moore*, Moore was not the *inventor* of what was 'stolen'. Rather, it was a product of nature (or something which someone else had *developed from* a product of nature) – albeit a part of nature with which he was intimately connected. Hence, *Moore* is a case of intellectual property theft only if we think that people have wide-ranging property rights in their own bodies, covering not only physical parts, but also intellectual property. We might, however, reasonably complain instead that Moore's spleen and other body parts and products were used as physical raw material in a production process without his consent, thereby breaching his rights over his body's physical parts.

The main ethical objection in all of these 'biopiracy' cases concerns not the commercialisation of genetic information *per se*, but rather exploitation and/or a failure to obtain proper consent, something which can occur with or without commercialisation. For this reason, I shall not pay a great deal of attention to biopiracy in the rest of the chapter, although issues relating to it will arise from time to time. In this respect, biopiracy is rather like organ theft. It serves as a useful reminder of what *can* happen if a commercial market isn't properly constrained and regulated, but it doesn't directly feed into an argument against patenting. So (as I said of organ theft) using biopiracy as a direct argument against DNA patenting in general would be like arguing against all employment on the grounds that there are some cases of slavery, or arguing against property because there are some cases of robbery. That said, if it could be shown that biopiracy is an inevitable, or a highly likely, consequence of permitting DNA patenting, then that would constitute an objection to it.

9.3 Contemporary regulation and practice

The rest of this chapter focusses more narrowly on the patenting of biological entities and, in particular, on the question of what special ethical issues are raised by DNA patenting, and of how compelling the moral arguments against this practice are. It is impossible to understand the complex issues raised by these questions without at least a basic grasp of some of the practical details. Section 9.3, therefore, aims to provide a brief description and analysis of contemporary regulation and practice and of how things came to be as they are.

(A) What is patenting and what is patentable?

The patent system aims to encourage the creation, commercial exploitation, and distribution of useful or otherwise desirable new inventions. Its origins can be traced as far back as the thirteenth century, and the first formal patent law is normally attributed to the Venetians, who in 1474 wrote the following in their patenting statute's preamble:[34]

> We have among us men of great genius, apt to invent and discover ingenious devices; and in view of the grandeur and virtue of our City, more such men come to us every day from diverse parts. Now, if provision were made for the works and devices discovered by such persons, so that others who may see them could not build them and take the inventor's honour away, more men would then apply their genius, would discover, and would build devices of great utility and benefit to our commonwealth.[35]

In most important respects, thinking about patenting has changed little in the last 500 years, and today, the very same argument as that offered by the Venetians is used to justify the patent system. Even the patenting of life forms isn't exactly new. The first known patent on a living organism was issued in Finland in 1843 and, in 1873, Pasteur was granted an American patent for a particular variety of yeast.[36]

The patent system involves granting and enforcing certain rights over intellectual property. These rights are quite limited, and holding a patent certainly can't be equated with fully-fledged ownership. Rather, a patent is a time-limited and conditional monopoly, granted and enforced by the state (or a state-sanctioned international organisation, such as the European Patent Office or the World Intellectual Property Organisation) on the use of an invention or design. A patent doesn't give its holder a right to produce, sell, or use the object in question. Rather, it just gives her a right to prevent others from doing so.

In virtually all jurisdictions, the object of a successful patent must be both *novel* and *inventive*. The *European Patent Convention*, for example, says that patents

> shall be granted for any inventions which are susceptible of industrial application, *which are new and which involve an inventive step*.[37]

Both novelty and inventiveness are to be understood primarily in terms of *the state of the art*, a term which refers to 'everything made available to the public by means of a written or oral description, by use, or in any other way'. So, roughly, the state of the art consists of that which is in the public domain.

An invention is *novel* if and only if it does not form part of the state of the art.[38] This is one reason why bodies involved in the Human Genome Project, such as the Sanger Centre in Cambridgeshire, publish their results daily on the internet.[39] By doing so, they make such knowledge part of the state of the art, thereby warding off patent claims by biotech companies. The idea of being *inventive*, or *involving an inventive step*, is slightly more complicated. One part of this requirement is that 'having regard to the state of the art' the invention must not be obvious 'to a person skilled in the art'.[40] Non-obviousness, however, is necessary but *not* sufficient for 'involving an inventive step', and certain kinds of non-obvious creation are not counted as inventions. In Europe, these include specifically:

(a) discoveries, scientific theories and mathematical methods; (b) aesthetic creations; (c) schemes, rules and methods for performing mental acts, playing games or doing business, and programs for computers; (d) presentations of information.[41]

This does not necessarily mean, however, that there cannot be *any* intellectual property rights in these types of thing, as they may be protected under separate copyright and trademark provisions.

(B) Patenting natural phenomena?

Recent developments in biotechnology have forced courts and legislators to address, or revisit, two fundamental questions about patenting. Is it possible (and, if so, under what circumstances) to patent *natural phenomena*? And is it possible to patent *modified organisms*?

One obvious reason for thinking that natural phenomena cannot be patented is the *inventive step requirement* and, in particular, the specific exclusion of 'discoveries' and 'scientific theories' from the category 'invention'. Natural phenomena are already 'out there' waiting to be discovered and so they cannot, one would think, be invented or patented. In principle, both European and US law support this view. For example, in a leading US case, *Diamond, Commissioner of Patents and Trademarks* v. *Chakrabarty* (henceforth, *Chakrabarty*), the US Supreme Court stated:

the laws of nature, physical phenomena and abstract ideas [are] not . . . patentable; a new mineral discovered in the earth or a new plant found in the wild is not patentable subject matter, and no patent could be obtained for Einstein's celebrated law or for the law of gravity, such discoveries being manifestations of nature which are free to all men and reserved exclusively to none.[42]

Chakrabarty is worth looking at in a little more detail, not only because of its intrinsic interest, but also because it had important implications for the way that US law views the patenting of biological material – and, ultimately, encouraged other parts of the world, notably Europe, to re-evaluate their positions.[43] Furthermore, the decision in *Chakrabarty* is believed by some commentators to have been 'a major factor in the phenomenal growth of the biotechnology industry'.[44]

The Supreme Court's view was that a patent should be granted to Ananda Chakrabarty, a microbiologist. Chakrabarty had 'invented' a bacterium which could break down crude oil in the event of a spill. There was no known naturally occurring bacterium with this capability. He created the new bacterium by introducing a naturally occurring strand of genetic material into an existing bacterium. His method was simply to culture together different strains of bacteria, in the hope that they would exchange genetic material, just as they might in nature. Chakrabarty believed at the outset that he hadn't *invented* anything and only filed for a patent after receiving legal advice[45]. Indeed, he

> was amazed at the Court's decision, since he had used common-place methods that also occur naturally to exchange genetic material between bacteria. 'I simply shuffled genes, changing bacteria that already existed', Chakrabarty told *People* magazine. 'It's like teaching your pet cat a few new tricks.'[46]

The main objection to Chakrabarty's original patent application was that previous US case law, especially *Funk Brothers Seed Co* v. *Kalo Inoculant Co*, had clearly established the doctrine that 'patents cannot issue for the discovery of the phenomena of nature'.[47] In *Funk Brothers*, this doctrine was used to justify denying Funk Brothers Seed Co. a patent for their 'invention', a mixture of different types of bacteria. The mixture was an effective inoculant for leguminous plants (so it had a clearly defined industrial application) and did not occur in nature. However, each bacterium in the mixture did occur naturally. The Supreme Court took the latter fact to be decisive. Merely mixing together natural products is not enough to justify a patent, even where these natural products have been put into a more useful form. Rather, a necessary condition for patentability is that the inventor must 'add something to nature's handiwork'. Similar arguments were heard in *Chakrabarty*. The objection was that he shouldn't be allowed a patent since (a) the most important parts of his invention, the existing bacteria and their genetic material, were phenomena of nature, and (b) the method for creating the invention was itself a natural process, one which he at most 'helped along'. Furthermore, *Chakrabarty* appears identical to *Funk Brothers* in important respects. For example, in both cases, naturally occurring things are usefully combined in ways which could have occurred naturally, given the right conditions.

In *Chakrabarty*, the Supreme Court reaffirmed the validity of the 'no phenomena of nature' doctrine, but held that Chakrabarty's invention was not a phenomenon of nature because human intervention, in particular his ingenuity and research, was involved in bringing it into being. So, while *merely discovering* a previously unknown natural phenomenon cannot generate a valid patent claim, 'goods that have been *transformed from their natural state* or ideas that have been *put to a practical end* are patentable'.[48] As the Supreme Court put it in this case, 'his discovery is not nature's handiwork, but his own'.

The importance of this case is that it introduces an extremely permissive understanding of the 'phenomena of nature' exclusion on patentability and permits the patenting of life forms even where (a) the level of human intervention involved in 'creating' them is minimal and (b) the invented life form results from merely replicating a natural process or substance. In practice, this means a substantial weakening of the 'no phenomena of nature' doctrine and a blurring of the related distinction between invention and discovery – at least in the biotechnology sector. Since *Chakrabarty*, there has been widespread DNA patenting. Resnik reports that

> Since the 1980s, the United States' (US) Patent and Trademark Office (PTO) has issued 2,330 patents on isolated and purified DNA sequences. The US government has the largest number of DNA patents (388), followed by Incyte Pharmaceuticals (356), University of California (265), SmithKline Beecham (197), and Genetech (175). The number of applications for DNA patents has risen dramatically in the last six years from less than 500 per year in 1994 to nearly 3000 in 1999.[49]

While, according to Sagoff,

> With few exceptions, the products of nature for which patents [were] issued were not changed, redesigned, or improved to make them more useful. Indeed, the utility of these proteins, genes, and cells typically depends on their functional equivalence with naturally occurring substances.[50]

Examples include Harvard University's patenting of GP120,[51] a naturally occurring protein on the coat of the human immunodeficiency virus; SyS-temix Inc's patenting of human bone marrow stem cells;[52] and Myriad Genetics' patenting of the breast and ovarian cancer gene, BRCA1.[53]

So is the patenting of natural phenomena now permitted? The answer is that while the patenting of natural phenomena *per se* is not allowed, the patenting of entities or processes closely connected to natural phenomena is. This includes techniques for isolating or testing for natural phenomena, ways of replicating natural phenomena, and ways of using natural phenomena. Resnik helpfully divides these patents into three categories. First, there are *composition of matter* or *structure* patents, which cover 'isolated and purified or modified' DNA sequences. Second, there are *function* patents, patents on using a DNA sequence in a particular way. Finally, there are *process* patents, patents on techniques for isolating, purifying, sequencing, analysing, synthesising, or modifying DNA.[54] Of these, function patents are perhaps the most controversial, both ethically and legally. One of the main issues concerns breadth. In other words, how narrow or specific must a function patent claim be in order to be valid? The problem with excessive breadth is that if a biotech company is able to obtain a sufficiently broad patent (i.e. one where the specified use is relatively vague and/or wide-ranging) on an application of a natural substance, this amounts to a *de facto* patent of the substance itself (since all or virtually all possible uses are covered). Much contemporary concern about biotech patents is about just this issue. Early American DNA patents 'were tied to extensive knowledge about the genes, including their role in specific diseases'.[55] However, in more recent times, they have become broader and more speculative.[56] As Harold Varmus, former head of the (US) National Institute of Health, puts it:

> Some of the issued patents have seemed very broad in their claims. Other issued patents appear to cover many possible gene functions that were only speculative at the time of submission. Moreover, patenting of incomplete genes and of gene variations implies that multiple parties may hold title to part or all of the same gene.[57]

So far, our discussion of regulation and practice has focussed almost exclusively on the US – not least because that is where the most dramatic (and, arguably, disturbing) developments have taken place. It is, however, worth saying something about the position in Europe. European law on DNA patenting comes from two main sources. The first is the European Union, in particular, the EC Directive on the Legal Protection of Biotechnological Inventions (98/44/EC), which was adopted by the Council and European Parliament on 6 July 1998. Since 30 July 2000, all member states of the European Union (EU) have had a duty to ensure that their domestic patent laws are compatible with it.[58] In many important respects, the directive simply brings Europe into line with the position in the US. For this reason, many see the directive as being mainly about ensuring that the European biotechnology industry is internationally competitive, rather than about enforcing ethical constraints through regulation.[59] The second source of European patent law is the *European Patent Convention* (revised in 2000) and the European Patent Office (EPO). The EPO is not a European Union body (and, similarly, the Convention is not an EU document). Rather, it was established by convention in 1977 as a freestanding supranational organisation. At present, its powers range over approximately twenty countries, not all of which are EU members. Hence, implementing EU directives is not, strictly speaking, part of the EPO's role (since EU directives don't, of course, apply to the non-EU signatories of the *European Patent Convention*).[60] That said, the EC Directive on the Legal Protection of Biotechnological Inventions (98/44/EC) and the *European Patent Convention* do share much of the same material, and so the distinction between the EU and the EPO needn't concern us too much for the present.

To turn now to the content of European law, the directive does prohibit certain kinds of patenting. For example, Article 4 says that plant and animal varieties and 'essentially biological processes' for producing plants and animals cannot be patented, and Article 5(1) says that

> The human body . . . and the simple discovery of one of its elements, including the sequence or partial sequence of a gene, cannot constitute patentable inventions.

However, the directive stops far short of banning DNA patenting, and a biological entity may be eligible for patenting if it meets the standard conditions, such as novelty and inventiveness. Furthermore, provided that the desired industrial application is disclosed from the outset, Article 5 allows that

> An element isolated from the human body or otherwise produced by means of a technical process, including the sequence or partial sequence of a gene, may constitute a patentable invention, even if the structure of that element is identical to that of a natural element.[61]

Similarly, Article 3 allows that

> Biological material which is isolated from its natural environment or produced by means of a technical process may be the subject of an invention *even if it previously existed in nature*.[62]

Taken together, these articles seem to go as far as *Chakrabarty*. For while, in theory, there is still a phenomena of nature exclusion, in practice, the exclusion is quite weak. Structure patents, function patents, and process patents all seem to be permitted.

(C) Modified organisms

So far, I've focussed solely on the question of whether and to what extent contemporary law permits the patenting of phenomena of nature. Before ending this section, though, it's worth saying something briefly about modified organisms. Can modified organisms be patented? The answer to this is (a slightly qualified) 'yes'. Almost by definition, modified organisms are inventions. Therefore, they are much less problematic, as far as the basic principles of patent law are concerned, than natural phenomena. For this reason, legal arguments against this kind of biotech patenting normally import more general moral or public policy considerations. For example, in *Chakrabarty*, the following argument (against granting the patent) was heard:

> The briefs present a gruesome parade of horribles. Scientists, among them Nobel laureates, are quoted suggesting that genetic research may pose a serious threat to the human race, or, at the very least, that the dangers are far too substantial to permit such research to proceed apace at this time. We are told that genetic research and related technological developments may spread pollution and disease, that it may result in a loss of genetic diversity, and that its practice may tend to depreciate the value of human life.[63]

The US Supreme Court rejected this, saying that it was 'without competence to entertain these arguments' and that these are political matters to be addressed by Congress.

The situation in Europe is a little different. Article 6 of the EC Directive on the Legal Protection of Biotechnological Inventions (98/44/EC) and Article 53 of the *European Patent Convention* prohibit the patenting of biotechnological inventions which are 'contrary to *ordre public* or morality', including processes for cloning humans, for altering the germ-line genetic identity of humans, and for modifying the genetic identity of animals in ways which 'are likely to cause them suffering without any substantial medical benefit to man or animal'.[64] Also, the European Patent Office announced in October 2000 that this '*ordre public* or morality' restriction would prevent them from granting patents on such things as 'mixed-species embryos'.[65] Presumably, the rationale for these exclusions is that granting such patents would encourage or endorse immoral behaviour on the part of patent holders.

9.4 Practical and utilitarian arguments

Moral arguments about DNA patenting can be divided into two broad categories. First, there are utilitarian arguments, focussing solely on the good or bad effects of the practice. Second, there are claims, and counter-claims, about the 'intrinsic' wrongness of DNA patenting, such as the argument that it is incompatible with a proper respect for human dignity. In this section, I assess arguments of the first kind, starting with the utilitarian case in favour of allowing DNA patenting, saving arguments of the second kind for subsequent sections.[66]

(A) The utilitarian case for DNA patenting

The main utilitarian argument for restricting access to goods through their commercialisation (i.e. through the use of private ownership and markets) is the *economic efficiency argument*. This has two parts: the *distributive efficiency argument* and the *productive efficiency argument*. Each one is a claim about a supposed advantage of commercialisation. The first (distributive efficiency) says that, when commercialisation is permitted in situations of scarcity,

> it [is] more likely that the good will be consumed by those who really value or need it – or at least value or need it more than others; prices . . . can help bring about a more efficient distribution, in the sense of one in which more desires are satisfied.[67]

The second (productive efficiency) says that, with commercialisation in place,

> we have an incentive to produce . . . goods that would not exist if they did not have the status of commodities. This incentive, how-ever, lasts only as long as there is a demand for such goods – so this is an incentive to produce enough of any given commodity to satisfy demand, but no more.[68]

It is not clear how, if at all, the distributive efficiency argument can be applied directly to intellectual property. The argument attempts to justify commercialisation by claiming that it is a good way of managing scarcity. However, since intellectual property is (as was mentioned in section 9.1) non-rivalrous, it cannot be scarce and, hence, the distributive efficiency argument cannot apply to it.[69]

In the case of intellectual property, then, the utilitarian argument must focus solely on productive efficiency: in particular, the argument from incentives. In other words, the justification is that by allowing patenting, we encourage people to benefit humankind by investing time and money in attempts to produce useful or otherwise desirable new compositions, designs, inventions, etc. This general argument can be applied in a straightforward way to DNA patenting. Allowing patenting, it's claimed, encourages biotechnology companies to invest in expensive, and potentially very beneficial, research and development. Haseltine and Scott offer us clear statements of this argument:

> Nowhere are patents more central to the creative process than in genetic drug development ... The biotechnology industry in the United States ... is on the threshold of a bonanza of genetic drugs and vastly greater relief for ill and aging populations around the world. Patent protection is the *sine qua non* of that bonanza. Discovering and developing a new gene-based pharmaceutical product in the United States requires years of commitment and immense capital resources – as much as $500 million. Without the possibility of recouping investment that is bestowed by patents, no biotechnology company would be able to raise the financing necessary to develop these products.[70]

> The patent system is designed to create incentives for invention, and nowhere is its role more apparent than in the case of genomic inventions. Existing patent guidelines, which have spurred the tremendous advances we've recently seen in medical research, must remain intact to ensure continued discovery. These revelations already have made a profound impact on the acceleration of drug development and the availability of new molecular diagnostic tests. The real world utility of these discoveries entitles them to patent protection.[71]

By the mid-1990s, private industry in the US alone was investing in excess of $100 billion per year in research and development, roughly half of which was spent in the biomedical sector.[72] Clearly, without the protection that patenting gives, companies would be unlikely to invest such huge sums in research.

The utilitarian argument in favour of permitting DNA patenting, then, can be broken down as follows:

1 Permitting DNA patenting is the best way of bringing about the development of genetic biotechnology.
2 The development of genetic biotechnology will have significant good effects (for example, medical treatments) and relatively few bad ones.
3 *Therefore* we ought to permit DNA patenting.

There are three kinds of objection to this argument, some of which also constitute positive arguments against DNA patenting. First, there are those which challenge the argument's validity – or its suppressed utilitarian premise – claiming that *even if* (1) and (2) are true, (3) does not follow, since there are non-utilitarian moral considerations to be taken into account. Some of these are discussed in section 9.5. Second, there are objections which dispute (1), claiming that patenting is not in fact the best way to engender biotechnological progress. These are discussed next. Third, there are objections which dispute (2), by claiming either that the alleged benefits of developments of biotechnology don't exist, or that these benefits are outweighed by the likely negative side-effects (either the side-effects of the technology itself or those of the patenting process).

(B) Biotechnological progress

Is patenting necessary for biotechnological progress, as Haseltine claims? There are two main arguments for thinking that it is not. The first states that, rather than boosting scientific progress, the widespread use of patenting in this area impedes it, by reducing the scientific community's access to information and suppressing academic freedom.[73] Consider, for example, these remarks:

> it is feared that the piles of patents deter and inhibit scientific inquiry. Any discovery now requires negotiating a complicated series of intellectual property suits.[74]

> I've been at conferences where we have been addressed by patent lawyers and told to stop showing our colleagues our notebooks, or to think twice about submitting an abstract at a meeting . . . It's a common experience at scientific meetings for people to withhold information because they have a patent pending. Progress is being slowed down.[75]

Furthermore, it's not just 'healthy' or 'positive' competition which accompanies the patenting process. There is also what we might term 'negative' competition – the use of patents by companies which have no interest in developing the product in question themselves and whose only interest is in preventing its development by competitors:

> what patent protection ensures is not technological development, but suppression of competition. Patents are as often used to prevent the development of new technologies as to exploit them.[76]

The second argument casts doubt on the claim that, without patenting, there would be no, or insufficient, investment in biotechnology. It does this by pointing out that there are other methods of funding such investment that are at least as good: most obviously, government funding. Clearly, public funding of this kind of scientific research is a real possibility and there have been some notable successes of this sort, such as national space programmes, weapons programmes, and multinational ventures like the human genome project.

As well as these general views about the relationship between patenting and biotechnological progress, there are more complex intermediate positions, which sanction some kinds of patenting, but not others. An example of this is the view of the Intellectual Property Rights Committee of HUGO (the Human Genome Organisation). HUGO has a 'generally positive attitude toward patenting',[77] but distinguishes 'patenting of *useful benefits derived from* genetic information' from 'patenting of short sequences from randomly isolated proteins of genes encoding proteins *of uncertain functions*'.[78] HUGO does not oppose the former. On the contrary, like Haseltine, it believes that such patents are necessary 'for securing adequate high risk investments in biology'.[79] However, it opposes the latter, since (it argues) such patents impede scientific research, by restricting access to basic information and to research tools. Information about DNA molecules and their sequences is what HUGO calls *pre-competitive*; it should be freely available in the public domain, in order to enable and stimulate research and development.

These biotechnological progress arguments (on both sides) rely heavily on empirical premises about which there's little agreement and which can't be assessed thoroughly here. (Indeed, such an assessment would fall way outside the ethicist's remit.) That said, it does seem to me that we should have quite serious reservations about DNA patenting's supposed ability to deliver an enhanced level of biotechnological progress, as well as some concerns about its stifling innovation. In particular, we should (with HUGO) be concerned about the ways in which some patents seek to limit access to basic information and research tools.

The main arguments for this view are clearly outlined in an extremely useful paper by Michael Heller and Rebecca Eisenberg, whose arguments I shall review briefly below.[80] The leading idea in their paper is 'the tragedy of the anti-commons':

> a resource is prone to underuse in a 'tragedy of the anticommons' when multiple owners each have a right to exclude others from a scarce resource and no one has an effective privilege of use.[81]

This idea is contrasted with 'the tragedy of the commons', in which (roughly) a scarce resource is *over*used because no one has the right to exclude others from accessing it. In one 'tragedy' there are too many property rights; in the other, too few. Heller and Eisenberg suggest that the 'tragedy of the anti-commons' model gives us a way of understanding certain problematic aspects of biotechnology patenting, and offer two specific examples: the patenting of gene fragments and RTLAs (reach-through licence agreements).

To look first at patenting gene fragments, the main problem here is that any given end product (for example, a pharmaceutical) may involve the use of numerous fragments, since 'property rights around gene fragments' are 'unlikely to track socially useful bundles of property rights in future commercial products'.[82] And if the required fragments each belong to a different patent holder, then it will be costly and difficult for (say) a pharmaceutical company to assemble the portfolio of rights needed to develop and market a practical commercial product. Indeed, the company may decide to pull out of such products altogether, fearful of high legal costs and prolonged delays. To use a musical analogy, allowing the patenting of gene fragments is a little like allowing thousands of people speculatively to claim copyright on musical fragments (consisting of, say, just two or three notes) and then expecting composers to negotiate with all these fragment-owners before creating and releasing a whole piece of music.

To turn now to RTLAs, these

> give the owner of a patented invention, used in upstream stages of research, rights in subsequent downstream discoveries. Such rights may take the form of a royalty on sales that result from use of the upstream research tool, an exclusive or nonexclusive licence on future discoveries, or an option to acquire such a licence.[83]

RTLAs can sometimes be appropriate for those researchers who need to use patented research tools but who have limited funds to pay for such use. Instead of paying an upfront fee, these researchers may offer the patent holder a royalty if a profitable downstream discovery or invention ensues. However, as Heller and Eisenberg point out, RTLAs can also contribute to the development of an anti-commons situation. For, as RTLAs become more widespread, the position of downstream researchers and their relationships both with upstream patent holders and with commercial organisations that might seek to purchase or otherwise exploit their discoveries will become progressively more complicated, and this in turn may put people off doing and investing in downstream research.

Problems like these aren't an inevitable or necessary part of biotechnology patenting. Indeed,

> In theory, in a world of costless transactions, people could always avoid commons or anticommons tragedies by trading their rights.[84]

In the real world, however,

> avoiding tragedy requires overcoming transaction costs, strategic behaviors, and cognitive biases of participants, with success more likely within close-knit communities than among hostile strangers. Once an anticommons emerges, collecting rights into usable private property is often brutal and slow.[85]

Heller and Eisenberg go on to describe in some detail different ways in which these factors function in the biotechnology sector. I'll briefly mention here just two examples: high transaction costs and cognitive bias.

Intellectual property transaction costs in the biotechnology sector are likely to be high for several reasons. One is the sheer complexity of what's patented. Another is that, given (a) the 'diverse set of techniques, reagents, DNA sequences, and instruments'[86] that might be patented, and (b) the fact that many upstream patents are speculative and of uncertain value, it will be hard to come up with a standard distribution or valuation scheme. This means costly case-by-case negotiation. These high transaction costs may lead to or perpetuate an anti-commons tragedy in the biotechnology area because some investors and researchers will decide (perhaps rationally) that the cost/profit ratio isn't sufficiently favourable and will pull out of the sector altogether.

Cognitive bias may exacerbate anti-commons problems because

> People consistently overestimate the likelihood that very low probability events of high salience will occur. For example, many travellers overestimate the danger of an airplane crash relative to the hazards of other modes of transportation.[87]

Another, perhaps more pertinent, example is the fact that people who buy lottery tickets often massively overestimate their chances of winning (which is one reason why they buy tickets and why lotteries can be profitable). Heller and Eisenberg argue that a similar bias affects the creators and owners of upstream biomedical research. Most upstream biomedical discoveries will have almost no downstream commercial value, but a small minority will turn out to have huge commercial potential. Which downstream discoveries are 'hits' can't generally be known in advance, and so the upstream researcher is rather like the lottery ticket purchaser: i.e. inclined to overestimate the chances of her discovery's being a 'winner'. This pushes up costs and/or prevents research and development from taking place in the following way, contributing to an anti-commons tragedy:

Imagine that one of a set of 50 upstream inventions will likely be the key to identifying an important new drug, the rest of the set will have no practical use, and a downstream product developer is willing to pay $10 million for the set. Given the assumption that no owner knows *ex ante* which invention will be the key, a rational owner should be willing to sell her patent for the probabilistic value of $200,000. However, if each owner overestimates the likelihood that her patent will be the key, then each will demand more than the probabilistic value, the upstream owners collectively will demand more than the aggregate market value of their inputs, the downstream user will decline the offers, and the new drug will not be developed.[88]

As I've said, these arguments rely on empirical premises which can't be assessed thoroughly here. Nonetheless, Heller and Eisenberg, by invoking the idea of the anti-commons tragedy, do seem to have provided a good *prima facie* case against the claim that unfettered patenting maximises biotechnological progress and in favour of something rather more like the 'moderate' HUGO position outlined above.

(C) Negative side-effects

In this subsection, I consider anti-patenting arguments which focus on patenting's alleged negative side-effects. The first of these is that DNA patenting is harmful because it drives up the cost of clinical testing and treatment, restricting access to beneficial new technologies. A poll of American laboratory directors, cited in the *Guardian* in December 1999, reported that one-quarter of them had received letters from patent lawyers instructing them to 'stop carrying out clinical tests designed to spot early warning signs for Alzheimer's disease, breast cancer and an array of other disorders'.[89] One company, Athena Diagnostics, allegedly sent out letters claiming that it had 'acquired exclusive rights to certain tests in the diagnosis of late-onset Alzheimer's disease'. Athena then offered to perform the tests itself, but for $195 per specimen – 'more than twice the price previously being charged by some university medical laboratories'. In a similar case, healthcare professionals protested when a corporation successfully patented the use of blood cells from the umbilical cord in various different therapeutic situations.[90]

However, in defending themselves against these accusations, the biotechnology companies might reasonably reinvoke the incentive and investment argument, claiming that, although the cost of some clinical tests and treatments is indeed raised by patenting, this is more than compensated for by corresponding increases in research and development expenditure, leading ultimately to more and better tests being available.

The second side-effects objection claims that DNA patenting should not be allowed because it leads to biopiracy. There seems little doubt that allowing DNA patenting *can* cause biopiracy. We know this because it has already done so in a number of cases. (Some such cases were mentioned in section 9.2.) However, what needs to be shown for this argument to work is not merely that biopiracy is a *possible* outcome, but that it is an inevitable, or almost inevitable, consequence of allowing patenting. For if inevitability is not proven, those in favour of patenting can simply respond by saying that there should be tougher anti-biopiracy regulations, rather than a complete ban on patenting. In the face of the practical impossibility of eliminating DNA patenting altogether, this is the kind of position that many of those with concerns about the behaviour of the bioprospectors have adopted of late. For example, a November 2000 document produced by RAFI (Rural Advancement Foundation International) contains 'ten points on piracy' – in effect, anti-piracy guidelines which scientists should follow and which should be built into laws and treaties.[91] Given the possibility of regulation and control, the biopiracy argument seems not to be terribly plausible, or at least not as an argument for an outright ban of DNA patenting.

The third side-effects objection is, in a sense, the opposite of an argument discussed earlier. That argument claimed that what is wrong with patenting is that it impedes scientific progress. This argument, on the other hand, claims that what is wrong with patenting is that it speeds up scientific 'progress' and that such *so-called* 'progress' is a bad thing.

This argument is normally motivated by thoughts about the risks, particularly environmental ones, posed by biotechnology.[92] As with the previous argument, though, it seems that this one will, at most, justify tougher regulation of the biotechnology sector, rather than a complete ban on patenting. This is partly because the relationship between patenting and danger is rather indirect. Some patents pose little risk and, conversely, it is possible to subject communities to bioenvironmental hazards without using the patenting system. It is also partly because it should be possible, within the patenting system, to distinguish (albeit imperfectly) inventions which are hazardous from those that are not. Presumably, this is one (though not the only) reason why the EC Directive on the Legal Protection of Biotechnological Inventions (98/44/EC) rules out patents on processes for cloning humans and for altering the germ-line genetic identity of humans.[93] These are seen as practices likely to harm society and so patent protection is not permitted.

Finally, there are arguments which appeal to less tangible side-effects, such as the effect that the patenting of life may have on the moral climate, on our attitudes to life-in-general, or to people.[94] Such concerns are undoubtedly consequence-based. Nonetheless, it seems to me that they overlap substantially with other deontological objections that I'll be considering later, such as worries about commodification and about dignity, so I won't pursue this idea further here.

(D) Summary and conclusions

Because of the difficult empirical issues involved, any conclusions to this section are inevitably somewhat tentative. That said, it does seem to me that the following conclusions can be drawn:

1   There is clearly a utilitarian case for DNA patenting: in particular, the incentives and investment argument.
2   This case is, however, at least partially overturned by a number of counter-arguments and objections. Of these, the most forceful are those which claim that patenting actually impedes scientific progress and that it drives up costs for researchers and therapists, thereby depriving patients of beneficial interventions. In particular, Heller and Eisenberg's idea that upstream biotechnology patents on research tools encourage the creation of a 'tragedy of the anti-commons' is persuasive.
3   Given (1) and (2), a 'moderate' position is tempting: one which sanctions some kinds of patenting, but not others. A case in point is the view of the Intellectual Property Rights Committee of HUGO, which has a 'generally positive attitude toward patenting',[95] but distinguishes 'patenting of *useful benefits derived from* genetic information' from 'patenting of short sequences from randomly isolated proteins of genes encoding proteins *of uncertain functions*'.[96] The view that only the former should be allowed appears to be a way of retaining some of the benefits of patenting (for example, incentives and investment) while avoiding a tragedy of the anti-commons.

9.5 Deontological objections

In this section, I'll consider some non-utilitarian objections to DNA patenting. The main claims assessed are that human DNA patenting (a) is, in morally relevant respects, like slavery; (b) involves the commodification of genes; and (c) involves the commodification of persons. These three claims are closely related to one another. However, they do differ in emphasis, in strength, and in plausibility.

(A) Slavery

According to the slavery argument, DNA patenting is wrong because it is morally equivalent to, or similar to, slavery:[97]

A new form of slavery is emerging in industrialised nations. The masters are biotechnology companies, and they own human genes.[98]

Not since it became illegal to own slaves in the 19th century have humans sought to extend ownership control so thoroughly over other organisms. Just as with slavery in the past, genetic owner-ship in our day means the ability to control organisms; i.e., the ability to sell the organism or manipulate its reproduction for profit.[99]

Claims like these will (or should) strike readers as fanciful and rhetorical, or at least as exaggerations. Furthermore, they will strike many people as offensive, in that they belittle the horrors of the slave trade. Nonetheless, this 'argument' really does get wheeled out, frequently and in all serious-ness, by participants in public debates about biotechnology. The 1995 *Relaxin* case is a good example. In this case, the Green Party opposed an application made to the European Patent Office by the Howard Florey Institute of Experimental Physiology and Medicine (Melbourne, Aus-tralia). It was claimed that the application covered a naturally occurring substance: 'the DNA sequence (i.e. the gene obtained from a human ovary) which codes for the hormone relaxin, which relaxes the uterus during childbirth'. The Green Party objected 'on the basis that to patent human genes was patenting "life" and therefore intrinsically immoral, and also that *patenting of human genes amounts to slavery* contrary to the fundamental human right to self-determination'.[100]

I won't spend a great deal of time on this argument, since it is seriously and obviously flawed. For it's not clear in what sense, if any, the patent-ing of a human bodily substance is 'equivalent' to slavery. The former is the granting of a limited property right in a kind of chemical. The latter is the ownership of an entire person. Of course, both practices involve property and humanity, but this is where the similarity ends. The wrong-ness of slavery (which I take not to be in doubt) is derived mainly from the fact that the slave is an autonomous, rational being who has rights to liberty and respect. Being owned by another person is, of course, incompatible with these rights. Hence, slavery is wrong. In addition, there are welfare arguments against slavery, since it is normally harmful, and justice arguments, since it involves exploitation. None of these con-siderations, however, applies directly at the level of biochemistry or genet-ics. For at these levels, we are not dealing with autonomous beings, or beings who could be harmed or treated unjustly. So the assertion that patenting genes, or other microbiological material, is morally equivalent to owning a slave is suspect. Also, as Resnik points out,

we should not forget . . . that patenting does not imply ownership. Thus, patenting a person would not be the same thing as owning a person. Patenting . . . only confers a right to exclude others from making, using, or marketing an invention. It does not give the patent holder positive rights to make, use, or market the invention, especially if these practices would violate laws. Thus, someone who had a patent on a human being would not have the same rights over that human as a slave owner. The patented person would still be free to make many life decisions, although he or she would probably not be able to reproduce or market his or herself without permission from the patent holder.[101]

There is, perhaps, a version of the slavery argument that does work against certain very extreme practices, though not ones which are realistic possibilities in the short term. What I have in mind here relates to some of the concerns which people have about human cloning. Imagine the following scenario. First, someone is allowed to patent a *full set* of human genes, the full unique genome of a particular individual. Second, through cloning technology, the patent holder produces large numbers of genetically identical humans, all of whom fall under this patent. Finally, the patent holder is granted a set of oppressive legal rights in relation to 'his' (or 'her') clones: for example, the ability to charge exorbitant fees for their 'use' of 'his' (or 'her') body-type, or the ability to remove a clone's body part on demand to sell for transplantation purposes. Such a scenario is equivalent to (or worse than) slavery, and so the slavery argument would work against practices like this.

This has little direct significance for the present 'real-world' debate on patenting, however, because no one is proposing to use cloned and patented human beings as slaves or (worse still) organ farms. However, it is the kind of scenario that opponents of patenting might use in a slippery-slope version of the slavery argument: the claim being that, although present practices are not equivalent to slavery, there is a substantial risk of their degenerating into slavery. This is indeed an argument worth taking seriously, although it remains weak insofar as it depends on an unproven empirical premise about risk.

(B) *The commodification of genes*

The issue is the commodification of life and the reduction of life to its commercial value.[102]

Hanson describes *commodification* as 'the commonest and most prominent objection to the patenting of biological materials'.[103] In Chapter 3, I offered the following account of commodification:

Fungiblisation is a type of objectification which involves wrong-fully treating persons as fungible. And commodification (in the normative sense) is a type of fungiblisation: more specifically, to commodify is to fungiblise through, or because of, commerce.

So, in order to see whether the commodification objection to DNA patent-ing works, we need to know whether DNA patenting involves treating DNA and/or persons as fungible, and (if it does) whether this constitutes wrongful fungiblisation (roughly, treating as fungible something which isn't fungible).

When biotech companies patent and use genetic material in product development, their attitude is likely to be highly instrumental. Almost by definition, their interest is exclusively in the genetic material's usefulness and functionality, its ability to deliver a certain outcome. They regard the material as *fungible* (because any other genetic material which delivered the same results would be just as good) and as *having only instrumental value* (because, for them, it is simply a means to an end). However, even if we allow that the companies have (and act on) this attitude, there is still some way to go before we have a successful commodification objection. For what needs to be shown is not only that genetic material is treated as if it were fungible and (merely) 'instrumental', but also that such treatment is wrong because, in fact, such material has dignity and non-instrumental value.

There are three main ways in which this might be done. First, we could appeal to the necessary connections that (allegedly) exist between human genes and humanity or personhood. For example, it might be argued that human genetic material is necessary for and/or constitutive of humanity or personhood and, therefore, that it possesses the same kind of intrinsic value as they do. Second, we could appeal to the cultural and symbolic importance of 'human genes'. Third, we could ground value claims about genes in an environmental, or environmenta*list*, philosophy.

The first argument states that because human beings have dignity and non-instrumental value, and because human genetic material is an essen-tial part of being human, such genetic material must also have dignity, etc. Hanson describes how a number of religious critics have propounded this style of argument (although it is not necessarily a religious argument). For example, he reports the views of Richard Land and C. Ben Mitchell of the Southern Baptist Convention's Christian Life Commission:

> even though a human being may share up to 95 percent of his or her genetic material with a nonhuman species, 'the image of God pervades human life in all of its parts' . . . any gene that belongs to the human genome, even if identical to genes of other species, has a status that is unique, intrinsically valuable, and, according to

some, sacred. Furthermore, all life, as created by God and thus a gift of God, has intrinsic value.[104]

Similarly, Brody claims that DNA sequences are *special body parts* because of their 'connection to the identity of the person'.[105]

What are we to make of this argument? The first thing to say is that insofar as it claims that the intrinsic value of human DNA is *entailed by* the intrinsic value of persons, it is fallacious. For it is quite possible for a thing (for example, a person) to have a property without one of its essential parts (for example, a person's genetic constitution) having that property. For example, that your brain is an essential part of you and that you are fat do not together entail that your brain is fat – and that the CPU is an essential part of my PC and that my PC is heavy do not together entail that the CPU is heavy.[106] So, similarly, that human genes are essential for being human and that humans have intrinsic value do not together entail that human genes have intrinsic value.

This, however, is based on a very unsympathetic reading of the argument, and there are more sophisticated understandings of it which we should consider. The really difficult issue that this argument needs to grasp is: what *exactly* is the relationship between persons and human DNA? And how does the value of the whole person come to reside, or be mirrored, in that person's DNA? Typically, proponents of such arguments make quite strong claims about the relationship between genes and identity, such as 'DNA ... is the point at which true identity (and self) can be determined'.[107] But how should such statements be interpreted? There are three main ways:

1 *An identity claim*: 'being me is the very same thing as having my genetic make-up'.
2 *A causal claim*: 'my genetic make-up made me how, or who, I am today'.
3 *An 'essentialist' claim*: 'having my genetic make-up is necessary for being me'.

No matter what interpretation is chosen, though, the argument is likely to fail. (1) can be discounted as false, since clearly someone else, a replicant or a twin, could have 'my' genes. For the same reason, it is not the case that my genetic make-up is sufficient for being me, or is my *'whole essence'*. (2) is reasonably plausible, at least if moderated to include a role for environmental factors. However, a causal claim is insufficient to underpin this kind of argument. For what is required is the idea that when you patent 'my' genes, you patent me – not merely that when you patent 'my' genes, you patent what 'caused me'. Finally, (3) is problematic both because it requires further disambiguation (in relation to the different senses of 'necessity') and because it rests on dubious meta-physical assumptions about the necessity of embodiment. And crucially, as we saw earlier, a thing's essential parts need not have the same properties as the thing itself.[108]

Let's turn now to the idea that human DNA has a special moral status because of its cultural and/or symbolic importance:

> the genome plays an important symbolic role in our current society: many people now regard a person's genome as a symbol of the person. Thus, I would say that the human genome has a 'special status' as a body part because of its causal role in human physiology ... and because it has acquired symbolic importance.[109]

There are at least two serious problems with this line of argument. The first, a practical one, is that even if we agree that a person's genome is a symbol of that person, it doesn't follow from this that small *parts* of the genome, of the kind that might realistically be patented, have any sort of symbolic importance:

> none of the parts of the genome are causally or symbolically con-nected to the whole person to the same degree that the whole genome is connected to the person.[110]

The second problem is a much more general philosophical concern about the extent to which we should base law and public policy on society's views about which things are symbolically important. The most compel-ling reason for taking symbolic importance into account is that, if we don't do so, we risk offending and upsetting people. Thus, one might argue (for example) that *even if* the symbolic importance attached to dead bodies is irrational (or non-rational), we should nonetheless take it ser-iously because, if we don't, then people will be offended by the (appar-ent) disrespect shown to their dead friends and relatives. But how far should this style of reasoning be allowed to take us? What if, for example, a widespread view in our society were that the knee is symbolically important and 'represents the whole person'? Would that give us grounds to prohibit artificial knee replacements? People's intuitions about this may vary, but I suspect that most of us would regard a prohib-ition on knee replacements in such circumstances as simply pandering to society's superstitious beliefs about knees (while harming people who need new knees in the process).

It is tempting at this point to make a distinction between what we might call *arguments from actual offence* and *arguments from reasonable offence*. Arguments from *actual* offence state that x should be banned because, as a matter of fact, many people are offended and/or upset by x. Arguments from *reasonable* offence state that x should be banned because (a) many people are offended and/or upset by x *and* (b) their being offended and/or upset by x is reasonable.[111] The main problem with arguments of the first kind is that they can generate highly counter-intuitive conclusions. For if the *mere fact* that most people are offended by the existence of a practice is supposed to justify a ban on that practice, then given (for example) a widespread taboo regarding homosexuality, such an argument could be (mis)used in an attempt to justify banning same-sex sex. Indeed (if this example doesn't work for you), arguments from actual offence could be used to justify bans on *absolutely anything*, as long as enough people were in fact offended. I take this to be a decisive objection to arguments of this sort.

Arguments from reasonable offence, however, are not vulnerable to the criticism just levelled at arguments from actual offence. For since (I presume) it would be unreasonable to be seriously offended by the existence (at least 'in private') of same-sex sex, arguments from reasonable offence would not justify banning it. Arguments from reasonable offence are, therefore, worth taking seriously. So, if it turns out that the symbolic importance attached to human DNA is reasonable (along with the resultant capacity to be offended or upset by DNA patenting), then there may be a sound argument from reasonable offence against gene patenting.

Once things are viewed in this light, however, the argument from symbolic importance, which was at the outset supposed to be an *independent* argument for restricting DNA patenting, seems to have lost much of its force and interest. For in order to know whether or not the argument is successful we need to know (in advance, so to speak) whether or not it is reasonable to attach symbolic value to DNA and to be offended or upset by DNA patenting. This, though, takes us straight back to the metaphysical issues that we were discussing just a short while ago. In particular, what is the *actual* (as opposed to merely symbolic) relationship between a person and her genetic constitution? It seems to me, then, that the argument from symbolic importance can't really add a lot to the debate. For symbolic importance *per se* can't be allowed to influence policy, as this may amount to legislators simply pandering to people's superstitious beliefs. But if we restrict ourselves to taking into account only reasonable beliefs about symbolic importance, then we're forced to revisit (and answer!) basic metaphysical questions in order to know which views to take seriously.

The third ('environmental') argument for genes having dignity and intrinsic value is harder to rebut, because a thorough assessment of it would mean engaging with some fundamental issues in environmental ethics (not something there is space to do in any detail here). Those who claim that human genetic material has dignity and intrinsic value need to say in virtue of what it is supposed to have these attributes. There are two main 'environmental' options: its contribution to *biodiversity* and its *organisational complexity*.

Appeals to biodiversity and complexity face a number of problems. Biodiversity is now almost universally seen as a good thing, and there is even a United Nations convention on biodiversity, signed by 157 governments in June 1992, which opens by declaring its recognition of

> the intrinsic value of biological diversity and of the ecological, genetic, social, economic, scientific, educational, cultural, recreational and aesthetic values of biological diversity and its components.[112]

However, it seems unlikely that biodiversity's popularity has a great deal to do with its (alleged) *intrinsic* value. Rather, the reason why people have a positive attitude towards it is its good effects or, more likely, the bad effects of eliminating it (such as the loss of potentially useful genetic resources and increased vulnerability to biological and climatic environmental hazards). Indeed, precisely what most contemporary defenders of biodiversity do is to point to how *instrumentally valuable* it is and to *what the consequences will be* if we diminish it. This is not incompatible with regarding it as intrinsically valuable, but, once the 'instrumental' considerations are stripped away, the claim that diversity *per se* is a good seems obscure and arbitrary. For it is hard to see what would lead one rationally to prefer more diversity to less; such a preference seems a mere whim. Similar considerations apply to complexity. As with diversity, it would be hard to justify (non-instrumentally) a preference for more rather than less. Why not prefer simplicity?

Another difficulty is that the commitment to biodiversity's being a good may well create ethical difficulties elsewhere in relation to biotechnology. What I have in mind here is genetic modification. Presumably, the creation of modified organisms must be seen by those who value biodiversity as *prima facie* good, at least insofar as it increases the amount of biodiversity in the world. This is an uncomfortable conclusion for the opponents of patenting, partly because many of them happen also to oppose genetic modification and, more importantly, because patenting may well be an effective mechanism for bringing about an increase in biodiversity – in which case, there would be a biodiversity argument *for* patenting.

It appears, then, that the anti-patenting arguments based on the (supposed) wrongness of commodifiying genes don't succeed, because the view that genes themselves have dignity and intrinsic value is unjustified. Hence, if there is a successful commodification objection to patenting, it must be based on the wrongness of commodifying some other type of entity, such as persons.

(C) The commodification of persons

So far, my focus has been almost exclusively on the claim that DNA patenting involves the wrongful commodification of DNA. The main problem with this claim is that it's hard to render plausible the idea that DNA itself has the sort of dignity and/or intrinsic value required to ground a commodification objection (in the moral sense of 'commodification' explicated in Chapter 3). Perhaps a more promising approach, then, is to focus instead on the commodification of persons, arguing that patenting DNA somehow wrongfully commodifies the person.

People whose objection to DNA patenting is that it commodifies persons face a problem which is the mirror image of that facing those who object that patenting commodifies DNA. For while it's almost universally accepted that persons have dignity and intrinsic value and ought not to be commodified, it's far from clear that DNA patenting actually involves the commodification of persons. This subsection therefore asks what reasons, if any, there are for thinking that DNA patenting involves the commodification of persons.

The first reason is that persons are to be identified with their genetic constitutions. There is, however, no need to consider this again here, since it was examined and rejected in the previous subsection.

The second reason is what I'll term the personal property argument. This draws on an idea from Margaret Radin, who talks of a continuum with entirely *personal* property at one end and entirely *fungible* property at the other. Personal property is 'involved in self-constitution' and is 'bound up with the self in a way that we understand as morally justifiable', while fungible property is external to and independent of the self.[113] At the fungible end of the continuum might be an investment in an overseas company, or a savings certificate, while (arguably) at the personal end are the 'contested commodities' such as one's own body and one's own reproductive and sexual capacities. (Things such as individuals' homes occupy interesting middle-ground positions.) Radin's view is that there are moral reasons not to separate personal property from 'the self':

> Since personal property is connected with the self, morally justifiably, in a constitutive way, to disconnect it from the person (from the self) harms or destroys the self.[114]

So the personal property argument states that we should not allow the commercial exploitation of genetic material because it is personal property and (following Radin) separating personal property from its owners is harmful.

Even if Radin's general view is accepted, there are still problems with the argument.[115] For it is not clear that genetic material is personal property or that the argument is applicable to some of the central DNA patenting cases. Whether a patent on genetic material involves taking away one's personal property rather depends upon what exactly is patented. If the full unique genome of a particular individual were patented non-consensually by a third party, in order to create clones, then that individual would probably have grounds for saying that something 'connected with her self' had been taken. Such a case would resemble 'breach of privacy' cases where someone finds that her likeness has been used in, say, a poster campaign. However, biotech patenting isn't generally like this. Compare, for example, the Moore case. Was a culture of cells producing lymphokines really connected with 'Moore's self'? This seems implausible. Moore may or may not have had (moral) property rights in what was patented. But, either way, the patent seems more like an investment in an overseas company (i.e. *fungible property*) than truly personal property. Similar considerations apply, but *a fortiori*, to patents on copies of widely occurring bodily substances, or gene fragments. These are personal to no one, since they are inside lots of us. So, while the personal property argument might work against some extreme practices (including, perhaps, biopirates' attacks on the traditional medicines), it is unlikely to work against biotech patenting as a whole because, in most cases, what is patented seems not to be very personal.

The third and final reason for thinking that DNA patenting would involve, or cause, the commodification of persons makes use of the displacement thesis (see section 3.6). The displacement thesis states that, even when different ways of valuing things (for example, instrumentally and 'as persons') don't logically contradict one another, they may nonetheless conflict psychologically. More specifically, instrumental valuation sometimes displaces other important modes of valuation in the human mind, encouraging us to see people as nothing more than means. If this were applied to the DNA patenting debate, the objection would be that valuing a person 'for her genes' encourages us (wrongfully) to ignore other important respects in which she is valuable (for example, 'as a person').

It's not difficult to think of cases in which one person values another purely genetically. A woman may 'instrumentalise' a prospective sperm donor, not caring about him as a person, but only about his IQ, physique, etc. – her assumption being that these features will be passed on genetically. Or a man (or couple) may similarly instrumentalise an egg donor, or a surrogate mother. Such cases are structurally just like ones in which biotech companies care only about a group's, or an individual's, unusual and potentially valuable genetic make-up; arguably, the biopiracy cases discussed in section 9.2 fall into this category. But is the existence of such cases a sufficient basis for a general argument against DNA patenting?

The answer is probably *no*. One reason for this is that (as I suggested in response to the personal property argument) many DNA patents are impersonal because they concern widely or universally occurring bodily substances. For these patents, there's little danger of any particular individual being commodified, since the substance in question will be so widely available that no individual will be valued simply for having it. (In this respect, intellectual property in the body differs from tangible property – for example, blood and kidneys – because there won't generally be a need to remove the thing in question *en masse*. Once the biotech companies have enough matter for research and development purposes, that's an end to it.)

But what about cases (such as *Moore*, or the exploited indigenous peoples) where individuals, or small groups, *do* have 'unique' genetic characteristics? Here there is, admittedly, a danger of commodification, since biotech companies' keenness to exploit the trait commercially may cause them to overlook (or deliberately ignore) the personhood of those to whom it belongs. However, to say this is to say little more than that there is a *possibility* of commodification, and this is (as we saw earlier) true whenever one person uses some feature of another – commercially or otherwise.

At this point, it's worth looking again at this quotation from Nussbaum:

> If I am lying around with my lover on the bed, and use his stomach as a pillow there seems to be nothing at all baneful about this, provided that I do so with his consent (or, if he is asleep, with a reasonable belief that he would not mind), and without causing him pain, provided, as well, that I do so in the context of a relationship in which he is generally treated as more than a pillow.[116]

Nussbaum's point here is that there's not normally anything wrong with using someone else's body, provided that (a) there is consent (or something similar – like hypothetical consent), (b) the use isn't harmful, and (c) the use takes place within a context in which the used person is 'treated as more than' an object of use. Applying this to DNA patenting, it seems to me that it's perfectly possible for DNA patenting to meet these three requirements, if it is carried out in the right way and within an ethically appropriate regulatory framework.

Take *Moore* as an example again. As I argued earlier, what was wrong in this case wasn't patenting *per se*, but rather the fact that Moore was deceived and so didn't validly consent – and, to a lesser extent, the fact that he was inconvenienced (by having to make extra trips to hospital and so on). So, in *Moore*, what's wrong is that conditions (a) and (b) (above) aren't met. (Whether (c) is met is unclear.) Hence, there's a case for saying that he was commodified, since he was (in some respects at least) treated as a *mere* biological commodity, instead of being granted the respect due to him as a person (the main expression of that lack of respect being the doctors' failure to obtain valid consent). Similar considerations apply to cases in which indigenous peoples are the victims of biopiracy. Often, biopirates – driven by their desire to exploit (commercially or otherwise) the genetic resources of the indigenous peoples – fail to obtain proper consent, care little about whether their victims are harmed, and don't operate within relationships in which their victims are treated as more than mere objects of use. Hence, there's a strong *prima facie* case for saying that biopirates commodify indigenous peoples. Indeed, this may well be an *a priori* truth, since in order to qualify as a bio*pirate* (as opposed to an 'innocent' scientist) some kind of harmful and/or disrespectful behaviour is required. But again, it isn't patenting *per se* which is disturbing, but rather the way in which the genetic information is extracted and used (non-consensually, harmfully, etc.)

We can concede, then, that human genetic biopiracy (at least typically, perhaps even necessarily) involves the commodification of persons. And we can also grant that, in the world as it is at present, there is a close link between DNA patenting, bioprospecting, and biopiracy. As RAFI put it,

> In the absence of clear and effective rules and processes within the community, within the country, and around the world, it is impossible to guarantee the integrity of the terms and conditions established through contractual arrangements [between bioprospectors and indigenous peoples] . . . therefore, all bioprospecting unavoidably risks becoming biopiracy.[117]

But, at least when we think about the long term, this only constitutes an objection to DNA patenting if it must inevitably (or almost inevitably) involve or cause biopiracy. And this seems improbable. For even if we take a distrustful view of biotech companies and believe that, left to their own devices, they will act as biopirates, the obvious solution is still not to prohibit DNA patents altogether, but rather to use regulation and enforcement to constrain the actions of the companies, to prevent them from treating indigenous peoples and others as mere commodities. Introducing sufficiently robust regulation and enforcement won't be easy and may take a considerable time. But, to give an idea of what such a system would look like, a sensible starting point and statement of principle is the 1992 *Convention on Biological Diversity*. This commits signatories to 'sharing equitably benefits arising from the use of traditional

knowledge' (preamble), 'sharing of the benefits arising out of the utilisation of genetic resources' (Article 1), and

> sharing in a fair and equitable way the results of research and
> development and the benefits arising from the commercial and
> other utilisation of genetic resources with the Contracting Party
> providing such resources. Such sharing will be upon mutually
> agreed terms.
>
> (Article 15.7)[118]

It also, crucially, contains an informed consent requirement:

> Access to genetic resources shall be subject to prior informed con-
> sent of the Contracting Party providing such resources.
>
> (Article 15.5)[119]

(D) Summary and conclusions

In section 9.5, we've considered a number of non-utilitarian objections to
DNA patenting. First, there was the claim that it is morally equivalent to,
or similar to, slavery. This was rejected on the grounds that patenting
DNA is fundamentally different from the fully-fledged ownership of a
whole human being. The latter involves having the legal right to disregard or violate another person's autonomy, whereas the former merely
involves having partial rights over the production of a particular substance. Second, we looked at the idea that DNA patenting involves the
commodification of human genetic material. The main problem with this
line of argument is that in order for a thing to be commod*ified*, in the
(required) pejorative sense, that thing must have morally relevant features in virtue of which it is not a (proper) commodity – more specifically,
features in virtue of which it ought not to be treated as fungible. And in
the case of human DNA, it is hard to see what those features might be.
Finally, we looked at the claim that DNA patenting involves the commodification of persons. We found that DNA patenting doesn't *necessarily*
involve the commodification of persons. However, it was conceded both
that human genetic biopiracy normally involves the commodification of
persons and that, in the 'real world', there is a close link between DNA
patenting, bioprospecting, and biopiracy. What policy recommendations
follow from this? One possibility is to stop DNA patenting altogether. A
less radical solution is to use regulation and enforcement to control
the behaviour of biotech companies, preventing them from treating
indigenous peoples and others as mere commodities.

9.6 Summary and conclusions

Chapter 9 has attempted to answer two questions. What ethical issues are raised by the patenting of human genetic material? And how strong are the moral arguments against this practice?

In response to the first question, we saw (in 9.1–3) that it's much harder to make sense of the ethico-legal issues relating to intellectual property in the human body than it is to make sense of those relating to tangible bodily products and services (like organ sale and surrogacy). This is partly because, for intellectual property, the moral objections we encounter are directed against various different targets, such as biopiracy, patenting phenomena of nature, patenting modified organisms, or patenting 'life' in general. And it's partly because biotech patents come in a number of importantly different forms – usefully categorised by Resnik as *structure* patents ('isolated and purified or modified' DNA sequences), *function* patents (using a DNA sequence in a particular way), and *process* patents (techniques for isolating, purifying, sequencing, analysing, synthesising, or modifying DNA).[120] In general terms, then, we can say that there are a large number of different ethical issues, corresponding to the distinctions just outlined. Thus, asking unqualified questions like 'should DNA patenting be permitted?' is best avoided, since we really need to know which particular kind of DNA patenting the questioner has in mind.

That said, the remaining sections (9.4 and 9.5) did, to a limited extent, ignore these distinctions, in order to scrutinise in more general and philosophical terms the styles of argument used by opponents of DNA patenting. These objections are divisible into two broad categories. There are utilitarian arguments, which appeal to the (allegedly) harmful effects of permitting patenting, and deontological ones, which typically claim that DNA patenting is, in some sense, 'intrinsically' wrong.

My conclusion in section 9.4 (which dealt with utilitarian arguments) was that, although there is a *prima facie* case for permitting DNA patenting (that patenting, arguably, vastly increases investment in biomedical science), this is outweighed by a number of objections. The most important of these was Heller and Eisenberg's idea that biotechnology patents on upstream research tools encourage the creation a 'tragedy of the anti-commons' and, in so doing, impede scientific progress and drive up costs for researchers and therapists. The utilitarian arguments, I concluded, point us towards a 'moderate' policy under which patents that seek to limit access to basic information and research tools are prohibited, while those on downstream inventions with immediate practical applications are permitted.

Section 9.5 considered three non-utilitarian objections to DNA patenting: that it is morally equivalent to slavery; that it involves the commodification of human genetic material; and that it involves the commodification of persons. The first two of these were rejected outright. The third, it was conceded, was worth taking seriously, but only insofar as there is a link between DNA patenting and biopiracy. For while there is no necessary connection between DNA patenting and the commodification of persons, biopiracy does often involve a failure properly to respect persons. It was argued, however, that what is justified is not a total ban on DNA patenting but rather the use of regulation and enforcement to manage the activities of biotech companies, stopping them from treating indigenous peoples and others as mere commodities.

My final conclusion therefore is that, while a complete ban on DNA patenting is not justified, two sets of restrictions are necessary: one to prevent an 'anti-commons' tragedy and the subsequent underuse of biotechnological resources, the other to prevent biopiracy and to ensure that indigenous peoples and others are treated with the respect that they deserve.

NOTES

1 INTRODUCTION

1 J. Mill, *On Liberty*, Ontario, Broadview Press, 1999.
2 M. Redfern (chair), *The Report of the Royal Liverpool Children's Inquiry*, London, The Stationery Office, 2001, http://www.rlcinquiry.org.uk/index.htm.
3 Ibid., para. 4.
4 Chief Medical Officer, *Report of a Census of Organs and Tissues Retained by Pathology Services in England*, London, The Stationery Office, 2001, http://www.doh.gov.uk/organcensus/index.htm, p. 7.
5 See Retained Organs Commission website, http://www.nhs.uk/retainedorgans/.

2 EXPLOITATION

1 A. Wertheimer, *Exploitation*, Princeton, NJ, Princeton University Press, 1996, p. 5.
2 Ibid., p. 6.
3 J. Feinberg, *Harmless Wrongdoing: The Moral Limits of the Criminal Law (Volume 4)*, New York, Oxford University Press, 1988, p. 177.
4 J. Schwartz, 'What's wrong with exploitation?', *Nous*, 1995, vol. 29, p. 176.
5 See also R. Arneson, 'Exploitation', in L. Becker (ed.), *Encyclopaedia of Ethics*, New York, Garland, 1992, p. 350; Wendler, 'Informed consent, exploitation and whether it is possible to conduct human subjects research without either one', *Bioethics*, 2000, vol. 14, pp. 310–39; Wertheimer, *Exploitation*, p. 5.
6 See also R. Goodin, 'Exploiting a situation and exploiting a person', in A. Reeve (ed.), *Modern Theories of Exploitation*, London, Sage, 1987, p. 167: 'there is nothing wrong (nothing necessarily wrong, anyway) with exploiting waves or rocks or sunlight'.
7 Similarly, Nancy Davis writes: 'The belief that it is wrong to use persons is one that is well entrenched in our moral thinking. In one form or another, it underlies a wide range of criticisms and analyses.' N. Davies, 'Using persons and common sense', *Ethics*, 1984, vol. 94, pp. 387–406.
8 O. O'Neill, 'Between consenting adults', *Philosophy and Public Affairs*, 1985, vol. 14, p. 252.
9 B. Williams, *Ethics and the Limits of Philosophy*, London, Fontana, 1985, p. 129.
10 In making this move I am very much in line with philosophical orthodoxy, as identified and criticised by Wood: 'Most philosophers who reflect on the concept of exploitation tend to follow the practice of dictionaries, distinguishing a "nonmoral" sense of "exploitation" from a "moral" sense, and taking the latter

222

sense to involve the idea of making use of someone or something unjustly or unethically. Since they suppose that it is only the latter "pejorative" meaning of the term which interests social critics, they provide what I ... call a "moralized" account of exploitation. That is, they suppose that the term "exploitation" (in the "pejorative" sense) already has wrongfulness built into its very meaning.' A. Wood, 'Exploitation', *Social Philosophy and Policy*, 1995, vol. 12, p. 137.

11 See Goodin, 'Exploiting a situation and exploiting a person', p. 167: 'While exploiting a person is a special case of exploiting a situation, it is a *very* special case. The two are interestingly different, most especially in that the former practice is inherently wrong in a way that the latter is not. Built into the concept of exploiting a person is a notion of "unfairness" (of "taking *unfair* advantage") which is out of place in talking of our treatment of mere situations.'

12 Ibid., p. 173.

13 Jonathan Wolff, 'Marx and exploitation', *Journal of Ethics*, 1999, vol. 3, p. 110.

14 Very few philosophers defend this position, one notable exception being Wood in his 'Exploitation'.

15 Schwartz, 'What's wrong with exploitation?', p. 176.

16 Wolff, 'Marx and exploitation', p. 110. Wolff is clearly right about 'ordinary thought' on this matter. However, it is still not obvious that using someone as a punch bag isn't, or couldn't be, exploitation – not least because, as Wertheimer notes, it may just be that any exploitation involved here is *occluded* by more serious and/or more noticeable wrongs. Wertheimer *Exploitation*, pp. 15–16.

17 Peter Singer is one of many to suggest that humans often wrongfully *exploit* non-human animals. P. Singer, *Practical Ethics*, Cambridge, Cambridge University Press, 1979, p. 288.

18 Wertheimer, *Exploitation*, p. 209.

19 J. Harris, *The Value of Life*, London, Routledge, 1985, p. 120. See also Goodin, 'Exploiting a situation and exploiting a person', p. 166:

> Lovers can exploit one another just as surely as can economic classes. Yet neither party in an affectionate relationship is functioning in any standard sense as a 'factor of production'. Nor, since neither party is creating valuable objects in any ordinary respect, does it in that context make much sense to define exploitation in the standard economics-based terms of receiving commodities which are less valuable than those one has created.

20 Harris, *The Value of Life*, p. 120.

21 For a discussion of these points see, for example: H. Klepper, 'Sexual exploitation and the value of persons', *Journal of Value Inquiry*, 1993, vol. 27, pp. 479–486; S. Marshall, 'Bodyshopping: the case of prostitution', *Journal of Applied Philosophy*, 1999, vol. 16, pp. 139–150.

22 Goodin, 'Exploiting a situation and exploiting a person', p. 172. My italics.

23 J. Sensat, 'Exploitation', *Nous*, 1984, vol. 18, p. 21.

24 Ibid.

25 Wolff, 'Marx and exploitation', p. 106.

26 Ibid., p. 115.

27 Wood, 'Exploitation', p. 137.

28 Ibid., p. 147.

29 See also the following:

The third element in exploitation is some redistribution of benefits and harms among the related parties. *The one essential feature here is that the exploiter himself is a gainer.*

(Feinberg, *Harmless Wrongdoing*, p. 192, my italics).

Persons are exploited if (1) others secure a benefit by (2) using them as a tool or resource so as (3) to cause them serious harm.

(S. Munzer, *A Theory of Property*, Cambridge, Cambridge University Press, 1990, p. 171)

30 Feinberg, *Harmless Wrongdoing*, p. 179, my italics.
31 Wertheimer, *Exploitation*, p. 208.
32 See also the following:

With respect to the dimension of value, A [the exploiter] must benefit from the transaction, for A would not *exploit* B if A were to *abuse* B without benefiting from the abuse . . . A can *abuse* B without exploiting B, as when A inflicts physical harm on B without benefiting from that imposition of harm . . . A can *discriminate* against B without exploiting B, as when A deprives B of an opportunity but does not gain from that deprivation in any important way . . . A can *oppress* B without exploiting B, as when A deprives B of freedom but does not gain from that deprivation of B's freedom.

(Wertheimer, *Exploitation*, p. 208)

33 Ibid., p. 17.
34 Ibid., p. 209.
35 Sensat, 'Exploitation', p. 31.
36 Ibid.
37 Goodin proposes a different formulation of the subjective benefit condition, claiming that exploitation 'is an act which, if successful, confers certain *perceived* benefits upon the exploiter'. I take it that the objections to the version which I discuss apply equally to Goodin's version. Goodin, 'Exploiting a situation and exploiting a person', p. 168.
38 Feinberg, *Harmless Wrongdoing*, p. 193.
39 Wertheimer, *Exploitation*, p. 210.
40 This also gives us a reason to reject Judith Farr Tormey's version of the benefit condition, according to which exploitation 'necessarily involves benefits or gains of some kind *to someone*'. J. Tormey, 'Exploitation, oppression and self-sacrifice', *Philosophical Forum*, 1974, vol. 206, p. 207 (my italics).
41 This form of words is borrowed from Sensat, 'Exploitation', p. 31.
42 Goodin, 'Exploiting a situation and exploiting a person', p. 171.
43 Wood, 'Exploitation', p. 142.
44 Wolff, 'Marx and exploitation', p. 111.
45 Wolff, thinking along similar lines, notes that: 'Exploitation of a person's circumstances is not sufficient for exploitation of that person . . . for there can be paternalistic exploitation of circumstances, and paternalism is not exploitation.' Ibid.
46 Wood, 'Exploitation', p. 142.
47 Ibid.

NOTES

3 OBJECTIFICATION, EXPLOITATION, AND COMMODIFICATION

1 I. Kant, 'Lectures on ethics', in H. Paton (ed.), *Groundwork of the Metaphysics of Morals*, London, Hutchinson, 1953, p. 165.
2 E. McLeod, 'Women working', cited in S. Marshall, 'Bodyshopping: the case of prostitution', *Journal of Applied Philosophy*, 1999, vol. 16, p. 145.
3 M. Nussbaum, 'Objectification', *Philosophy and Public Affairs*, 1995, vol. 24, p. 256.
4 Ibid., p. 257.
5 Ibid., p. 258.
6 Radin suggests a distinction between 'severable, fungible "objects"' and 'the realm of autonomous, self-governing "persons"'. M. Radin, 'Reflections on objectification', *Southern California Law Review*, 1991, vol. 65, p. 349.
7 Nussbaum, 'Objectification', p. 257.
8 Radin, 'Reflections on objectification', p. 345. See also:

> Consider the social 'bad' of objectification. This concept derives from a Kantian worldview, in which persons are subjects and not objects. The person is a moral agent, autonomous and self-governing. An object is a nonperson, not treated as a self-governing moral agent. When we use the term 'objectification' pejoratively, as in 'objectification of persons', we mean, roughly, 'what a Kantian moral reasoner would not want us to do'.
>
> (M. Radin, *Contested Commodities*, Cambridge, MA, Harvard University Press, 1996, p. 155)

9 That ethical concerns about objectification and commodification can be understood in Kantian terms is widely noted in the literature. See, for example, N. Naffine, 'The legal structure of self-ownership: or the self-possessed man and the woman possessed', *Journal of Law and Society*, 1998, vol. 25, p. 199.
10 I. Kant (translated by L. Beck), *Foundations of the Metaphysics of Morals*, Indianapolis, Bobbs-Merrill, 1959, p. 47.
11 Ibid., p. 53.
12 J. Burley and J. Harris, 'Human cloning and child welfare', *Journal of Medical Ethics*, 1999, vol. 25, p. 108. See also J. Harris, 'Goodbye Dolly? The ethics of human cloning', *Journal of Medical Ethics*, 1997, vol. 23, pp. 353–360.
13 Nussbaum, 'Objectification', p. 288.
14 André Gallois has pointed out to me that there are possible counter-examples to the principle that anyone who adopts an entirely instrumental attitude towards X, in so doing, regards X as fungible. This is because sometimes X will be the only possible object with the 'relevant causal powers'. In such cases, X may be fully instrumentalised but viewed as irreplaceable-in-principle. In these unusual cases, I'd have to concede that instrumentalisation and fungibilisation 'come apart'. However, for virtually all practical (and ethical) purposes, the link posited here holds.
15 Radin, *Contested Commodities*, p. 120.
16 E. Anderson, 'Is women's labor a commodity?', *Philosophy and Public Affairs*, 1990, vol. 19, p. 72.
17 Nussbaum, 'Objectification', p. 264.
18 A. Wood, 'Exploitation', *Social Philosophy and Policy*, 1995, vol. 12, p. 141.
19 Anderson, 'Is women's labor a commodity?', p. 92. Davies also tells us that the 'conviction that there is something wrong with using persons has formed the background and, in some cases, the framework of much recent moral

philosophy'. N. Davies, 'Using persons and common sense', *Ethics*, 1984, vol. 94, p. 387.

20 M. Warnock *et al.*, *Report of the Committee of Enquiry into Human Fertilisation and Embryology*, section 8.17.

21 J. Harris, *The Value of Life*, London, Routledge, 1985, p. 143.

22 Nussbaum, 'Objectification', p. 266.

23 Elizabeth Anderson, *Value in Ethics and Economics*, Cambridge, MA, Harvard University Press, p. 154.

24 Nussbaum, 'Objectification', p. 265.

25 S. Millns, 'Dwarf-throwing and human dignity: a French perspective', *Journal of Social Welfare and Family Law*, 1996, vol. 18, p. 375.

26 Ibid., p. 376.

27 The 'other things being equal' phrase is mainly here just to screen out the fact that A may simultaneously be doing something else to B in virtue of which A fails fully to respect B as an 'end'.

28 P. Manga, 'A commercial market for organs. Why not?', *Bioethics*, 1987, vol. 1, p. 325.

29 D. Resnik, 'The commodification of human reproductive materials', *Journal of Medical Ethics*, 1998, vol. 24, p. 388.

30 M. Wilkinson and A. Moore, 'Inducements revisited', *Bioethics*, 1999, vol. 13, p. 122.

31 M. Radin, 'Market-inalienability', *Harvard Law Review*, 1987, vol. 100, p. 1859.

32 The *Sun* is an English tabloid newspaper. Page 3 normally contains pictures of 'topless' young women.

33 B. Brecher, 'The kidney trade: or, the customer is always wrong', *Journal of Medical Ethics*, 1990, vol. 16, p. 122.

34 See S. Wilkinson, 'Commodification arguments for the legal prohibition of organ sale', *Health Care Analysis*, 2000, vol. 8, p. 192.

35 Radin, 'Reflections on objectification', p. 347.

36 Radin, 'Market-inalienability', p. 1932; Radin, 'Reflections on objectification', p. 348.

37 Wilkinson, 'Commodification arguments for the legal prohibition of organ sale', p. 195.

38 Ibid.

39 Radin, *Contested Commodities*, p. 118.

40 Ibid.

41 Ibid.

42 A. Davies, 'Labelled encounters and experiences: ways of seeing, thinking about and responding to uniqueness', *Nursing Philosophy*, 2001, vol. 2, pp. 101–111.

43 Marshall, 'Bodyshopping', p. 145.

44 Radin, *Contested Commodities*, p. 120.

45 'Two different objects can't occupy the same space at the same time' may not, strictly, be true, but it will suffice for our present purposes.

46 S. Kripke, *Naming and Necessity*, Oxford, Blackwell, 1980.

47 See, for example, Naffine, 'The legal structure of self-ownership', pp. 193–212.

4 HARM

1 J. Feinberg, *Harmless Wrongdoing: The Moral Limits of the Criminal Law*, New York, Oxford University Press, 1988, vol. 4, p. 176.

2 J. Mill, *On Liberty*, Ontario, Broadview Press, 1999.
3 A. Buchanan, *Ethics, Efficiency and the Market*, Oxford, Clarendon Press, p. 87.
4 Similarly,

> now some have argued that exploitation must always be harmful . . .
> [but] if exploitation were always harmful, it would be a less interest-
> ing phenomenon, for it would be much more obvious why it is wrong
> and its moral force would be much less in doubt.
>
> (A. Wertheimer, 'Two questions about surrogacy and exploitation',
> *Philosophy and Public Affairs*, 1992, vol. 21, p. 213)

And

> The moral force of harmful and nonconsensual exploitation is rela-
> tively unproblematic. Whatever the added moral importance of the
> gain to A from the harm to B, it is certainly at least *prima facie* wrong
> for A to harm B, and it seems that the state is at least *prima facie*
> justified in prohibiting it.
>
> (A. Wertheimer, *Exploitation*, Princeton, NJ, Princeton University
> Press, 1999, p. 13)

5 Wertheimer, *Exploitation*, p. 13.
6 Wertheimer, 'Two questions', p. 223.
7 J. Wolff, 'Marx and exploitation', *Journal of Ethics*, 1999, vol. 3, p. 113.
8 See J. Feinberg, *Harm to Others: The Moral Limits of the Criminal Law*, New York, Oxford University Press, 1984, vol. 1.
9 Ibid., p. 32.
10 Ibid., p. 33.
11 Ibid., p. 34.
12 Wertheimer, *Exploitation*, p. 172.
13 This list is not meant to be exhaustive. Working out which possible worlds are 'closest' can be a complicated matter and has vexed philosophical minds far greater than mine.
14 Wertheimer agrees: 'there are good theoretical reasons to understand the notion of harm by reference to a normative baseline'. Wertheimer, *Exploitation*, p. 172.
15 J. Harris, 'The Marxist conception of violence', *Philosophy and Public Affairs*, 1974, vol. 3, p. 192. See also J. Harris, *Violence and Responsibility*, London, Routledge & Kegan Paul, 1980, p. 24.
16 Distinguishing non-arbitrarily between acts and omissions is, of course, notoriously difficult.
17 See Feinberg, *Harm to Others*, pp. 159–163, for a more detailed discussion of the distinction between omissions and 'other inactions'.
18 Ibid., p. 159.
19 Wolff, 'Marx and exploitation', p. 113.
20 Wertheimer, *Exploitation*, p. 23.
21 S. Millns, 'Dwarf-throwing and human dignity: a French perspective', *Journal of Social Welfare and Family Law*, 1996, vol. 18, p. 375.
22 Feinberg, *Harm to Others*, p. 34.
23 See Wertheimer, *Exploitation*, p. 24, for a more sophisticated version of this style of argument.
24 Feinberg, *Harm to Others*, p. 33.

5 CONSENT

1 R. Goodin, 'Exploiting a situation and exploiting a person', in A. Reeve (ed.), *Modern Theories of Exploitation*, London, Sage, 1987, p. 174.
2 I am grateful to David McNaughton for a particularly useful discussion of this point.
3 A. Wertheimer, *Exploitation*, Princeton, NJ, Princeton University Press, 1996, pp. 15–16.
4 A. Wood, 'Exploitation', *Social Philosophy and Policy*, 1995, vol. 12, p. 149 (my italics). See also A. Wertheimer, 'Two questions about surrogacy and exploitation', *Philosophy and Public Affairs*, 1992, vol. 21, p. 223.
5 Wood, 'Exploitation', p. 142.
6 R. Gillon, *Philosophical Medical Ethics*, Chichester, Wiley, 1986, p. 113.
7 R. Faden and T. Beauchamp, 'The concept of informed consent', in T. Beauchamp and L. Walters (eds), *Contemporary Issues in Bioethics*, Belmont, CA, Wadsworth, 1994 (4th edition), p. 149.
8 As ever, things are not as straightforward as I suggest. For a more detailed discussion of drunken consent to sexual relations see A. Wertheimer, 'Intoxicated consent to sexual relations', *Law and Philosophy*, 2001, vol. 20, pp. 373–401.
9 Another fascinating concept which plays a similar consent-invalidating role is manipulation. Unfortunately, there is not space to consider this in detail here and, in any case, it has only a minor role in the body commodification debate.
10 J. Harris, *The Value of Life*, London, Routledge, 1985, p. 143.
11 J. Schwartz, 'What's wrong with exploitation?', *Nous*, 1995, vol. 29, p. 162.
12 Harris, *The Value of Life*, p. 120.
13 Wood, 'Exploitation', p. 149.
14 Ibid., p. 148.
15 Wertheimer, *Exploitation*, p. 226.

6 COERCION

1 G. Dworkin, *The Theory and Practice of Autonomy*, Cambridge, Cambridge University Press, 1988, p. 14.
2 G. Dworkin, 'Acting freely', *Nous*, 1970, vol. 4, p. 367.
3 Michael Kligman and Charles Culver, 'An analysis of interpersonal manipulation', *Journal of Medicine and Philosophy*, 1992, vol. 17(2), pp. 173–197.
4 J. Greene, 'Coercion: description or evaluation?', *International Journal of Applied Philosophy*, 1996, vol. 10, p. 7.
5 This discussion of coercion is, of necessity, relatively brief and cannot do justice to the many complexities associated with the topic. There is a not insubstantial philosophical literature on coercion, of which the following are examples: L. Alexander, 'Zimmerman on coercive wage offers', *Philosophy and Public Affairs*, 1983, vol. 12, pp. 160–164; C. Carr, 'Coercion and freedom', *American Philosophical Quarterly*, 1988, vol. 15, pp. 59–67; M. Gilbert, 'Agreements, coercion and obligation', *Philosophy and Public Affairs*, 1993, vol. 103, pp. 679–706; Martin Gunderson, 'Threats and coercion', *Canadian Journal of Philosophy*, 1979, vol. 9, pp. 247–259; R. Nozick, 'Coercion', in S. Morgenbesser, P. Suppes, and M. White (eds), *Philosophy, Science and Method: Essays in Honor of Ernest Nagel*, New York, St Martin's Press, 1969, pp. 440–472; C. Ryan, 'The normative concept of coercion', *Mind*, 1980, vol. 89, pp. 481–498; P. Wilson, 'Ryan on coercion', *Mind*, 1982, vol. 91, pp. 257–263; A. Wertheimer, *Coercion*, Princeton, NJ, Princeton University Press, 1988; D. Zimmerman, 'Coercive wage offers',

Philosophy and Public Affairs, 1981, vol. 10, pp. 121–145; D. Zimmerman, 'More on coercive wage offers: a reply to Alexander', *Philosophy and Public Affairs*, 1983, vol. 12, pp. 165–171.

6 Greene writes: 'in most but not all instances, claiming that a policy is coercive is taken to be equivalent to claiming, or at any rate implying, that it is wrong'. Greene, 'Coercion: description or evaluation?', p. 7.

7 Wertheimer, *Coercion*, p. xi.

8 Dworkin, *The Theory and Practice of Autonomy*, p. 14. See also G. Dworkin, 'Compulsion and moral concepts', *Ethics*, 1968, vol. 78, p. 229.

9 Of course, the extent to which I am relieved of responsibility depends partly on the seriousness of the threat and partly on the consequences of acceding to it. Hence, it might be argued that I am obliged to opt for Tiddles's death in order to protect innocent children. Nonetheless, the general point still stands.

10 A. Wertheimer, 'Two questions about surrogacy and exploitation', *Philosophy and Public Affairs*, 1992, vol. 21, p. 213.

11 Dworkin, 'Acting freely', p. 383.

12 Ibid.

13 Dworkin, *The Theory and Practice of Autonomy*, p. 18.

14 Ibid., p. 15.

15 Wertheimer, *Coercion*, p. xi. See also M. Gorr, 'Toward a theory of coercion', *Canadian Journal of Philosophy*, 1986, vol. 16, pp. 383–406; Greene, 'Coercion: description or evaluation?'

16 Ryan, 'The normative concept of coercion', p. 485.

17 Greene, 'Coercion: description or evaluation?', p. 12, my italics.

18 Ibid., my italics.

19 Ibid., p. 13.

20 Ibid., p. 14.

21 In fact, the points may be subtly different, but that need not bother us for the present.

22 Ryan, 'The normative concept of coercion', p. 483.

23 Ibid.

24 Wertheimer, *Coercion*, p. 204.

25 Wertheimer makes similar points in a number of places: 'if offers and threats were intertranslatable, we could view the paradigmatic armed robber case as one in which, having threatened to kill B, the robber is now offering B the benefit of life in exchange for B's money'. A. Wertheimer, *Exploitation*, Princeton, NJ, Princeton University Press, 1996, p. 136.

26 Wertheimer's national health plan case is another example of this. See Wertheimer, *Coercion*, p. 208.

27 Nozick, 'Coercion', p. 449, my italics.

28 Ibid., p. 447.

29 Ibid., p. 450.

30 Wertheimer, *Coercion*, p. 209.

7 ORGANS FOR SALE

1 Carl Becker, 'Money talks, money kills – the economics of transplantation in Japan and China', *Bioethics*, 1999, vol. 13, p. 241. See also D. Josefson, 'Two arrested in US for selling organs for transplantation', *British Medical Journal*, 7 March 1998, vol. 316, p. 723, http://www.bmj.com.

2 Also, Cameron and Hoffenberg report that

the death penalty may be applied currently in China for at least 68 offences, including discharging a firearm, embezzlement, rape, car theft, and drug dealing. The number of executions in China now exceeds twofold all of the other judicial executions performed throughout the world today, even though Chinese account for only one fifth of humankind . . . a number of organizations, including the Transplantation Society, the European Renal Association, and the Asian Transplantation Society, have . . . made statements condemning the use of executed prisoners' organs, adding the threat of expulsion from the society for any member found to be engaged in performing or facilitating this practice.

(J. Cameron and R. Hoffenberg, 'The ethics of organ transplantation reconsidered: paid organ donation and the use of executed prisoners as donors', *Kidney International*, 1999, vol. 55, p. 728)

3 'Group works for end to desperate practice of organ selling', *CNN.com*, 14 November 1999, http://www5.cnn.com/ASIANOW/south/9911/14/organ. selling/index.html; J. Siegel-Itzkovich, ' "Sale of organs" to be investigated', *British Medical Journal*, 20 January 2001, vol. 322, p. 128, http://www.bmj.com; J. Siegel-Itzkovich, 'Israel investigates organ sales', *British Medical Journal*, 9 November 1996, vol. 313, p. 1167, http://www.bmj.com.

4 J. Radcliffe-Richards *et al.*, 'The case for allowing kidney sales', *Lancet*, 27 June 1998, vol. 351, p. 1950.

5 Astrid and Ronald Guttmann note that

All Western nations have laws banning the sale of organs and tissues. Some of these laws are of older origin, adopted to protect against the commercialisation of other organs, as in Italy, whereas other nations, such as Great Britain, passed the law in response to incidents of sale of kidneys for transplantation.

(A. Guttmann and R. Guttmann, 'Attitudes of health care professionals and the public towards the sale of kidneys', *Journal of Medical Ethics*, 1993, vol. 19, p. 149)

6 Radcliffe-Richards *et al.*, 'The case for allowing kidney sales', p. 1950. In Great Britain in 1999, 4,794 people were waiting for kidney transplants, while only 1,626 transplant operations were carried out. In the same year, an estimated 44,000 US citizens were waiting for kidney transplants. *BBC News*, 'Kidney sale on web halted', 3 September 1999, http://news.bbc.co.uk/1hi/sci/tech/437504.stm. Also worthy of note is the fact that

the results of living donor kidney transplantation are better than those of cadaveric transplantation. The half life of a cadaveric kidney is about eight years, which compares poorly with averages of 12 and 26 years for living donor kidneys matched for one and two haplotypes respectively.

(M. Nicholson and J. Bradley, 'Renal transplantation from living donors', *British Medical Journal*, 13 February 1999, vol. 318, pp. 409–410, http://www.bmj.com)

7 It is also a subject on which there is a huge philosophical and legal-theoretic literature. See, for example, J. Bickenbach, 'Law and morality', *Law and Philosophy*, 1989, vol. 8, pp. 291–300; P. Devlin, *The Enforcement of Morals*, London, Oxford University Press, 1965; R. Dworkin (ed.), *The Philosophy of Law*,

London, Oxford University Press, 1977; R. Dworkin, 'Law, Devlin and the enforcement of morality', *Yale Law Journal*, 1966, vol. 75, pp. 986–1005; H. Hart, *Law, Liberty and Morality*, London, Oxford University Press, 1963; H. Hart, *Essays in Jurisprudence and Philosophy*, Oxford, Clarendon Press, 1983; N. Unwin, 'Morality, law, and the evaluation of values', *Mind*, 1985, vol. 94, pp. 538–549; D. Welch (ed.), *Law and Morality*, Philadelphia, Fortress Press, 1987.

8 A more sophisticated consequentialist case against organ sale may, of course, be made: for example, one might believe that the benefits in terms of lives saved, etc. are outweighed by the negative social consequences of body commodification.

9 S. Wilkinson, 'Commodification arguments for the legal prohibition of organ sale', *Health Care Analysis*, 2000, vol. 8, pp. 189–201.

10 Sue Lloyd-Roberts reports that the only significant exceptions are China and Iran. S. Lloyd-Roberts, 'How big business bankrolls the sick trade in human body parts', *Independent on Sunday*, 8 July 2001, p. 20. See also Cameron and Hoffenberg, 'The ethics of organ transplantation reconsidered', p. 725; Radcliffe-Richards *et al.*, 'The case for allowing kidney sales', p. 1950.

11 These include the World Health Organisation, the Transplantation Society, and the European Renal Association. Cameron and Hoffenberg, 'The ethics of organ transplantation reconsidered', p. 725.

Opposition to organ sale isn't, however, total, or even confined to academic commentary. For example, in 1998, a group of experts (including 'physicians from the United States, Canada, England, and Oman') writing on behalf of the International Forum for Transplant Ethics published a paper in *The Lancet* which argued that the ban on kidney sales should be reversed or at least looked at again. See Radcliffe-Richards *et al.*, 'The case for allowing kidney sales', p. 1950; 'Experts call for debate on kidney sales', *BBC News*, 26 June 1998, http://news.bbc.co.uk/hi/english/health/newsid_120000/120805.stm; V. Baskerville, 'Panel encourages debate on legalizing kidney sales', *Transplant News Network*, 15 July 1998, http://www.centerspan.org/tnn/98071502.htm.

12 Guttmann and Guttmann, 'Attitudes of health care professionals and the public towards the sale of kidneys', pp. 148–153.

13 World Medical Association, *Statement on the Live Organ Trade* (adopted by the 37th World Medical Assembly, Brussels, Belgium, October 1985), http://www.wma.net/e/policy/17-m_e.html.

14 World Medical Association, *Statement on Human Organ and Tissue Donation and Transplantation* (adopted by the 52nd WMA General Assembly, Edinburgh, Scotland, October 2000), http://www.wma.net/e/policy/17–180_e.html.

15 Astrid and Ronald Guttmann report that 'the practice of paid, unrelated donation is flourishing in a number of developing countries, such as Brazil, Egypt and India where endemic poverty ensures vast numbers of willing donors'. Guttmann and Guttmann, 'Attitudes of health care professionals and the public towards the sale of kidneys', p. 149. Kahn reports that

> there is increasingly open discussion of an international black market that connects eager-to-buy patients with ready-to-sell donors. This shadowy market exists because of increasingly desperate patients who can't afford the years it takes to make their way up waiting lists for cadaver organs.
>
> (J. Kahn, 'ISO healthy kidney; top dollar paid', CNN website, 29 May 2001, http://www3.cnn.com/2001/HEALTH/05/29/ethics.matters/index.html)

16 Cameron and Hoffenberg, 'The ethics of organ transplantation reconsidered', p. 725; P. Kandela, 'India: kidney bazaar', *Lancet*, 22 June 1991, vol. 337, p. 1534.
17 'Group works for end to desperate practice of organ selling', *CNN.com*.
18 V. Walia, 'Racketeers cheat kidney donors', *Tribune* website, 6 October 1999, http://www.tribuneindia.com/99oct06/head3.htm.
19 Ibid.
20 'Group works for end to desperate practice of organ selling', *CNN.com*.
21 We should, however, bear in mind that organ sale wasn't (at least before prohibition) universally condemned by the Indian medical establishment. Guttmann and Guttmann, writing in the early 1990s, tell us that

> Some [Indian] physicians see this practice as providing a service to both the recipient and the donor, and as the only alternative until a cadaveric programme can be established. Others see the practice as unethical, unregulatable and a hindrance to the development of a cadaveric programme. The Indian doctors are, however, unanimous in their condemnation of the [extremely hostile] Western reaction, as being formulated in the vacuum of the reality of the situation in India.
>
> (Guttmann and Guttmann, 'Attitudes of health care professionals and the public towards the sale of kidneys', p. 149)

22 Lloyd-Roberts, 'How big business bankrolls the sick trade in human body parts'.
23 'Lottery winner: I'd rather have new kidney', *BBC News*, 29 March 2000, http://news.bbc.co.uk/hi/english/uk/newsid_694000/694837.stm; 'Kidney plea by lottery winner', *Guardian*, 30 March 2000, http://www.guardian.co.uk/Archive/Article/0,4273,3980015,00.html.
24 M. McLeod, 'Kidneys for sale after £4m win', *Guardian*, 31 March 2000, http://www.guardian.co.uk/Archive/Article/0,4273,3980667,00.html.
25 A similar incident was reported in December 1998 when 'a graduate student at George Mason University advertised a kidney for sale on Yahoo! Inc.'s auction site. The posting, which the student said in an e-mail was an "end of the semester" prank, offered the organ for $5,000,000.' L. Bowman, 'Kidneys for sale on the Web', ZDNet UK website, 15 December 1998, http://news.zdnet.co.uk/story/0,,s2070235,00.html.
26 *BBC News*, 'Kidney sale on web halted'.
27 Nicholson and Bradley, 'Renal transplantation from living donors', p. 409.
28 Cameron and Hoffenberg, 'The ethics of organ transplantation reconsidered'.
29 Cameron and Hoffenberg, 'The ethics of organ transplantation reconsidered'. Organ sale is compared to 'risky labour' by a number of authors, for example, J. Harris, *The Value of Life*, London, Routledge, 1985, pp. 142–145; S. Wilkinson and E. Garrard, 'Bodily integrity and the sale of human organs', *Journal of Medical Ethics*, 1996, vol. 22, pp. 334–339.
30 J. Keown, 'The gift of blood in Europe: an ethical defence of EC directive 89/381', *Journal of Medical Ethics*, 1997, vol. 23, p. 96. Richard Titmuss's book *The Gift Relationship: From Human Blood to Social Policy* (London, Allen and Unwin, 1970) is undoubtedly the best-known work on this topic, i.e. on the 'altruism argument' for not commercialising blood donation. For further discussions see, for example, K. Arrow, 'Gifts and exchanges', *Philosophy and Public Affairs*, 1972, vol. 1, pp. 343–362; L. Siminoff and K. Chillag, 'The fallacy of the "gift of life"', *Hastings Center Report*, 1999, vol. 29, pp. 34–41; J. Schwartz, 'Blood and altruism', *The Public Interest*, 1999, vol. 136, pp. 35–51; P. Singer, 'Altruism and

commerce: a defense of Titmuss against Arrow', *Philosophy and Public Affairs*, 1973, vol. 2, pp. 312–320.

31 M. Brazier, 'Regulating the reproduction business?', *Medical Law Review*, 1999, vol. 7, p. 186.

32 HFEA (Human Fertilisation and Embryology Authority), *Eighth Annual Report and Accounts*, Norwich, The Stationery Office, 1999, p. 28, http://www.hfea.gov.uk.

33 Siminoff and Chillag, 'The fallacy of the "gift of life"', p. 34.

34 Cameron and Hoffenberg, 'The ethics of organ transplantation reconsidered', p. 726. Cameron and Hoffenberg don't support this; they are merely reporting it.

35 H. McLachlan, 'The unpaid donation of blood and altruism: a comment on Keown', *Journal of Medical Ethics*, 1998, vol. 24, p. 253.

36 Ibid.

37 Arrow, 'Gifts and exchanges', p. 350.

38 B. Brecher, 'Organs for transplant: donation or payment?', in R. Gillon (ed.), *Principles of Health Care Ethics*, Chichester, John Wiley and Sons, 1994, p. 996.

39 Shortly after the incident described above, such trading, along with various related activities (for example, advertising) was criminalised throughout Great Britain under the Human Organ Transplants Act 1989.

40 Brecher, 'Organs for transplant: donation or payment?', p. 993.

41 Cameron and Hoffenberg, 'The ethics of organ transplantation reconsidered', pp. 724–732.

42 Several writers make this suggestion. See, for example, R. Sells, 'Transplants', in Gillon, *Principles of Health Care Ethics*, p. 1020.

43 G. Abouna *et al.*, 'The negative impact of paid organ donation' in W. Land and J. Dossetor (eds), *Organ Replacement Therapy: Ethics, Justice, Commerce*, Berlin, Springer-Verlag, 1991, p. 167. See also Sells, 'Transplants', p. 1020. Keown makes a similar claim about blood: 'to allow payment would not only *encourage* donation for non-altruistic motives, but might also *discourage* unpaid donation'. Keown, 'The gift of blood in Europe', p. 97.

44 J. Harvey, 'Paying organ donors', *Journal of Medical Ethics*, 1990, vol. 16, p. 119.

45 Department of Health website, http://www.doh.gov.uk/ultra.htm#what.

46 Cameron and Hoffenberg, 'The ethics of organ transplantation reconsidered', p. 726.

47 M. Wilkinson and A. Moore, 'Inducements revisited', *Bioethics*, 1999, vol. 13, p. 123.

48 R. Gillon, 'Commerce and medical ethics', *Journal of Medical Ethics*, 1997, vol. 23, p. 68.

49 P. Short, 'Organ donations don't keep up with those wanting transplants', American Medical Association website, 7 June 2001, http://www.ama-assn.org.

50 World Medical Association, *Statement on Human Organ and Tissue Donation and Transplantation*.

51 M. Wilkinson and A. Moore, 'Inducement in research', *Bioethics*, 1997, vol. 11(5), pp. 373–389.

52 Nuffield Council on Bioethics, *The Ethics of Clinical Research in Developing Countries*, London, Nuffield Council on Bioethics, October 1999, p. 14, http://www.nuffieldfoundation.org/fileLibrary/pdf/clinicaldiscuss1.pdf (my italics).

53 Some philosophers, notably John Harris, argue that it is not possible to give a reductive account of the distinction between 'due' and 'undue' influence,

because these ideas are themselves basic moral concepts (source: discussion at the University of Manchester School of Law, 6 March 2002).

54 The 'offeree' is the person to whom the offer is made.

55 A. Lynne (director), *Indecent Proposal*, Paramount Pictures, 1993.

56 In *Indecent Proposal*, it's not absolutely clear that David and Diana don't *need* the money, since they have admittedly fallen on hard times before meeting John Gage in Las Vegas. However, unlike some of the Indian kidney sellers, they certainly don't need the money in order to avoid death, and so this is still, I'd argue, a case of the second kind – one in which the concerns about voluntariness are more to do with the size of the offer than the desperation of the offeree.

57 Ananova, 'All is fair in love and money, reveals survey', 11 October 2000, http://www.ananova.com/news/story/sm_82744.html.

58 Ananova, 'Britons would have sex for cash, survey says', 12 November 2000, http://www.ananova.com/news/story/sm_114136.html.

59 There's a huge philosophical literature on the nature of temptation, irresistible desires, and the relationship between temptation and free will. See, for example, J. Bigelow, 'Temptation and the will', *American Philosophical Quarterly*, 1990, vol. 27, pp. 39–49; J. Day, 'Temptation', *American Philosophical Quarterly*, 1993, vol. 30, pp. 175–181; J. Day, 'Bribery and corruption: more about temptation', *Journal of Social Philosophy*, 1996, vol. 27, pp. 168–175; J. Fulda, 'The mathematical pull of temptation', *Mind*, 1992, vol. 101, pp. 305–308; P. Hughes, 'Temptation and the manipulation of desire', *Journal of Value Inquiry*, 1999, vol. 33, pp. 371–379; A. Mele, 'Irresistible desires', *Nous*, 1990, vol. 24, pp. 455–472; A. Nuyen, 'The nature of temptation', *Southern Journal of Philosophy*, 1997, vol. 35, pp. 91–103.

60 Wilkinson and Moore, 'Inducement in research', p. 377.

61 This isn't presented as a general theory of freedom. Rather it is an account of just one of the many ways in which the word 'freedom' is used. By way of an aside, this understanding of freedom might account for why we're generally more inclined to think of the offeree as unfree in desperate offeree cases than in enormous offer cases. It's because desperate offerees are much more likely to have no other means available of achieving their fundamental goals – and because 'enormous offers' often appeal to non-fundamental goals, such as the desire for luxury goods.

62 G. Dworkin, *The Theory and Practice of Autonomy*, Cambridge, Cambridge University Press, 1988, p. 15.

63 We should really attribute autonomy (or the lack of it) to persons and/or to the ways in which they relate to their desires. So, as I say, calling a *desire* 'autonomous' should be taken as no more than useful shorthand.

64 S. Bosely, 'Net surfers lie to hide addiction', *Guardian*, 30 September 1999, http://www.guardian.co.uk/Archive/Article/0,4273,3907514,00.html; U. Kenny, 'Hooked on addiction', *Observer*, 18 February 2001, http://www.guardian.co.uk/Archive/Article/0,4273,4137839,00.html; M. Mills, 'Hooked on the exercise high', *Guardian*, 24 October 2000, http://www.guardian.co.uk/Archive/Article/0,4273,4080695,00.html; J. Pollard, 'Are you addicted to your job?', *Observer*, 1 October 2000, http://www.guardian.co.uk/Archive/Article/0,4273,4070350,00.html; H. Welford, 'Net-aholics anonymous', *Guardian*, 30 September 1999, http://www.guardian.co.uk/Archive/Article/0,4273,3907230,00.html.

65 J. Moss and S. King, 'Prostitution – how women sleep rough', National Homeless Alliance (UK) website, 30 April 2001, http://www.nha.org.uk/db/20010430125019.

66 P. Hughes, 'Exploitation, autonomy, and the case for organ sales', *International Journal of Applied Philosophy*, 1998, vol. 12, p. 90.
67 J. Harvey, 'Paying organ donors', *Journal of Medical Ethics*, 1990, vol. 16, p. 118.
68 Department of Health, *Unrelated Live Transplant Regulatory Authority Report 1995–1998*, London, Department of Health, 1999, http://www.doh.gov.uk/ultrarep.htm.
69 Wilkinson and Moore, 'Inducement in research', p. 378.
70 Kahn, 'ISO healthy kidney; top dollar paid'.
71 Cameron and Hoffenberg, 'The ethics of organ transplantation reconsidered', p. 726. Note that here Cameron and Hoffenberg are simply reporting this argument, not endorsing it.
72 Hughes, 'Exploitation, autonomy, and the case for organ sales', p. 94.
73 Cameron and Hoffenberg, 'The ethics of organ transplantation reconsidered', p. 727.
74 Ibid.
75 Gillon, 'Commerce and medical ethics', p. 68.

8 BABIES FOR SALE?

1 R. Ber, 'Ethical issues in gestational surrogacy', *Theoretical Medicine and Bioethics*, 2000, vol. 21, p. 153.
2 Tessa Jowell, Public Health Minister (England), quoted in BBC News Online, 'Health review proposes regulation for surrogacy', 16 October 1999, http://news.bbc.co.uk/hi/english/health/newsid_192000/192611.stm.
3 COTS (Childlessness Overcome Through Surrogacy), 'What motivates women to be surrogates?' (online article), http://www.surrogacy.org.uk/faqs.htm#motive.
4 M. Brazier, A. Campbell, and S. Golombok, *Surrogacy: Review for Health Ministers of Current Arrangements for Payments and Regulation*, London, The Stationery Office, 1998. Henceforth, Brazier.
5 Andrea Dworkin, *Right-wing Women*, London, Women's Press, 1983, p. 36. The literature contains numerous mentions of the comparison with prostitution. See, for example, Ber, 'Ethical issues in gestational surrogacy'; J. Harris, *The Value of Life*, London, Routledge, 1985, p. 138; A. Niekerk and L. Zyl, 'The ethics of surrogacy: women's reproductive labour', *Journal of Medical Ethics*, 1995, vol. 21, pp. 345–9; Richard Posner, *Sex and Reason*, Cambridge, MA, Harvard University Press, 1992, ch. 15.
6 S. Wilkinson, 'Commodification arguments for the legal prohibition of organ sale', *Health Care Analysis*, 2000, vol. 8, pp. 189–201.
7 On this point, John Harris perceptively remarks: 'the moral objections to prostitution *per se* are without foundation and ... the primitive reaction against it has somehow "rubbed off" on our attitudes to the practice or possibility of womb leasing'. *The Value of Life*, p. 138.
8 M. Freeman, 'Does surrogacy have a future after Brazier?', *Medical Law Review*, 1999, vol. 7, p. 2.
9 M. Freeman, 'Is surrogacy exploitative?', in Sheila McLean (ed.), *Legal Issues in Human Reproduction*, Aldershot, Dartmouth, 1989, p. 165.
10 Freeman, 'Does surrogacy have a future after Brazier?', p. 12.
11 BBC News Online, 'UK surrogacy network founder resigns', 22 May 1999, http://news.bbc.co.uk/hi/english/uk/newsid_350000/350100.stm. See also K. Cotton and D. Winn, *Baby Cotton: For Love and Money*, London, Dorling Kindersley, 1985.

12 Quoted in BBC News Online, 'UK surrogacy network founder resigns'.
13 M. Warnock *et al.*, *Report of the Committee of Inquiry into Human Fertilisation and Embryology*, London, HMSO, 1984. Henceforth, Warnock.
14 See especially sections 8.18 and 8.19 of Warnock.
15 A first-rate example of this is Harris, *The Value of Life*.
16 From time to time, such cases are reported in the news media, usually when something goes wrong. One recent case was that of Helen Beasley, a 26-year-old from Shrewsbury (England), who – it was reported – agreed to act as a surrogate for a San Franciscan couple, whom she met over the internet, in return for $20,000. The commissioning couple 'allegedly backed out of the contract when they discovered she was carrying twins and not the one baby they had agreed'. BBC News Online, 'Surrogate fights to stop twins sale', 15 August 2001, http://news.bbc.co.uk/hi/english/health/newsid_1491000/1491926.stm. See also BBC News Online, 'Couple denies surrogate abortion claim', 14 August 2001, http://news.bbc.co.uk/hi/english/health/newsid_1489000/1489956.stm; BBC News Online, 'US Couple bids for surrogate twins', 13 August 2001, http://news.bbc.co.uk/hi/english/health/newsid_1488000/1488358.stm; BBC News Online, 'Surrogate mother pushes for adoption', 12 August 2001, http://news.bbc.co.uk/hi/english/health/newsid_1485000/1485494.stm.
17 Brazier, 1.6–12.
18 Other cases of interest include the following:

> Police are considering a possible charge of obtaining money by deception against a 29 year old British surrogate mother who refused to hand over a baby commissioned by a childless couple. Angela Richardson was arrested and released on bail by Derbyshire police after a complaint from Greg and Deborah White ... The divorced mother of two from Derby was allegedly paid £4000 to have the child for the Whites but decided to keep him when he was born last August. Miss Richardson had simultaneously been in touch with two surrogacy organisations. She underwent artificial insemination for the Whites in November 1995 through Childlessness Overcome Through Surrogacy. The following month she flew to Stockholm to be inseminated for a Swedish couple under the aegis of the Surrogacy Parenting Centre. She reportedly told the Swedish couple that the baby was lost.
>
> (C. Dyer, 'Surrogate mother refuses to give up baby', *British Medical Journal*, 25 January 1997, vol. 314, p. 250)

> *Bionews* (31 May 1999, http://www.progress.org.uk/) reports the following case: *Surrogacy Scam*: A tabloid investigation uncovered an illegal surrogacy business last week. Undercover *Mirror* journalists discovered a couple offering £10,000 in cash to fertile women willing to become surrogate mothers. It is also understood that the couple offer a commission to anyone who introduces them to potential surrogates.

19 Brazier, executive summary, 3.
20 Brazier, 1.5.
21 Ibid., 5.25
22 Ibid.
23 Warnock, 8.11.

24 Judge Richard N. Parslow, Jr, quoted in G. Annas, 'Crazy making: embryos and gestational mothers', *Hastings Center Report*, January 1991, vol. 21, p. 36.

25 Another example is Elizabeth Anderson, who claims that the actions of surrogacy brokers (for example, agencies) are 'morally on a par with baby selling'. E. Anderson, 'Why commercial surrogate motherhood unethically commodifies women and children: reply to McLachlan and Swales', *Health Care Analysis*, 2000, vol. 8, p. 25.

26 In the case of partial surrogacy, of course, surrogates may also be egg sellers, but I'll leave the egg-selling dimension to one side for now so as to avoid unnecessarily complicating matters. It should also be noted that the moral status of egg selling is much less clear than that of baby selling (on the assumption that the latter is obviously wrong). So establishing that paid partial surrogates are egg sellers (which seems plausible) may not in any case have much significance for the argument. For we're as unclear about the moral status of egg selling as we are about that of commercial surrogacy.

27 R. Kornegay, 'Is commercial surrogacy baby-selling?', *Journal of Applied Philosophy*, 1990, vol. 7, p. 46.

28 Kornegay, 'Is commercial surrogacy baby-selling?', p. 45. In the passage quoted, Kornegay merely reports this view without endorsing it.

29 B. Oxman, 'California's experiment in surrogacy', *Lancet*, 6 May 1993, vol. 341, p. 1468.

30 Kornegay, 'Is commercial surrogacy baby-selling?', p. 45 (my italics).

31 Ibid., p. 49 (my italics).

32 Posner also supports (a), by appealing to a distinction between selling a baby and selling one's parental rights:

> The surrogate mother no more 'owns' the baby than the father does. What she sells is not the baby but her parental rights, and in this respect she is no different from a woman who agrees in a divorce proceeding to surrender her claim to custody of the children of the marriage in exchange for some other concession from her husband.
> (R. Posner, 'The ethics and economics of surrogate motherhood', *Journal of Contemporary Health Law and Policy*, 1989, vol. 5, p. 29)

33 E. Anderson, 'Is women's labor a commodity?', *Philosophy and Public Affairs*, 1990, vol. 19, p. 76.

34 H. McLachlan and J. Swales, 'Babies, child bearers and commodification: Anderson, Brazier *et al.*, and the political economy of commercial surrogate motherhood', *Health Care Analysis*, 2000, vol. 8, pp. 3–4.

35 Harris, *The Value of Life*, p. 139.

36 I use 'happy' and 'happiness' here (and throughout this chapter) as a shorthand for (positive) quality of life.

37 That said, as this book was being completed, research was presented at the annual conference of the European Society of Human Reproduction and Embryology in Vienna suggesting that 'parents of children born following the use of a surrogate have better parenting skills and show more warmth towards their children than those in non-surrogacy families'. The research, it is claimed, also 'shows that children born to surrogates show no differences in emotional and psychological well-being when compared to other children'. *Bionews*, 2 July 2002, http://www.progress.org.uk/.

See also 'Surrogate couples "make better parents"', BBC News Online, 2 July 2002, http://news.bbc.co.uk/1/hi/health/2069469.stm; J. Meek, 'Surrogacy "leads to better parenting"', *Guardian*, 1 July 2002, www.guardian.co.uk/

uk_news/story/0,3604,747098,00.html; 'Infant steps', *The Times*, 1 July 2002, www.timesonline.co.uk/article/0,,542-343120,00.html.

38 Brazier, executive summary, 2.

39 Anderson, 'Is women's labor a commodity?', p. 76.

40 V. Munroe, 'Surrogacy and the construction of the maternal–foetal relationship: the feminist dilemma examined', *Res Publica*, 2001, vol. 7, p. 18. And according to Brazier,

> 4.11 – children born through surrogacy differ from adopted and assisted reproduction children in ways that may be detrimental to their emotional well-being as they grow up. It is not known, for example, how a child will feel about having been created for the purpose of being given away to other parents or, if the surrogate mother remains in contact with the family, what the impact of two mothers will be on his or her social, emotional and identity development through childhood and into adult life, particularly in families where the surrogate mother is also the genetic mother of the child.

41 Posner, 'The ethics and economics of surrogate motherhood', p. 25.

42 There is another philosophical question too: does the mere fact that we know relatively little about the welfare of children born of commercial surrogacy arrangements justify banning, or officially discouraging, commercial surrogacy? The authors of Brazier, which contains talk of the state's obligation to act on the 'precautionary principle' and of society's duty to 'minimise risk', appear to think that the answer is *yes*. This – in particular, issues relating to the meaning and application of the 'precautionary principle' – is a fascinating topic, but not one which we need to engage with here. This is because, in what follows, I argue that knowing that surrogates' children have below average quality lives wouldn't be sufficient to justify laws which ban or discourage surrogacy. So, *a fortiori*, merely fearing that surrogates' children have below average quality lives isn't enough to justify these anti-surrogacy measures.

43 See S. Sheldon and S. Wilkinson, 'Termination of pregnancy for reason of foetal disability: are there grounds for a special exception in law?', *Medical Law Review*, 2001, vol. 9, pp. 85–109.

44 H. Kuhse and P. Singer, *Should the Baby Live?*, Oxford, Oxford University Press, 1985, p. 158 (my italics).

45 J. Glover, *Fertility and the Family: the Glover Report on Reproductive Technologies to the European Commission*, London, Fourth Estate, 1989, p. 129. As I've suggested, these cases are all controversial and contestable. For a more detailed discussion of these arguments see Sheldon and Wilkinson, 'Termination of pregnancy for reason of foetal disability'.

46 J. Harris, 'The welfare of the child', *Health Care Analysis*, 2000, vol. 8, p. 33.

47 In English law, an interesting parallel case is section 13(5) of the Human Fertilisation and Embryology Act 1990. This states that a woman must not be provided with infertility treatment services unless 'the welfare of any child who may be born as a result of the treatment (including the need of that child for a father)' has been taken into account. Here, as in surrogacy cases, it would seem that 'welfare of the child' considerations ought always to support existence rather than non-existence, except in those extremely rare cases where the future child will have a horrendously painful and/or miserable life (a 'life not worth living'). However, in practice, section 13(5) is applied much more restrictively than this, and the Human Fertilisation and Embryology

Authority's guidance to clinics 'enjoins clinicians to take into account factors such as the would-be parents' commitment to having and bringing up a child; their ability to provide a stable and supportive environment; their future ability to look after or provide for a child's needs and the possibility of any risk of harm to their child'. E. Jackson, 'Conception and the irrelevance of the welfare principle', *Modern Law Review*, 2002, vol. 65, p. 181.

48 A. Campbell, 'Surrogacy, rights and duties: a partial commentary', *Health Care Analysis*, 2000, vol. 8, pp. 38–39 (my italics).
49 L. Purdy, 'Surrogate mothering: exploitation or empowerment?', *Bioethics*, 1989, vol. 3, p. 28.
50 T. Appleton, *Surrogacy*, Cambridge, IFC Resource Centre, 2000, p. 2. Usually the absence of a uterus is because of 'removal of all or part of the womb due to medical complications'; more rarely, it is due to congenital absence.
51 Warnock, 8.17.
52 See again Sheldon and Wilkinson, 'Termination of pregnancy for reason of foetal disability'.
53 J. Glover, *Causing Death and Saving Lives*, Harmondsworth, Penguin, 1977, p. 148.
54 Campbell, 'Surrogacy, rights and duties', p. 38.
55 Warnock, 8.17.
56 There's a very real possibility of commissioning couples being exploited by surrogates. I don't, however, discuss that here, partly for reasons of space, and partly because the *main* (i.e. most prevalent) exploitation argument against commercial surrogacy concerns the exploitation of the surrogates themselves.
57 Anderson, 'Is women's labour a commodity?', p. 238.
58 C. Erin and J. Harris, 'Surrogacy', *Baillière's Clinical Obstetrics and Gynaecology*, 1991, vol. 5, p. 628.
59 A. Wertheimer, 'Two questions about surrogacy and exploitation', *Philosophy and Public Affairs*, 1992, vol. 21, p. 217.
60 Brazier, executive summary, 4.
61 L. Andrews, 'Surrogate motherhood: the challenge for feminists', *Law, Medicine and Health Care*, 1988, vol. 16, p. 75.
62 J. Oakley, 'Altruistic surrogacy and informed consent', *Bioethics*, 1992, vol. 6, p. 273.
63 Ber, 'Ethical issues in gestational surrogacy', p. 158.
64 Oakley, 'Altruistic surrogacy and informed consent', p. 274.
65 See Andrews, 'Surrogate motherhood: the challenge for feminists' (p. 75) for a critique of this argument.
66 Anderson, 'Is women's labor a commodity?', p. 87.
67 Ibid., p. 85.
68 A. Wood, 'Exploitation', *Social Philosophy and Policy*, 1995, vol. 12, p. 148.
69 Appleton, *Surrogacy*, p. 7.
70 Brazier, 5.15.
71 B. Brecher, 'Surrogacy, liberal individualism and the moral climate', in J. Evans (ed.), *Moral Philosophy and Contemporary Problems*, Cambridge, Cambridge University Press, 1987, p. 195.
72 Ber, 'Ethical issues in gestational surrogacy', p. 159.
73 Brecher, 'Surrogacy, liberal individualism and the moral climate', p. 196.
74 Andrews, 'Surrogate motherhood: the challenge for feminists', p. 74.
75 Brecher, 'Surrogacy, liberal individualism and the moral climate', p. 188.
76 Ibid., p. 197.
77 Anderson, 'Is women's labor a commodity?', p. 80.

78 McLachlan and Swales, 'Babies, child bearers and commodification', p. 7 (my italics).
79 Anderson, 'Why commercial surrogate motherhood unethically commodifies women and children', p. 23.
80 Ibid.
81 Brecher, 'Surrogacy, liberal individualism and the moral climate', p. 184.
82 Ibid., p. 195.

9 PATENTING LIFE

1 D. Resnik, 'The morality of human gene patents', *Kennedy Institute of Ethics Journal*, 1997, vol. 7, p. 44.
2 M. Bunting, 'The debate nobody wants: gene patenting', *Guardian*, 31 May 2001, http://www.guardian.co.uk/Archive/Article/0,4273,4195342,00.html.
3 A. Moore, 'Owning genetic information and gene enhancement techniques: why privacy and property rights may undermine social control of the human genome', *Bioethics*, 2000, vol. 14, p. 99.
4 Resnik, 'The morality of human gene patents', p. 45. See also D. Resnik, 'DNA patents and scientific discovery and innovation: assessing benefits and risks', *Science and Engineering Ethics*, 2001, vol. 7, pp. 29–62.
5 A. Alexandra and A. Walsh, 'Exclusion, commodification, and plant variety rights legislation', *Agriculture and Human Values*, 1997, vol. 14, p. 313.
6 Moore, 'Owning genetic information and gene enhancement techniques', p. 99.
7 See, for example, F. Charatan, 'US religious groups oppose gene patents', *British Medical Journal*, 1995, vol. 310, pp. 1351–1355; M. Hanson, 'Religious voices in biotechnology: the case of gene patenting', *Hastings Center Report*, 1997, vol. 27, pp. 1–23; M. Sagoff, 'Patented genes: an ethical appraisal', *Issues in Science and Technology*, 1998, vol. 14, pp. 33–37. See also the following Greenpeace website: http://www.greenpeace.org/~geneng.
8 A consultation exercise commissioned by the Human Genetics Commission suggests that there is 'public concern over the issue of patenting of gene sequences'. See Human Genetics Commission, *Work Plan 2000/2001*, paras 48–55, http://www.hgc.gov.uk/business_work.htm. The Nuffield Council on Bioethics is also taking a keen interest in this area, and a discussion paper from the Council on the ethics of patenting DNA and proteins was published in 2001. See http://www.nuffield.org/bioethics.
9 See *Bionews*, 6 March 2000, http://www.progress.org.uk.
10 *Bionews*, 6 March 2000. See also J. Meek, 'Patenting our genes', *Guardian*, 26 June 2000, http://www.guardian.co.uk/Archive/Article/0,4273,4033782,00.html.
11 One issue that I won't be able to discuss here is whether something is an 'organism type' if and only if it is a species.
12 *Funk Bros Seed Co v. Kalo Co*, 333 US, pp. 130–132.
13 See, for example, A. Barnett, 'Patent allows creation of man–animal hybrid', *Observer*, 26 November 2000, http://www.guardian.co.uk/Archive/Article/0,4273,4096677,00.html.
14 I am grateful to David Resnik for this point.
15 Resnik, 'DNA patents and scientific discovery and innovation', p. 37.
16 Leandra Zalabata, an Arahuaco spokesperson, quoted in L. Andrews and D. Nelkin, *Body Bazaar: The Market for Human Tissue*, New York, Crown, 2001, p. 73.
17 The term 'biopiracy' is now widely used. See, for example, G. Dutfield,

'Bioprospecting or biopiracy?', *Biofutur*, 2000, vol. 204, pp. 42–45; R. Nash, 'Who benefits from biopiracy?', *Phytochemistry*, 2001, vol. 56, pp. 403–405; V. Shiva, *Biopiracy: The Plunder of Nature and Knowledge*, Totnes, Green Books, 1998.

18 Another interesting internet resource is the website of RAFI, the Rural Advancement Foundation International, http://www.rafi.org. From here, a large number of detailed reports on (alleged) biopiracy can be downloaded. RAFI was renamed the Action Group on Erosion, Technology and Concentration, or ETC (pronounced etcetera) in September 2001.

19 Greenpeace, 'Patents on life: biopiracy' (online article), http://www.greenpeace.org/~geneng/reports/pat/intrpat3.htm.

20 M. Thom, 'Broad coalition challenges patents on life' (press release), 6 June 1995, http://www.rz.uni-frankfurt.de/~ecstein/gen/biolib/320.

21 Greenpeace, 'Patents on life: human patenting' (online article), http://www.greenpeace.org/~geneng/reports/pat/intrpat7.htm. For an ethicist's critical assessment of this project see D. Resnik, 'The Human Genome Diversity Project: ethical problems and solutions', *Politics and the Life Sciences*, 1999, vol. 18, pp. 15–24. An informative discussion can also be found in Andrews and Nelkin, *Body Bazaar: The Market for Human Tissue*, ch. 3. Another example is reported by Caplan and Merz:

> the [US] government filed and received a patent on the genes of a member of the Hagahai tribe in Papua New Guinea, some of whom have an unusual resistance to leukaemia. This set off an international contretemps, with Third World nations protesting against exploitation of their national genomic resources by avaricious scientists from economically privileged nations.
>
> (A. Caplan and J. Merz, 'Patenting gene sequences', *British Medical Journal*, 1996, vol. 312, p. 926)

See also F. Powledge, 'Patenting piracy and the global commons', *Bioscience*, 2001, vol. 51, pp. 273–277.

22 Andrews and Nelkin, *Body Bazaar: The Market for Human Tissue*, p. 65.

23 Greenpeace, 'Patents on life: human patenting'.

24 Andrews and Nelkin, *Body Bazaar: The Market for Human Tissue*, p. 64.

25 M. Thom, 'Broad coalition challenges patents on life'.

26 Andrews and Nelkin, *Body Bazaar: The Market for Human Tissue*, p. 65.

27 National Cancer Institute website, http://www.niaid.nih.gov/daids/dtpdb/004414.htm.

28 K. Perry, 'Getting a fair price for indigenous remedies', *Guardian*, 21 December 2000, http://www.guardian.co.uk/Archive/Article/0,4273,4108742,00.html.

29 Note, however, that according to *Cancerweb*,

> The NCI is very aware of the contributions made by various countries around the world in permitting the evaluation of their natural resources for anticancer and anti-AIDS activity. The contractors collecting samples for NCI collaborate closely with source country institutions. The results of anticancer and anti-AIDS testing of samples from a source country are provided to that country's scientific community. Scientists of source countries are invited to NCI laboratories to collaborate in the study of active samples collected in their countries or gain experience in NCI screening methods. The NCI funds these visits and provides technical training lasting up to 12

months, and also promotes technology transfer. Should a drug from a particular country advance to commercial use, NCI will require the pharmaceutical company marketing the drug to negotiate, directly with the country, terms of compensation to that country.

(http://www.graylab.ac.uk/cancernet/600733.html)

30 Perry, 'Getting a fair price for indigenous remedies'.
31 There are many complex and technical issues relating both to commercial and non-commercial uses of personal genetic information. See, for example, the Human Genetics Commission's consultation paper, 'Whose hands on your genes?' (November 2000), http://www.hgc.gov.uk/business_consultations2.htm.
32 51 Cal. 3d 120 (1990).
33 E. Gold, *Body Parts: Property Rights and the Ownership of Human Biological Materials*, Washington, DC, Georgetown University Press, 1996, p. 24.
34 B. Reid, *A Practical Guide to Patent Law*, London, Sweet and Maxwell, 1993, p. 1.
35 Reprinted in *Journal of the Patent Office Society*, 1948, vol. 30, p. 176.
36 R. Hoedmaekers, 'Human gene patents: core issues in a multi-layered debate', *Medicine, Health Care and Philosophy*, 2001, vol. 4, pp. 211–221.
37 *Convention on the Grant of European Patents (European Patent Convention)*, 10th edn, European Patent Office, 2000, Article 52, p. 72 (my italics). Available online: http://www.european-patent-office.org.
38 Ibid., Article 54(1).
39 See http://www.sanger.ac.uk and http://www.wellcome.ac.uk. See also BBC, 'Plan to block patenting of human genes', 20 September 1999, http://news.bbc.co.uk/hi/english/sci/tech/newsid_452000/452293.stm; K. Perry, 'The key players', *Guardian*, 26 June 2000, http://www.guardian.co.uk/Archive/Article/0,4273,4033843,00.html.
40 *European Patent Convention*, Article 56.
41 Ibid., Article 52(2).
42 *Diamond, Commissioner of Patents and Trademarks* v. *Chakrabarty*, 447 U.S. 303 (decided: 16/6/80).
43 Dworkin and Kennedy report that one of the main driving forces behind the European Union's attempt to produce a directive on biotechnology during the 1990s was a desire to stop European biotechnology companies from lagging behind the US and Japan. G. Dworkin and I. Kennedy, 'Human tissue: rights in the body and its parts', *Medical Law Review*, 1993, vol. 1, p. 316.
44 T. Dickenson (Under Secretary, US Department of Commerce), *FDCH Congressional Testimony (Patenting Inventions Developed from the Genome Project)*, 13 July 2000.
45 Resnik, 'DNA patents and scientific discovery and innovation', p. 34.
46 Sagoff, 'Patented genes: an ethical appraisal', p. 37.
47 *Funk Bros Seed Co* v. *Kalo Co*, 333 US at 130–132.
48 Gold, *Body Parts*, p. 81.
49 Resnik, 'DNA patents and scientific discovery and innovation', p. 30.
50 Sagoff, 'Patented genes: an ethical appraisal', p. 37.
51 Ibid.
52 S. Brownlee, 'Staking claims on the human body', *U.S. News and World Report*, 18 November 1991, vol. 111, pp. 89–91.
53 V. Griffith, 'Call for tougher standards', *Financial Times (FT.com)*, 13 July 2000, http://news.ft.com/home/uk/.
54 Resnik, 'DNA patents and scientific discovery and innovation', p. 34. See also

D. Resnik, 'DNA patents and human dignity', *Journal of Law, Medicine, and Ethics*, 2001, vol. 29, pp. 152–165.

55 Griffith, 'Call for tougher standards'.
56 See also an April 2000 statement by HUGO (the Human Genome Organisation) which expresses concern about broad patents, recommending that '[patent] claims of the broad "having" and "comprising" type, which cover not only the disclosed DNA sequence and its use but also products "having" or "comprising" that sequence, [should] be allowed only exceptionally'. HUGO, 'Statement on patenting of DNA sequences: in particular response to the European Biotechnology Directive', April 2000, http://www.hugo-international.org/hugo/, p. 1.
57 Quoted in Griffith, 'Call for tougher standards'.
58 The Patent Office (UK), *Legal Protection of Biotechnological Inventions: A Consultation Paper on Implementation in the United Kingdom of EC Directive 98/44/EC*, London, Department of Trade and Industry, 5 April 2000.
59 See, for example, Anon, 'Churches say no to gene patenting', *Christian Century*, 13 September 2000, vol. 117, pp. 899–901.
60 The formal relationship between the Directive and the Convention is described in Rule 23b (Chapter VI) of the Convention, which states that 'Directive 98/44/EC of 6th July 1998 on the legal protection of biotechnological inventions shall be used as a supplementary means of interpretation.'
61 European Parliament and Council Directive 98/44/EC of 6th July 1998 on the Legal Protection of Biotechnological Inventions, 5(2).
62 Ibid.
63 *Diamond, Commissioner of Patents and Trademarks* v. *Chakrabarty*, 447 U.S. 303 (decided: 16 June 1980).
64 Barnett, 'Patent allows creation of man–animal hybrid.' See also *European Patent Convention*, Article 63(1).
65 Barnett, 'Patent allows creation of man–animal hybrid.'
66 I use the term 'utilitarian' here in a broad sense to refer to arguments which are solely or mainly about effects. One can use such arguments without, in general, being a utilitarian (without thinking that maximising the good, for example happiness, is all that matters morally).
67 Alexandra and Walsh, 'Exclusion, commodification, and plant variety rights legislation', p. 315.
68 Ibid., p. 316.
69 In case this is misunderstood, I'm *not* suggesting that it is impossible for good ideas to be in short supply, or that there cannot be such things as 'knowledge-rich' and 'knowledge-poor' societies. What is claimed, rather, is that once something is invented, it makes no sense to say that this invention, *qua* abstract object, is in short supply. However, what can (of course) be in short supply are the tangibles required for the instantiation and transmission of intellectual property, such as books, computers and teachers.
70 W. Haseltine, 'The case for gene patents', *Technology Review*, September/October 2000, p. 59.
71 R. Scott (Incyte Genomics), *FDCH Congressional Testimony (Patenting Inventions Developed from the Genome Project)*, 13 July 2000.
72 Resnik, 'DNA patents and scientific discovery and innovation', p. 44.
73 A World Health Organisation (WHO) report notes that 'Patenting has the potential to impede international collaboration, especially between developing and developed countries, to the ultimate detriment of service delivery to those with genetic disorders.' WHO, *Proposed International Guidelines on Ethical*

Issues in Medical Genetics and Genetic Services: Report of a WHO Meeting on Ethical Issues in Medical Genetics, December 1997, http://www.who.int/ncd/hgn/hgnethic.htm.

74 Bunting, 'The debate nobody wants: gene patenting'.

75 J. Borger, 'Rush to patent genes stalls cures for disease', *Guardian*, 15 December 1999, http://www.guardian.co.uk/Archive/Article/0,4273,3941983,00.html.

76 Jonathan King and Doreen Stabinsky, 'Genes, cells and organisms are not corporate property', http://hornacek.coa.edu/dave/Reading/patents.html.

77 HUGO, 'Statement on patenting of DNA sequences', p. 1.

78 HUGO, 'Statement on patenting issues related to early release of raw sequence data', 1997, http://www.gene.ucl.ac.uk/hugo/ip1997.htm, p. 1. My italics.

79 Ibid.

80 M. Heller and R. Eisenberg, 'Can patents deter innovation? The anticommons in biomedical research', *Science*, 5 January 1998, vol. 280, pp. 698–701.

81 Ibid., p. 699.

82 Ibid.

83 Ibid.

84 Ibid.

85 Ibid.

86 Ibid.

87 Ibid., p. 700.

88 Ibid.

89 Borger, 'Rush to patent genes stalls cures for disease'.

90 King and Stabinsky, 'Genes, cells and organisms are not corporate property'.

91 RAFI, 'Call to dialogue or call to 911?' (online article), 2 November 2000, http://www.rafi.org.

92 In September 1999, the Parliamentary Assembly of the Council of Europe recommended that 'neither plant, animal nor human derived genes, cells, tissue or organs' should be subject to patents. One of the reasons cited was their belief that 'patents of living organisms could threaten biodiversity'. See 'Council of Europe opposed to gene patenting', *Bionews*, 4 October 1999, http://www.progress.org.uk.

93 EC Directive on the Legal Protection of Biotechnological Inventions (98/44/EC), Article 6.

94 See B. Brecher, 'Surrogacy, liberal individualism and the moral climate', in J. Evans (ed.), *Moral Philosophy and Contemporary Problems*, Cambridge, Cambridge University Press, 1987, p. 184.

95 HUGO, 'Statement on patenting of DNA sequences', p. 1.

96 Ibid.

97 The slavery argument is sometimes also used against other practices, notably cloning.

98 P. Fannin, 'Patent critics try to stop human gene slave trade', *The Age*, 19 March 2000, http://www.theage.com.au/news/20000319/A17591–2000Mar18.html.

99 T. Weiskel, 'The contested morality of biotechnology', *ENN (Environmental News Network)*, 18 November 1999, http://www.enn.com/features/1999/11/111899/weiskel_7085.asp.

100 Nuffield Council on Bioethics, *Human Tissue: Ethical and Legal Issues*, London, Nuffield Council on Bioethics, 1995, p. 91. See also L. Bentley and B. Sherman, 'The ethics of patenting: towards a transgenic patent system', *Medical Law Review*, 1995, vol. 3, p. 280.

101 Resnik, 'DNA patents and human dignity', p. 157. Caplan and Merz make a similar point:

it is hard to equate assigning a patent to a DNA strip with ownership of a human body. Selling bodies into slavery is exploitative, because our personal identity is so intimately tied to our bodies. It is not so obviously a violation of the human spirit to assign rights to exclusive use and development over a segment of chromosome 13 to a government agency or a biotechnology concern.

(Caplan and Merz, 'Patenting gene sequences', p. 926)

102 Bishop Kenneth Carder of the United Methodist Church, quoted in Hanson, 'Religious voices in biotechnology: the case of gene patenting', p. 8.
103 Hanson, 'Religious voices in biotechnology: the case of gene patenting', p. 8.
104 Ibid.
105 Resnik, 'DNA patents and human dignity', p. 159.
106 CPU: Central Processing Unit, the most important constituent of a computer's microprocessor, which performs calculations and executes instructions.
107 Nelkin and Lindee, quoted in Hanson, 'Religious voices in biotechnology: the case of gene patenting', p. 4.
108 I am, of course, skimming over lots of difficult issues in metaphysics and the philosophy of mind here.
109 Resnik, 'DNA patents and human dignity', pp. 159–160.
110 Ibid., p. 160.
111 See S. Sheldon and S. Wilkinson, 'Female genital mutilation and cosmetic surgery: regulating non-therapeutic body modification', *Bioethics*, 1997, vol. 12, p. 282.
112 *Convention on Biological Diversity*, 5 June 1992, http://www.biodiv.org/doc/legal/cbd-en.pdf.
113 M. Radin, *Contested Commodities*, Cambridge, MA, Harvard University Press, 1996, pp. 57–58.
114 Ibid., pp. 59–60.
115 Space restrictions prevent me from providing a proper critical consideration of Radin's influential ideas here. I should, however, note that her philosophical views about the self and personal property do seem to me to be problematic in a number of respects.
116 M. Nussbaum, 'Objectification', *Philosophy and Public Affairs*, 1995, vol. 24, p. 265.
117 RAFI, 'Call to dialogue or call to 911?'.
118 *Convention on Biological Diversity*.
119 Ibid.
120 Resnik, 'DNA patents and scientific discovery and innovation', p. 34. See also Resnik, 'DNA patents and human dignity', p. 153.

INDEX